English Phonetics and Phonology

A practical course
Second edition

Peter Roach
Professor of Phonetics
University of Reading

CAMBRIDGE
UNIVERSITY

D0307486

PUBLISHED BY THE PRESS SYNDICATE OF THE UNIVERSITY OF CAMBRIDGE
The Pitt Building, Trumpington Street, Cambridge CB2 1RP, United Kingdom

CAMBRIDGE UNIVERSITY PRESS
The Edinburgh Building, Cambridge CB2 2RU, United Kingdom
40 West 20th Street, New York, NY 10011–4211, USA
10 Stamford Road, Oakleigh, Melbourne 3166, Australia

First published 1983
Eighth printing 1989
Second edition 1991
Eighth printing 1998

Printed in the United Kingdom at the University Press, Cambridge

Library of Congress catalogue card number: 90–28674

British Library cataloguing in publication data
Roach, Peter *1943–*
English phonetics and phonology: a practical course. – 2nd ed.
1. English language. Phonetics
1. Title
421.5

ISBN 0 521 40718 4
ISBN 0 521 40719 2 Set of 2 cassettes
(ISBN 0 521 28252 7 Student's Book first edition)
(ISBN 0 521 28253 5 Tutor's Book first edition)

VN

Contents

Contents

List of symbols used

1. Symbols for phonemes

ɪ	as in 'pit' pɪt	iː	as in 'key' kiː
e	as in 'pet' pet	ɑː	as in 'car' kɑː
æ	as in 'pat' pæt	ɔː	as in 'core' kɔː
ʌ	as in 'putt' pʌt	uː	as in 'coo' kuː
ɒ	as in 'pot' pɒt	ɜː	as in 'cur' kɜː
ʊ	as in 'put' pʊt		

ə   as in 'about, 'upper'
    əbaʊt, ʌpə

eɪ	as in 'bay' beɪ	əʊ	as in 'go' gəʊ
aɪ	as in 'buy' baɪ	aʊ	as in 'cow' kaʊ
ɔɪ	as in 'boy' bɔɪ		

ɪə   as in 'peer' pɪə
eə   as in 'pear' peə
ʊə   as in 'poor' pʊə

p	as in 'pea' piː	b	as in 'bee' biː
t	as in 'toe' təʊ	d	as in 'doe' dəʊ
k	as in 'cap' kæp	g	as in 'gap' gæp
f	as in 'fat' fæt	v	as in 'vat' væt
θ	as in 'thing' θɪŋ	ð	as in 'this' ðɪs
s	as in 'sip' sɪp	z	as in 'zip' zɪp
ʃ	as in 'ship' ʃɪp	ʒ	as in 'measure' meʒə
h	as in 'hat' hæt		
m	as in 'map' mæp	l	as in 'led' led
n	as in 'nap' næp	r	as in 'red' red
ŋ	as in 'hang' hæŋ	j	as in 'yet' jet
		w	as in 'wet' wet
tʃ	as in 'chin' tʃɪn	dʒ	as in 'gin' dʒɪn

2. *Non-phonemic symbols*

i   as in 'react', 'happy' riækt, hæpi

u   as in 'to each' tu iːtʃ

ʔ   glottal stop

ʰ   aspiration, as in 'pin' pʰɪn

ˌ   syllabic consonant, as in 'button' bʌtn̩

3. *Stress and intonation*

| tone-unit boundary

‖   pause

'   primary stress, as in 'open' 'əʊpən

ˌ   secondary stress, as in 'ice cream' ˌaɪsˈkriːm

Tones: ˎfall

        ˏrise

        ˅fall-rise

        ˄rise-fall

        ˗level

'   stressed syllable in head, high pitch, as in 'please ˎdo

ˌ   stressed syllable in head, low pitch, as in ˌplease ˎdo

·   stressed syllable in tail, as in ˎmy ·turn

↑   extra pitch height, as in ↑ˎmy ·turn

vii

Preface to the second edition

I am very glad to have had the opportunity to make some improvements to *English Phonetics and Phonology*, though since it has become widely used as a course-book I have tried not to make a lot of fundamental changes. Many of the improvements have been made in response to feedback from users around the world. The most obvious change is that there is no longer a separate book for tutors: this book contained most of the information about further reading and alternative approaches, and this information was not sufficiently accessible to student readers. There is now just one book and the "Tutor's Book" information is given in the form of notes at the end of each chapter. In doing this I have left out the general discussion that was in the Tutor's Book about pronunciation teaching methods: I feel that this is a subject that does not really belong in this book, and is better dealt with elsewhere; I have, however, included some specific notes for teachers after most of the chapters. I have also taken the opportunity to include some written exercises at the end of each chapter: these are not meant to give a comprehensive test on the material in the chapter, but to give a little useful practical follow-up. I have not made any changes to the tape exercises.

Of the other changes, some are simply terminological changes and re-phrasing of various points. Many excellent books and papers have appeared since 1983, and reference is made to these. There have been some changes in the practice and terminology of general phonetics (particularly arising out of the Kiel Congress of the International Phonetic Association in 1989 and the subsequent revision of the Association's recommendations), and finally there are places where as a result of discussing and reading my views on some of the issues presented in the first edition have developed in new directions.

I hope that the new edition will continue to serve the needs of newcomers to a subject that can at times be difficult but ought to be enjoyable and interesting most of the time.

Thanks

The material in this course was originally developed over more than ten years, and during that period many people helped me. The first time I actually wrote out a full version was when I was teaching (on leave from Reading University) in the Department of English at the University of Seville, Spain, for the academic year 1975–6. For this valuable experience my thanks are chiefly due to Professor Antonio Garnica and to Reading University, but I would also like to thank the staff of the Seville Department of English and the British Council in Madrid for their assistance.

I am extremely glad that Cambridge University Press arranged for this course to be tested before publication in a number of institutions around the world concerned with English language teaching at an advanced level. The trials have resulted in a large amount of valuable comments and suggestions based on practical experience, and I am very grateful to the testers for the work they devoted to this task. I must make special mention of three testers. Dr Roger Bowers, of The British Council, wrote a detailed and penetrating critique of the course that was enormously valuable; however, his connection with the course goes back further than that, as he gave me encouragement, material and ideas when we were colleagues in the Department of Linguistic Science at Reading University. It has been useful to me to have the critical comments of Professor Garnica of Seville, whose role in the early development of the course was mentioned above and who tested it in its later form. I am also very glad that a colleague at Leeds University, David Taylor of the Overseas Education Unit, was able to try the course out with a group of overseas teachers of English. I would like to thank all the other testers: The British Council in Athens and in Naples, The University of Strasbourg, The University of Sussex (School of European Studies) and The Cultura Inglesa, São Paulo.

I have received a lot of help and encouragement from colleagues at Reading University and at Leeds University, where I owe a particular debt to Marion Shirt for her detailed reading of two drafts of the course. I am also grateful to all the students I have taught, both on degree courses and on Summer Schools; I have learned a lot from them.

The cassettes that accompany the course include material provided by Tony Fox, Patrick Leach, Doreen Lucas and David Maguire. I am very grateful to Eric Brearley for making the recordings and to my wife

Helen, who has helped me in so many ways in addition to being the "other voice" on the cassettes.

I would like to acknowledge some of the help I have had in preparing this second edition. Joanne Kenworthy of the Polytechnic of East London has given me invaluable advice, and I would like to thank her particularly. I have had many useful comments on the first edition from Tom Baldwin, Caroline Henton, Jack Windsor Lewis and Linda Taylor, and helpful discussion on a number of points with Bill Hardcastle, Peter Ladefoged, John Laver, Celia Scully and John Wells. I have been glad to have the advice of Annemarie Young of Cambridge University Press on many occasions during the preparation of this edition. I wish I could thank individually all the other people who have written or spoken to me about the book and given me ideas for improving it. Finally, I am grateful as before to my wife (and friend and colleague) Helen for all she has done for me.

How to use this book

The first thing to remember about this book is that it is intended to be a *course*. It is designed to be read from beginning to end, and is therefore different from a reference book. Most readers of the book are expected either to be studying in a college or university, or to be practising English language teachers. The readers can be divided into groups as follows:

Firstly, they will be either a) students using the course under the direction of a tutor in charge of their course, or b) working through the course as individuals.

Secondly, they will be either i) native speakers of a language other than English, or ii) native speakers of English.

Finally, they will be either 1) teachers of English (or being trained to be such), or 2) students of English or linguistics and phonetics.

The course is intended to be used by all of these groups (if you multiply them together you get eight categories, and you should be able to place yourself in one of them); most of the material in the course has at some time or other been used by people of all eight categories, but it is necessary to use the course differently in these different circumstances.

Each chapter is followed by short additional sections, which you may choose not to use. Firstly, there is a section of notes on problems and further reading: this tells you how you can go further in studying the areas discussed in the chapter. Secondly, where relevant, there are brief notes for teachers about pronunciation teaching and the use of the taped practice material. Finally, there are some written exercises which test your understanding of the material in the chapter. Answers to the questions are given near the end of the book (pp. 229–39).

The course includes *cassettes* containing practical exercise material; there are 19 Tape Units which correspond to Chapters 2–20 of this book. When there is a relevant exercise on the cassettes, the symbol ⊑▭⊐ is placed in the margin with a reference to the exercise, e.g. ⊑▭⊐ TU1, Ex 1 indicates Tape Unit 1, Exercise 1. If you are in category (i) (a non-native speaker of English), every Tape Unit ought to be relevant to you, though the relevance of any particular exercise will depend on your particular native language. If you are in category (ii), only some of the exercises will be relevant: those on intonation are the most likely to be worth studying. If possible the cassettes should be used in a language laboratory, where a tutor can correct mistakes for you and where you can record your voice in exercises where you have to speak, but they are still of value when used on an ordinary cassette recorder.

The way in which this book is designed to be used by readers in category (a) is the following:

i) All the students in a class read a chapter of this book.

ii) The students then have a class with the tutor in charge of this part of their course. This provides an opportunity to discuss the material in the chapter, and for the tutor to check if difficult points have been understood, to provide additional explanation and examples if necessary and possibly to recommend further reading.

iii) If the students are not native speakers of English it is expected that they will then have a session working on the Tape Unit corresponding to the chapter they have read and discussed.

iv) The group then goes on to the next chapter.

If you are working through the course individually you will of course arrange your own way of proceeding; the only important point here is that it would not be advisable to use the Tape Units without first reading the relevant chapters in the book.

The book begins with an Introduction, and there is no Tape Unit corresponding to this. Please read the Introduction, whatever category you come into, since it explains the purpose of the course and presents a number of basic points that are important for understanding the material that follows.

1 Introduction

You probably want to know what the purpose of this course is, and what you can expect to learn from it. An important purpose of the course is to explain how English is pronounced in the accent normally chosen as the standard for people learning the English spoken in England. If this was the only thing the course did, a more suitable title would have been "English Pronunciation". However, at the comparatively advanced level at which this course is aimed it is usual to present this information in the context of a general theory about speech sounds and how they are used in language; this theoretical context is called **phonetics and phonology**. Why is it necessary to learn this theoretical background? The same question arises in connection with grammar: at lower levels of study one is concerned simply with setting out how to form grammatical sentences, but people who are going to work with the language at an advanced level as teachers or researchers need the deeper understanding provided by the study of grammatical theory and related areas of linguistics. The theoretical material in the present course is necessary for anyone who needs to understand the principles regulating the use of sounds in spoken English.

The nature of phonetics and phonology will be explained as the course progresses, but one or two basic ideas need to be introduced at this introductory stage. In any language we can identify a small number of regularly used sounds (vowels and consonants) that we call **phonemes**; for example, the vowels in the words 'pin' and 'pen' are different phonemes, and so are the consonants at the beginning of the words 'pet' and 'bet'. Because of the notoriously confusing nature of English spelling it is particularly important to learn to think of English pronunciation in terms of phonemes rather than letters of the alphabet; one must be aware, for example, that the word 'enough' begins with the same vowel phoneme as that at the beginning of 'inept' and ends with the same consonant as 'stuff'. We often use special **symbols** to represent speech sounds; using the symbols chosen for this course, the word 'enough' would be written (**transcribed**) as ɪnʌf. A list of the symbols is given on p. ix.

The first part of the course is mainly concerned with identifying and describing the phonemes of English. Chapters 2 and 3 deal with vowels and Chapter 4 with some consonants. After this preliminary contact with the practical business of how some English sounds are pronounced, the fifth chapter looks at the phoneme and at the use of symbols in a theoretical way, while the corresponding Tape Unit revises the material of Chapters 2–4. After the phonemes of English have been introduced, the rest of the course goes on to look at larger units of speech such as the syllable and at aspects of speech such as **stress** (which could be roughly described as the relative strength of a syllable) and **intonation** (the use of the pitch of the voice to convey meaning). It would be a mistake to think that phonemes are studied first because they are the most important aspect of speech; the reason is simply that, in my experience, courses which begin with matters such as stress and intonation and deal with phonemes later are found more confusing by the students who use them.

You will have to learn a number of technical terms; you will find that when they are introduced in order to be defined or explained, they are printed in **bold type**. This has already been done in this Introduction in the case of, for example, **phoneme, phonetics** and **phonology**. Another convention to remember is that when words used as examples are given in spelling form, they are enclosed in single quotes (see for example 'pin', 'pen', etc.). Double quote marks are used where quote marks would normally be used; see, for example, "English Pronunciation" above.

Languages have different **accents**: they are pronounced differently by people from different geographical places, from different social classes, of different ages and different educational backgrounds. The word "accent" is often confused with **dialect**. We use the word "dialect" to refer to a variety of a language which is different from others not just in pronunciation but also in such matters as vocabulary, grammar and word-order. Differences of accent, on the other hand, are pronunciation differences only.

This course is not written for people who wish to study American pronunciation. The accent that we concentrate on and use as our **model** is the one that is most often recommended for foreign learners studying British English. It is most familiar as the accent used by most announcers and newsreaders on serious national and international BBC broadcasting channels. It has for a long time been identified by the rather quaint name **Received Pronunciation** (usually abbreviated to its initials, **RP**). The pronunciation of English in America is different from most accents found in Britain. There are exceptions to this – you can find accents in parts of Britain that sound American, and accents in America that sound English. But the pronunciation that you are likely to hear from most Americans does sound noticeably different from RP.

In talking about accents of English, the foreigner should be careful about the difference between **England** and **Britain**; there are many different accents in England, but the range becomes very much wider if the accents of Scotland, Wales and Northern Ireland (Scotland and

Wales are included in Britain and with Northern Ireland form the **United Kingdom**) are taken into account. Within the accents of England, the distinction that is most frequently made by the majority of English people is between **Northern** and **Southern**. This is a very rough division, and there can be endless argument over where the boundaries lie, but most people on hearing a pronunciation typical of someone from Lancashire, Yorkshire or other counties further north would identify it as "Northern". This course deals almost entirely with RP. There is, of course, no implication that other accents are inferior or less pleasant-sounding; the reason is simply that RP is the accent that has always been chosen by British teachers to teach to foreign learners, and is the accent that has been most fully described and has been used as the basis for textbooks and pronouncing dictionaries.

If you are a native speaker of English and your accent is different from RP you should try, as you work through the course, to note what your main differences are for purposes of comparison. I am not, of course, suggesting that you should try to change your pronunciation to RP! If you are a learner of English you are recommended to concentrate on RP initially, though when you have worked through the course and become familiar with this you will probably find it an interesting exercise to listen analytically to other accents of English, to see if you can identify the ways in which they differ from RP and even to learn to pronounce some examples of different accents yourself.

Notes on problems and further reading

I feel that if we had a completely free choice of model accent it would be possible to find more suitable ones: many Scottish and Irish accents, for example, have a much more straightforward relationship between spelling and sounds than does RP, and have simpler vowel systems, and would therefore be easier for most foreign learners to acquire. Unfortunately, the majority of English teachers would be reluctant to learn to speak in the classroom with such an accent, so this is not a practical possibility.

For introductory reading on English pronunciation, see O'Connor (1980), pp. 5–6; Brown (1990), pp. 12–13; Gimson (1989), pp. 83–8. For a discussion of the status of RP, see Abercrombie (1965). For those who want to know more about British accents, a simple introduction is Hughes and Trudgill (1987); undoubtedly the major work on all accents of English is Wells (1982), which is a very valuable source of information (see especially pp. 117–18 and 279–301 on RP). A recent book that has caused a certain amount of controversy is Honey (1989), which discusses the importance of accents (and RP in particular) in education, politics and social life. I disagree with many of the views expressed, but the book is interesting to read.

A problem area that has received a lot of attention is the choice of symbols for representing English phonemes. In the past, many different conventions have been proposed and students have often been confused by finding that the symbols used in one book are different from the ones they have learned in another. The symbols used in this book are in almost every respect those devised by A. C. Gimson for the *English Pronouncing Dictionary* (14th edition) and used in his *Introduction to the Pronunciation of English* (1989). These symbols are now used in most modern works on English pronunciation published in Britain, and can therefore be looked on as a *de facto* standard. Although good arguments can be made for some alternative symbols, the advantages of having a common set of symbols for pronunciation teaching materials and pronunciation entries in dictionaries are so great that it would be very regrettable to go back to the confusing diversity of earlier years.

The subject of symbolization is returned to in Chapter 5, section 5.2.

Notes for teachers

Pronunciation teaching is not popular all the time with teachers and language-teaching theorists, and in recent years it has been fashionable to treat it as a rather outdated activity. It has been claimed, for example, that it attempts to make learners try to sound like native speakers of RP, that it discourages them through difficult and repetitive exercises and that it fails to give importance to **communication**. A good example of this attitude is to be found in Brown and Yule (1983), pp. 26–7. The criticism is misguided, I believe. No pronunciation course that I know has ever said that learners must try to speak perfect RP; to claim this mixes up **models** with **goals**: the *model* chosen is RP, but the *goal* is normally to develop the learner's pronunciation sufficiently to permit effective communication with native speakers. Pronunciation exercises can be difficult, of course, but if we eliminate everything difficult from our teaching, we may end up doing very little beyond getting students to play little communication games. It is, incidentally, quite incorrect to suggest that the classic works on pronunciation and phonetics teaching concentrated on mechanically perfecting vowels and consonants: Jones (1956), for example, writes " 'Good' speech may be defined as a way of speaking which is clearly intelligible to all ordinary people. 'Bad' speech is a way of talking which is difficult for most people to understand ... A person may speak with sounds very different from those of his hearers and yet be clearly intelligible to all of them, as for instance when a Scotsman or an American addresses an English audience with clear articulation. Their speech cannot be described as other than 'good'."

There are many different and well-tried methods of teaching and testing pronunciation, many of which are used in this book. I do not feel that it is suitable in this book to go into a detailed analysis of these methods, but there is an excellent treatment of the subject in Kenworthy (1987). Gimson (1989) also discusses pronunciation teaching (chapter 12), and Brown and Yule (1983) contains some interesting ideas.

2 The production of speech sounds

2.1 Articulators above the larynx

All the sounds we make when we speak are the result of muscles contracting. The muscles in the chest that we use for breathing produce the flow of air that is needed for almost all speech sounds; muscles in the larynx produce many different modifications in the flow of air from the chest to the mouth. After passing through the larynx, the air goes through what we call the **vocal tract**, which ends at the mouth and nostrils. Here the air from the lungs escapes into the atmosphere. We have a large and complex set of muscles that can produce changes in the shape of the vocal tract, and in order to learn how the sounds of speech are produced it is necessary to become familiar with the different parts of the vocal tract. These different parts are called **articulators**, and the study of them is called **articulatory phonetics**.

Fig. 1 is a diagram that is used frequently in the study of phonetics. It represents the human head, seen from the side, displayed as though it had been cut in half. You will need to look at it carefully as the articulators are described, and you will often find it useful to have a mirror and a good light placed so that you can look at the inside of your mouth.

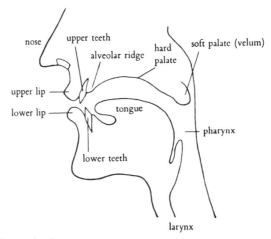

Fig. 1 The articulators

i) The **pharynx** is a tube which begins just above the larynx. It is about 7 cm long in women and about 8 cm in men, and at its top end it is divided into two, one part being the back of the mouth and the other being the beginning of the way through the nasal cavity. If you look in your mirror with your mouth open, you can see the back of the pharynx.

ii) The **velum** or **soft palate** is seen in the diagram in a position that allows air to pass through the nose and through the mouth. Yours is probably in that position now, but often in speech it is raised so that air cannot escape through the nose. The other important thing about the velum is that it is one of the articulators that can be touched by the tongue. When we make the sounds k and g the tongue is in contact with the lower side of the velum, and we call these **velar** consonants.

iii) The **hard palate** is often called the "roof of the mouth". You can feel its smooth curved surface with your tongue.

iv) The **alveolar ridge** is between the top front teeth and the hard palate. You can feel its shape with your tongue. Its surface is really much rougher than it feels, and is covered with little ridges. You can only see these if you have a mirror small enough to go inside your mouth (such as those used by dentists). Sounds made with the tongue touching here (such as t and d) are called **alveolar**.

v) The **tongue** is, of course, a very important articulator and it can be moved into many different places and different shapes. It is usual to divide the tongue into different parts, though there are no clear dividing lines within the tongue. Fig. 2 shows the tongue on a larger scale with these parts shown: **tip**, **blade**, **front**, **back** and **root**. (This use of the word "front" often seems rather strange at first.)

vi) The **teeth** (upper and lower) are usually shown in diagrams like Fig. 1 only at the front of the mouth, immediately behind the lips. This is for the sake of a simple diagram, and you should remember that most speakers have teeth to the sides of their mouths, back almost to the soft palate. The tongue is in contact with the upper side teeth for many speech sounds. Sounds made with the tongue touching the front teeth are called **dental**.

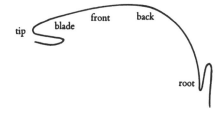

Fig. 2 Sub-divisions of the tongue

vii) The **lips** are important in speech. They can be pressed together (when we produce the sounds p, b), brought into contact with the teeth (as in f, v), or rounded to produce the lip-shape for vowels like uː. Sounds in which the lips are in contact with each other are called **bilabial**, while those with lip-to-teeth contact are called **labiodental**.

The seven articulators described above are the main ones used in speech, but there are three other things to remember. Firstly, the larynx (which will be studied in Chapter 4) could also be described as an articulator – a very complex and independent one. Secondly, the **jaws** are sometimes called articulators; certainly we move the lower jaw a lot in speaking. But the jaws are not articulators in the same way as the others, because they cannot themselves make contact with other articulators. Finally, although there is practically nothing that we can do with the nose and the nasal cavity, they are a very important part of our equipment for making sounds (what is sometimes called our **vocal apparatus**), particularly nasal consonants such as m, n. Again, we cannot really describe the nose and the nasal cavity as articulators in the same sense as (i) to (vii) above.

2.2 **Vowel and consonant**

The words **vowel** and **consonant** are very familiar ones, but when we study the sounds of speech scientifically we find that it is not easy to define exactly what they mean. The most common view is that vowels are sounds in which there is no obstruction to the flow of air as it passes from the larynx to the lips. A doctor who wants to look at the back of a patient's mouth often asks the patient to say "ah"; making this vowel sound is the best way of presenting an unobstructed view. But if we make a sound like s or d it can be clearly felt that we are making it difficult or impossible for the air to pass through the mouth. Most people would have no doubt that sounds like s and d should be called consonants. However, there are many cases where the decision is not so easy to make. One problem is that some English sounds that we think of as consonants, such as the sounds at the beginning of the words 'hay' and 'way', do not really obstruct the flow of air more than some vowels do. Another problem is that different languages have different ways of dividing their sounds into vowel and consonant; for example, the usual sound produced at the beginning of the word 'red' is felt to be a consonant by most English speakers, but in some other languages (some dialects of Chinese, for example) the same sound is treated as one of the vowels.

If we say that the difference between vowels and consonants is a difference in the way that they are produced, there will inevitably be some cases of uncertainty or disagreement; this is a problem that cannot be avoided. It is possible to establish two distinct groups of sounds (vowels and consonants) in another way. Consider English words beginning with the sound h; what sounds can come next after this h? We find that most of the sounds we normally think of as vowels can follow (for example e in the word 'hen'), but practically none of the sounds we class as consonants. Now think of English words beginning with the two sounds bɪ; we find many cases where a consonant can follow (for example d in the word 'bid', or l in the word 'bill'), but hardly any cases where a vowel may follow. What we are doing here is looking at the different contexts and positions in which particular sounds can occur; this is the study of the **distribution** of the sounds, and is of great importance in phonology. Study of the sounds found at the beginning and end of English words has shown that two groups of sounds with quite different patterns of distribution can be identified, and these two groups are those of vowel and consonant. If we look at the vowel–consonant distinction in this way, we must say that the most important difference between vowel and consonant is not the way that they are made, but their different distributions. Of course, the distribution of vowels and consonants is different for each language.

There are many interesting theoretical problems connected with the vowel–consonant distinction, but we will not return to this question. For the rest of this course it will be assumed that the sounds are clearly divided into vowels and consonants.

We begin the study of English sounds in this course by looking at vowels, and it is necessary to say something about vowels in general before turning to the vowels of English. We need to know in what ways vowels differ from each other. The first matter to consider is the shape and position of the tongue. It is usual to simplify the very complex possibilities by describing just two things: firstly, the vertical distance between the upper surface of the tongue and the palate, and secondly the part of the tongue, between front and back, which is raised highest. Let us look at some examples:

i) Make a vowel like the iː in the English word 'see' and look in a mirror; if you tilt your head back slightly you will be able to see that the tongue is held up close to the roof of the mouth. Now make an æ vowel (as in the word 'cat') and notice how the distance between the surface of the tongue and the roof of the mouth is now much greater. The difference between iː and æ is a difference of **tongue height**, and we would describe iː as a relatively **close** vowel and æ as a relatively **open** vowel. Tongue height can be changed by moving the tongue up or down, or moving the lower jaw up or down. Usually we use some combination of the two sorts of movement, but when drawing side-of-the-head diagrams such as Fig. 1 and Fig. 2 it is usually found simpler to illustrate tongue shapes for vowels as if tongue height was altered by tongue movement alone, without any accompanying jaw movement. So we would illustrate the tongue height difference between iː and æ as in Fig. 3.

ii) In making the two vowels described above, it is the front part of the tongue that is raised. We could therefore describe iː and æ as comparatively **front** vowels. By changing the shape of the tongue we can produce vowels in which a different part of the tongue is the highest point. A vowel in which the back of the tongue is the highest point is called a **back** vowel. If you make the vowel in the word 'calm', which we write phonetically as ɑː, you can see that the back of the tongue is raised. Compare this with æ in front of a mirror; æ is a front vowel and ɑː is a back vowel. The vowel in 'too' (uː) is also a comparatively back vowel, but compared with ɑː it is close.

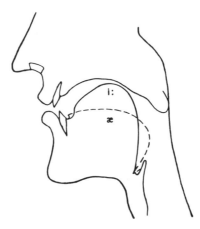

Fig. 3 Tongue positions for iː and æ

So now we have seen how four vowels differ from each other; we could show this in a simple diagram (Fig. 4). However, this diagram is rather inaccurate. Phoneticians need a very accurate way of classifying vowels, and have developed a set of vowels, arranged in a close–open, front–back diagram like Fig. 4, which are not the vowels of any

	Front	Back
Close	iː	uː
Open	æ	ɑː

Fig. 4 Extreme vowel positions

particular language. These **cardinal vowels** are a standard reference system, and people being trained in phonetics have to learn to make them accurately and recognise them correctly. If you learn the cardinal vowels, you are not learning to make English sounds, but you *are* learning about the range of vowels that the human vocal apparatus can make, and also learning a useful way of describing, classifying and comparing vowels. They are recorded at the end of Cassette 2.

It has become traditional to locate cardinal vowels on a four-sided figure (quadrilateral) of the shape seen in Fig. 5 (the design used here is the one recommended by the International Phonetic Association in 1989). The exact shape is not really important – a square would do quite well – but we will use the traditional shape. The vowels on Fig. 5 are the so-called **primary** cardinal vowels; these are the vowels that are most familiar to the speakers of most European languages, and there are other cardinal vowels (**secondary cardinal vowels**) that sound less

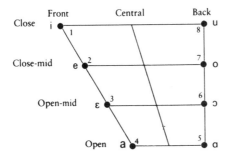

Fig. 5 Primary cardinal vowels

familiar. Cardinal vowel no. 1 has the symbol [i], and is defined as the vowel which is as close and as front as it is possible to make a vowel without obstructing the flow of air enough to produce friction noise; friction noise is the sort of hissing sound that one hears in consonants like s or f. Cardinal vowel no. 5 has the symbol [ɑ] and is defined as the most open and back vowel that it is possible to make. Cardinal vowel no. 8 [u], is fully close and back and no. 4 [a], is fully open and front. After establishing these extreme points, it is possible to put in intermediate points (vowels no. 2, 3, 6 and 7). Many students when they hear these vowels find that they sound strange and exaggerated; you must remember that they are *extremes* of vowel quality. It is useful to think of the cardinal vowel framework like a map of an area of country that you are interested in. Obviously, if the map is to be useful to you it must cover all the area; but if it covers the whole area of interest it must inevitably go a little way beyond that and include some places that you might never want to go to. However, it is still important to know where the edges of the map are drawn. When you are familiar with these extreme vowels, you have (as mentioned above) learned a way of describing, classifying and comparing vowels. For example, we can say that the English vowel æ (the vowel in 'cat') is not as open as cardinal vowel no. 4 [a]. (In this course cardinal vowels will always be printed within square brackets to distinguish them clearly from English vowel sounds.)

We have now looked at how we can classify vowels according to their tongue height and their frontness or backness. There is another important variable of vowel quality and that is **lip-rounding**. Although the lips can have many different shapes and positions, we will at this stage consider only three possibilities. These are:

i) **Rounded**, where the corners of the lips are brought towards each other and the lips pushed forwards. This is most clearly seen in cardinal vowel no. 8 [u].

ii) **Spread**, with the corners of the lips moved away from each other, as for a smile. This is most clearly seen in cardinal vowel no. 1 [i].

iii) **Neutral**, where the lips are not noticeably rounded or spread. The noise most English people make when they are hesitating (written 'er') has neutral lip position.

Now, using the principles that have just been explained, we will examine some of the English vowels.

2.3 **English short vowels**

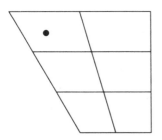

TU 2,
Exs 1–4

English has a large number of vowel sounds; the first ones to be examined are short vowels. The symbols for these short vowels are: ɪ, e, æ, ʌ, ɒ, ʊ. Short vowels are only *relatively* short; as we shall see later, vowels can have quite different lengths in different contexts.

Each vowel is described in relation to the cardinal vowels.

ɪ (example words: 'bit', 'pin', 'fish') The diagram shows that, though this vowel is in the close front area, compared with cardinal vowel no. 1 [i] it is more open, and nearer in to the centre. The lips are slightly spread.

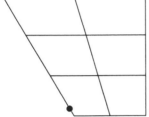

e   (example words: 'bet', 'men', 'yes')
This is a front vowel between cardinal vowel no. 2 [e] and no. 3 [ɛ]. The lips are slightly spread.

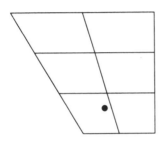

æ   (example words: 'bat', 'man', 'gas')
This vowel is front, but not quite as open as cardinal vowel no. 4 [a]. The lips are slightly spread.

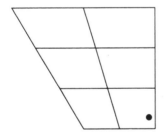

ʌ   (example words: 'but', 'some', 'rush')
This is a central vowel, and the diagram shows that it is more open than the open-mid tongue height. The lip position is neutral.

o   (example words: 'pot', 'gone', 'cross')
This vowel is not quite fully back, and between open-mid and open in tongue height. The lips are slightly rounded.

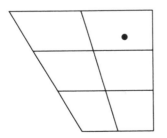

ʊ   (example words: 'put', 'pull', 'push')
The nearest cardinal vowel is no. 8 [u], but it can be seen that ʊ is more open and nearer to central. The lips are rounded.

There is one other short vowel, for which the symbol is ə. This central vowel, which is called **schwa**, is a very familiar sound in English; it is heard in the first syllable of the words 'about', 'oppose', 'perhaps', for example. Since it is different from the other vowels in several important ways, we will study it separately in Chapter 9.

Notes on problems and further reading

One of the most difficult aspects of phonetics at this stage is the large number of technical terms that have to be learned. Every phonetics textbook gives a description of the articulators, and I will not attempt to list all of them. Two useful introductions are Ladefoged (1982), chapter 1, and O'Connor (1973), chapter 2. I would recommend Hardcastle (1976), chapter 5, to anyone wishing to go into a more detailed study of this subject.

The best-known discussion of the vowel–consonant distinction is by Pike (1943), pp. 66–79. He suggests that since the two approaches to the distinction produce such different results we should use new terms: sounds which do not obstruct the airflow (traditionally called "vowels") should be called *vocoids*, and sounds which do obstruct the airflow (traditionally called "consonants") should be called *contoids*. This leaves the terms "vowel" and "consonant" for use in labelling phonological elements according to their distribution and their role in syllable structure. While vowels are usually vocoids and consonants are usually contoids, this is not always the case: for example, j in 'yet' and w in 'wet' are (phonetically) vocoids but function (phonologically) as consonants.

A study of the distributional differences between vowels and consonants in English is described in O'Connor and Trim (1953); a briefer treatment is in Gimson (1989), pp. 29–31 and 54–5.

The classification of vowels has a large literature. I would recommend Jones (1975), chapter 8, Ladefoged (1982), pp. 11–14 and Abercrombie (1967), pp. 55–60 and chapter 10. Ladefoged, in a series of studies, has examined experimentally most of the fundamental principles of vowel classification and his findings are summarised in Ladefoged (1967), pp. 50–142. The International Phonetic Association has recently revised its vowel classification system: see *Journal of the International Phonetic Association*, vol. 19, no. 2 (1989). It is much easier to understand the Cardinal Vowel system if you can hear the vowels themselves. I have included a recording of my pronunciation of the eight "Primary Cardinal Vowels" on Cassette 2, after the end of Tape Unit 20; it is not a good idea to mix up the study of these vowels with practice on English vowels. In a more thorough presentation of the vowels I would have avoided using the notion of "Primary" vowels, since what makes them primary is to a large extent the fact that they are particularly familiar to speakers of the European languages that have been dominant in the development of contemporary phonetics, and we should try not to be influenced by such subjective factors. Consequently, at a more advanced level of study it is better to refer to vowels on the Cardinal Vowel quadrilateral simply by their tongue position and lip configuration.

Written exercises

1. On the diagram provided, various articulators are indicated by numbered arrows (a–e). Give the names for the articulators.

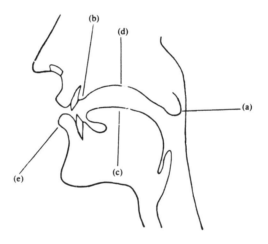

2. Using the descriptive labels introduced for vowel classification, say what the following Cardinal Vowels are:

    a) u   *b)* e   *c)* a   *d)* i   *e)* o

3. Draw a vowel quadrilateral and indicate on it the correct places for the following English vowels:

    a) æ   *b)* ʌ   *c)* ɪ   *d)* e

4. Write the symbols for the vowels in the following words:

    a) bread   *b)* rough   *c)* foot   *d)* hymn
    e) pull   *f)* cough   *g)* mat   *h)* friend

3 Long vowels, diphthongs and triphthongs

3.1 Long and short vowels

In Chapter 2 the short vowels were introduced. In this chapter we look at other types of English vowel sound. The first to be introduced here are the five **long vowels**; these are the vowels which tend to be longer than the short vowels in similar contexts. It is necessary to say "in similar contexts" because, as we shall see later, the length of all English vowel sounds varies very much according to context (such as the type of sound that follows them) and the presence or absence of stress. To remind you that these vowels tend to be long, the symbols consist of one vowel symbol plus a length-mark made of two dots ː. Thus we have: iː, ɜː, ɑː, ɔː, uː. We will now look at these long vowels individually.

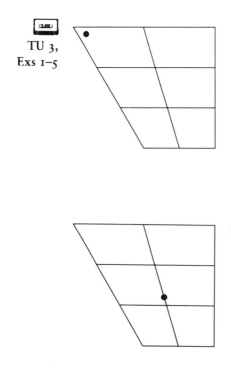

TU 3,
Exs 1–5

iː (example words: 'beat', 'mean', 'peace')
This vowel is nearer to cardinal vowel no. 1 [i] (that is, it is more close and front) than the short ɪ vowel of 'bid', 'pin', 'fish' described in Chapter 2. Although the tongue shape is not much different from cardinal vowel no. 1, the lips are only slightly spread and this results in a rather different vowel quality.

ɜː (example words: 'bird', 'fern', 'purse')
This is a central vowel which is well-known in most English accents as a hesitation sound (spelt 'er'), but which many foreigners find difficult to copy. The lip position is neutral.

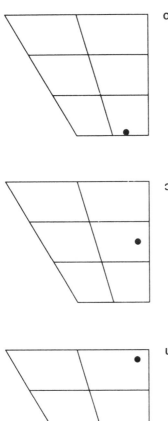

ɑː (example words: 'card', 'half', 'pass')
This is an open vowel in the region of cardinal vowel no. 5 [ɑ], but not as back as this. The lip position is neutral.

ɔː (example words: 'board', 'torn', 'horse')
The tongue height for this vowel is between cardinal vowel no. 6 [ɔ] and no. 7 [o]. This vowel is almost fully back and has quite strong lip-rounding.

uː (example words: 'food', 'soon', 'loose')
This vowel is not very different from cardinal vowel no. 8 [u], but it is not quite so back nor so close, and the lips are only moderately rounded.

You may have noticed that these five long vowels are different from the six short vowels described in Chapter 2 not only in length but also in quality. If we compare some similar pairs of long and short vowels, for example ɪ with iː, or ʊ with uː, or æ with ɑː, we can see distinct differences in quality (resulting from differences in tongue shape and position, and lip position) as well as in length. For this reason, all the long vowels have symbols which are different from those of short vowels; you can perhaps see that the long and short vowel symbols would still all be different from each other even if we omitted the length mark, so it is important to remember that the length mark is used not because it is essential but because it helps learners to remember the length difference. Perhaps the only case where a long and short vowel are closely similar in quality is that of ə and ɜː; but ə is a special case, as we shall see later.

3.2 **Diphthongs**

TU 3,
Exs 6 & 7

RP has a large number of **diphthongs**, sounds which consist of a movement or **glide** from one vowel to another. A vowel which remains constant and does not glide is called a **pure vowel**, and one of the most common pronunciation mistakes that result in a learner of English having a "foreign" accent is the production of pure vowels where a diphthong should be pronounced.

In terms of length, diphthongs are like the long vowels described above. Perhaps the most important thing to remember about all the diphthongs is that the first part is much longer and stronger than the second part; for example, most of the diphthong aɪ (as in the words 'eye', 'I') consists of the a vowel, and only in about the last quarter of the diphthong does the glide to ɪ become noticeable. As the glide to ɪ happens, the loudness of the sound decreases. As a result, the ɪ part is shorter and quieter. Foreign learners must, therefore, always remember that the last part of English diphthongs must not be made too strongly.

The total number of diphthongs is eight. The easiest way to remember them is in terms of three groups divided as in this diagram:

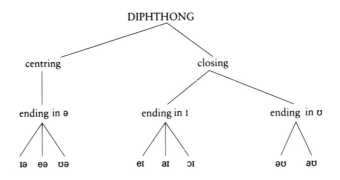

The **centring** diphthongs glide towards the ə (schwa) vowel, as the symbols indicate.

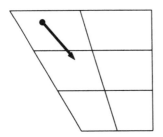

ɪə   (example words: 'beard', 'Ian', 'fierce')
The starting point is a little closer than ɪ in 'bit', 'bin'.

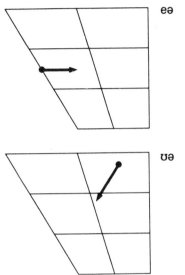

eə (example words: 'aired', 'cairn', 'scarce')
This diphthong begins with the same vowel sound as the e of 'get', 'men'.

ʊə (example words: 'moored', 'tour')
This has a starting point slightly closer than ʊ in 'put', 'pull'.

The **closing** diphthongs have the characteristic that they all end with a glide towards a closer vowel. Because the second part of the diphthong is weak, they often do not reach a position that could be called close. The important thing is that a glide from a relatively more open towards a relatively more close vowel is produced.

Three of the diphthongs glide towards ɪ, as described below:

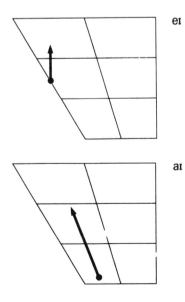

eɪ (example words: 'paid', 'pain', 'face')
The starting point is the same as the e of 'get', 'men'.

aɪ (example words: 'tide', 'time', 'nice')
This diphthong begins with an open vowel which is between front and back; it is quite similar to the ʌ of the words 'cut', 'bun'.

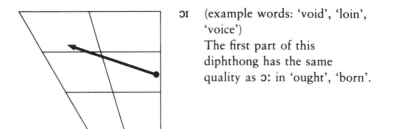

ɔɪ (example words: 'void', 'loin', 'voice')
The first part of this diphthong has the same quality as ɔː in 'ought', 'born'.

Two diphthongs glide towards ʊ, so that as the tongue moves closer to the roof of the mouth there is at the same time a rounding movement of the lips. This movement is not a large one, again because the second part of the diphthong is weak.

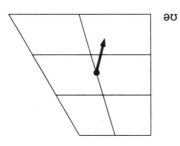

əʊ (example words: 'load', 'home', 'most')
The vowel position for the beginning of this is the same as for the "schwa" vowel ə, as found in the first syllable of the word 'about'. The lips may be slightly rounded in anticipation of the glide towards ʊ, for which there is quite noticeable lip-rounding.

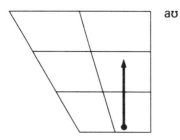

aʊ (example words: 'loud', 'gown', 'house')
This diphthong begins with a vowel similar to ɑː but a little more front. Since this is an open vowel, a glide to ʊ would necessitate a large movement. Usually in English the glide towards ʊ begins but is not completed, the end of the diphthong being somewhere between close-mid and open-mid in tongue height. There is only slight lip-rounding.

3.3 Triphthongs

TU 3,
Ex 8

The most complex English sounds of the vowel type are the **triphthongs**. They can be rather difficult to pronounce, and very difficult to recognise. A triphthong is a glide from one vowel to another and then to a third, all produced rapidly and without interruption. For example, a careful pronunciation of the word 'hour' begins with a vowel quality similar to ɑː, goes on to a glide towards the back close rounded area (for which we use the symbol ʊ), then ends with a mid-central vowel (schwa, ə). We use the symbols aʊə to represent the way we pronounce 'hour', but this is not always an accurate representation of the pronunciation.

The triphthongs can be looked on as being composed of the five closing diphthongs described in the last section, with ə added on the end. Thus we get:

$$eɪ + ə = eɪə \qquad əʊ + ə = əʊə$$
$$aɪ + ə = aɪə \qquad aʊ + ə = aʊə$$
$$ɔɪ + ə = ɔɪə$$

The principal cause of difficulty for the foreign learner is that in present-day English the extent of the vowel movement is very small, except in very careful pronunciation. Because of this, the middle of the three vowel qualities of the triphthong (that is, the ɪ or ʊ part) can hardly be heard and the resulting sound is difficult to distinguish from some of the diphthongs and long vowels.

We will not go through a detailed description of each triphthong. This is partly because there is so much variation in the amount of vowel movement according to how slow and careful the pronunciation is, and also because the "careful" pronunciation can be found by looking at the description of the corresponding diphthong and adding ə to the end. However, to help identify these triphthongs, some example words are given below:

eɪə 'layer', 'player'   əʊə 'lower', 'mower'
aɪə 'liar', 'fire'   aʊə 'power', 'hour'
ɔɪə 'loyal', 'royal'

Notes on problems and further reading

Long vowels and diphthongs can be seen as a group of vowel sounds that are consistently longer *in a given context* than the short vowels

23

described in the previous chapter. Some writers (particularly Americans) give the label **tense** to long vowels and diphthongs and **lax** to the short vowels. This is done (and explained) in Jakobson and Halle (1964), Chomsky and Halle (1968) and many others.

As I mentioned in the notes on Chapter 1, the choice of symbols has tended to vary from book to book, and this is particularly noticeable in the case of length-marks for long vowels (this issue comes up again in Chapter 5, section 5.2); you could read Gimson (1989), section 4; two works which are opposed to length-marks are Brown (1990) and Windsor Lewis (1975b), but at the present time the transcription with length-marks seems to be an agreed standard.

The phonemes iː and uː are usually classed as long vowels; it is worth noting that most English speakers pronounce them with something of a diphthongal glide, so that a possible alternative transcription could be ɪi and ʊu respectively. This is not normally proposed, however.

It seems that triphthongs in RP are in a rather unstable state, resulting in the loss of some distinctions: in the case of some speakers, for example, it is not easy to distinguish between 'tyre' taɪə, 'tower' taʊə and 'tar' tɑː. BBC newsreaders often pronounce 'Ireland' as ɑːlənd, particularly in the context 'Northern Ireland'. Gimson (1964) has suggested that a change in the phonemic system of RP is in progress in this area.

Notes for teachers

I mention above that iː and uː are often pronounced as slightly diphthongal: although this glide is often noticeable, I have never found it helpful to try to teach foreign learners to pronounce iː and uː in this way. Foreign learners who wish to get close to the RP model should be careful not to pronounce the "r" that is usually found in the spelling corresponding to ɑː, ɔː and ɜː ('ar', 'or', 'er').

Most of the essential pronunciation features of the diphthongs are described in Chapter 3. Two additional points are worth making, I feel. The diphthong ʊə is included, but this is not used as much as the others – many English speakers use ɔː in words like 'moor', 'mourn', 'tour'. However, I feel that it is preferable for foreign learners to learn this diphthong to ensure the maximum distinctiveness of words in pairs like 'moor' and 'more', 'poor' and 'paw'. The other diphthong that requires comment is əʊ. English speakers seem to be especially sensitive to the quality of this diphthong, particularly to the first part. It often happens that foreign learners, having understood that the first part of the diphthong is not a back vowel, exaggerate this by using a vowel that is too front, producing a diphthong like [eʊ]; unfortunately, this gives the impression of a "posh" accent – it sounds like someone trying to copy an upper-class pronunciation, since [eʊ] for əʊ is very noticeable in the speech of the Royal Family.

Written exercises

1. On the vowel diagram given below, indicate the glides for the diphthongs in the following words:

    a) fright   c) clear

    b) home   d) cow

2. Write the symbols for the long vowels in the following words:

    a) broad   d) learn   g) err

    b) ward   e) cool   h) seal

    c) calf   f) team   i) curl

3. Write the symbols for the diphthongs in the following words:

    a) tone   d) way   g) hair

    b) style   e) beer   h) why

    c) out   f) coil   i) they

4 Voicing and consonants

4.1 The larynx

We begin this chapter by studying the **larynx**. The larynx has several very important functions in speech, but before we can look at these functions we must examine its anatomy and physiology, that is, how it is constructed and how it works.

The larynx is in the neck; it has several parts, shown in Fig. 6. Its main structure is made of **cartilage**, a material that is similar to bone but less hard. If you press down on your nose, the hard part that you can feel is cartilage. The larynx's structure is made of two large cartilages. These are hollow and are attached to the top of the **trachea**; when we breathe, the air passes through the trachea and the larynx. The front of the larynx comes to a point and you can feel this point at the front of your neck – particularly if you are a man and/or slim. This point is commonly called the **Adam's Apple**.

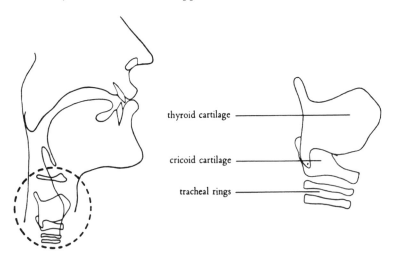

thyroid cartilage

cricoid cartilage

tracheal rings

Fig. 6 The larynx

Inside the "box" made by these two cartilages are the **vocal folds**, two thick flaps of muscle rather like a pair of lips; an older name for these is **vocal cords**. Looking down the throat is difficult to do, and requires special optical equipment, but Fig. 7 shows in diagram form the most important parts. At the front the vocal folds are joined together and fixed to the inside of the thyroid cartilage. At the back they are attached to a pair of small cartilages called the **arytenoid cartilages** so that if the arytenoid cartilages move, the vocal folds will move too.

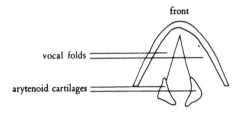

Fig. 7 The inside of the larynx seen from above

The arytenoid cartilages are attached to the top of the cricoid cartilage but they can move so as to move the vocal folds apart or together (Fig. 8). We use the word **glottis** to refer to the opening between the vocal folds. If the vocal folds are apart we say that the glottis is open; if they are pressed together we say that the glottis is closed. This seems quite

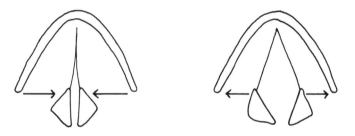

Fig. 8 Arytenoid cartilages causing closing and opening of the glottis

simple, but in fact we can produce a very complex range of changes in the vocal folds and their positions. These changes are often important in speech. Let us first look at four easily recognisable states of the vocal folds; it would be useful to practise moving your vocal folds into these different positions.

i) Wide apart.
   The vocal folds are wide apart for normal breathing and usually during voiceless consonants like p, f, s (Fig. 9a). Your vocal folds are probably apart now.
ii) Narrow glottis.
   If air is passed through the glottis when it is narrowed as in Fig. 9b,

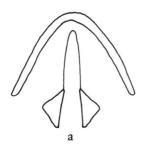
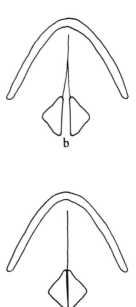
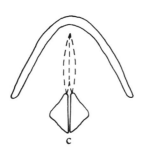

Fig. 9 Four different states of the glottis

the result is a fricative sound for which the symbol is h. The sound is not very different from a whispered vowel. It is called a **voiceless glottal fricative.** (Fricatives are discussed in more detail in Chapter 6.) Practise saying **ahahahahaha** – alternating between this state of the vocal folds and that described in (iii) below.

iii) Position for vocal fold vibration.

When the edges of the vocal folds are touching each other, or nearly touching, air passing through the glottis will usually cause **vibration** (Fig. 9c). Air is pressed up from the lungs and this air pushes the vocal folds apart so that a little air escapes. As the air flows quickly past the edges of the vocal folds, the folds are brought together again. This opening and closing happens very rapidly and is repeated regularly, averaging roughly between two and three hundred times per second in a woman's voice and about half that rate in adult men's.

iv) Vocal folds tightly closed.

The vocal folds can be firmly pressed together so that air cannot pass between them (Fig. 9d). When this happens in speech we call it **a glottal stop** or **glottal plosive,** for which we use the symbol ?. You can practise this by coughing gently; then practise the sequence **aʔ aʔaʔaʔaʔa.**

4.2   **Respiration and voicing**

Section 4.1 referred several times to air passing between the vocal folds. The normal way for this air flow to be produced is for some of the air in the lungs to be pushed out; when air is made to move out of the lungs we say that there is an **egressive pulmonic airstream**. All speech sounds are made with some movement of air, and the egressive pulmonic is by far the most commonly found in the languages of the world. There are other ways of making air move in the vocal tract, but they are not usually relevant in the study of English pronunciation, so we will not discuss them here.

How is air moved into and out of the lungs? It is important to know something about this, since it will make it easier to understand many aspects of speech, particularly the nature of stress and intonation. The lungs are like sponges that can fill with air, and they are contained within the **rib cage** (Fig. 10). If the rib cage is lifted upwards and outwards there is more space in the chest for the lungs and they expand, with the result that they take in more air. If we allow the rib cage to return to its rest position quite slowly, some of the air is expelled and can be used for producing speech sounds. If we wish to make the egressive pulmonic airstream continue without breathing in again (for example when saying a long sentence and not wanting to be interrupted) we can make the rib cage press down on the lungs so that more air is expelled.

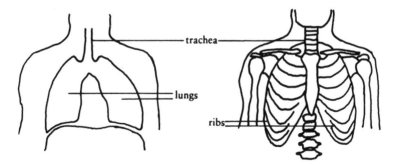

Fig. 10 The lungs and the rib cage

In talking about making air flow into and out of the lungs, the process has been described as though the air was free to pass with no obstruction. But as we saw in Chapter 2, to make speech sounds we must obstruct the air flow in some way – breathing by itself makes very little sound. We obstruct the airflow by making one or more obstructions or **strictures** in the vocal tract, and one place where we can make a stricture is in the larynx, by bringing the vocal folds close to each other as described in the previous section. Remember that there will be no vocal fold vibration unless the vocal folds are in the correct position and the air below the vocal folds is under enough pressure to be forced through the glottis.

If the vocal folds vibrate we will hear the sound that we call **voicing** or **phonation**. There are many different sorts of voicing that we can produce – think of the differences in the quality of your voice between singing, shouting and speaking quietly, or think of the different voices you might use reading a story to young children in which you have to read out what is said by characters such as giants, fairies, mice or ducks; many of the differences are made with the larynx. We can make changes in the vocal folds themselves – they can, for example, be made longer or shorter, more tense or more relaxed or be more or less strongly pressed together. The pressure of the air below the vocal folds (the **subglottal pressure**) can also be varied. Three main differences are found:

i) Variations in **intensity** – we produce voicing with high intensity for shouting, for example, and with low intensity for speaking quietly.

ii) Variations in **frequency** – if the vocal folds vibrate rapidly, the voicing is at high frequency; if there are fewer vibrations per second the frequency is lower.

iii) Variations in **quality** – we can produce different-sounding voice qualities, such as those we might call harsh, breathy, murmured or creaky.

We will consider the ways in which we make use of these variables in later chapters.

4.3 Plosives

A **plosive** is a consonant articulation with the following characteristics:

– One articulator is moved against another, or two articulators are moved against each other, so as to form a stricture that allows no air to escape from the vocal tract. The stricture is, then, total.

– After this stricture has been formed and air has been compressed behind it, it is **released**, that is, air is allowed to escape.

– If the air behind the stricture is still under pressure when the plosive is released, it is probable that the escape of air will produce noise loud enough to be heard. This noise is called **plosion**.

– There may be voicing during part or all of the plosive articulation.

To give a complete description of a plosive consonant we must describe what happens at each of the following four phases in its production:

i) The first phase is when the articulator or articulators move to form the stricture for the plosive. We call this the **closure phase**.
ii) The second phase is when the compressed air is stopped from escaping. We call this the **hold phase**.
iii) The third phase is when the articulators used to form the stricture are moved so as to allow air to escape. This is the **release phase**.
iv) The fourth phase is what happens immediately after (iii), so we will call it the **post-release phase**.

4.4 English plosives

English has six plosive consonants, **p, t, k, b, d, g**. The glottal plosive **ʔ** occurs frequently but it is of less importance, since it is usually just an alternative pronunciation of **p, t** or **k** in certain contexts.

The plosives have different places of articulation. **p** and **b** are bilabial; the lips are pressed together (Fig. 11). **t** and **d** are alveolar; the tongue blade is pressed against the alveolar ridge (Fig. 12). Normally

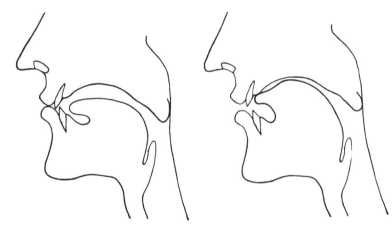

Fig. 11 Bilabial articulation   Fig. 12 Alveolar articulation

the tongue does not touch the front teeth as it does in the dental plosives found in many languages. **k** and **g** are velar; the back of the tongue is pressed against the area where the hard palate ends and the soft palate begins (Fig. 13).

p, t and **k** are always voiceless. **b, d** and **g** are sometimes fully voiced, sometimes partly voiced and sometimes voiceless; we will consider what they should be called in 4.5 below.

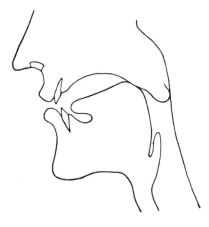

Fig. 13 Velar articulation

All six plosives can occur at the beginning of a word (**initial position**), between other sounds (**medial position**) and at the end of a word (**final position**). To begin with we will look at plosives preceding vowels (CV, where C stands for a consonant and V stands for a vowel), between vowels (VCV) and following vowels (VC). We will look at more complex environments in later chapters.

TU 4,
Ex 1

i)   Initial position (CV)
The closure phase for **p, t, k** and **b, d, g** takes place silently. During the hold phase there is no voicing in **p, t, k**; in **b, d, g** there is normally very little voicing – it begins only just before the release. If the speaker is pronouncing an initial **b, d** or **g** very slowly and carefully there may be voicing during the entire hold phase (the plosive is then **fully voiced**), while in rapid speech there may be no voicing at all.

The release of **p, t, k** is followed by audible plosion, that is, a burst of noise. There is then, in the post-release phase, a period during which air escapes through the vocal folds, making a sound like **h**. This is called **aspiration**. Then the vocal folds come together and voicing begins. The release of **b, d, g** is followed by weak plosion, and this happens at about the same time as, or shortly after, the beginning of voicing. The most noticeable and important difference, then, between initial **p, t, k** and **b, d, g** is the aspiration of the voiceless plosives **p, t, k**. The different phases of the plosive all happen very rapidly, of course, but the ear distinguishes clearly between **p, t, k** and **b, d, g**. If English speakers hear a fully voiced initial plosive they will hear it as one of **b, d, g** but will notice that it does not sound quite natural. If they hear a voiceless unaspirated plosive they will also hear that as one of **b, d, g**, because it is aspiration, not voicing which distinguishes initial p, t, k from b, d, g. Only when they hear a voiceless aspirated plosive will they hear it as one of p, t, k; experiments have shown that we perceive aspiration when there is a delay between the sound of plosion and the beginning (or **onset**) of voicing.

In initial position b, d, g cannot be preceded by any consonant, but p, t, k may be preceded by s. When one of p, t, k is preceded by s it is unaspirated. From what was said above it should be clear that the unaspirated p, t, k of the initial combinations sp, st, sk have the sound quality that makes English speakers perceive a plosive as one of b, d, g; and if a tape recording of a word beginning with one of sp, st, sk is heard with the s removed, an initial b, d or g *is* heard by English speakers.

ii) Medial position (VCV)

The pronunciation of p, t, k and b, d, g in medial position depends to some extent on whether the syllables preceding and following the plosive are stressed. In general we can say that a medial plosive may have the characteristics either of final or of initial plosives.

iii) Final position (VC)

TU 4,
2 & 3

Final b, d, g normally have little voicing; if there is voicing, it is at the beginning of the hold phase. p, t, k are, of course, voiceless. The plosion following the release of p, t, k and b, d, g is very weak and often not audible. The difference between p, t, k and b, d, g is primarily the fact that vowels preceding p, t, k are much shorter. The shortening effect of p, t, k is most noticeable when the vowel is one of the long vowels or diphthongs.

4.5 Fortis and lenis

Are b, d, g voiced plosives? The description of them makes it clear that it is not very accurate to call them "voiced"; in initial and final position they are scarcely voiced at all, and any voicing they may have seems to have no perceptual importance. Some phoneticians say that p, t, k are produced with more force than b, d, g, and that it would therefore be better to give the two sets of plosives (and some other consonants) names that indicate that fact; so the voiceless plosives p, t, k are sometimes called **fortis** (meaning 'strong') and b, d, g are then called **lenis** (meaning 'weak'). It is probably true that p, t, k are produced with more force (though nobody has really proved it – **force of articulation** is very difficult to define and measure). On the other hand, the terms fortis and lenis are difficult to remember. Despite this, we shall follow the practice of many books and use these terms.

The plosive phonemes of English can be presented in the form of a table as shown below:

	PLACE OF ARTICULATION		
	bilabial	alveolar	velar
FORTIS ("voiceless")	p	t	k
LENIS ("voiced")	b	d	g

Tables like this can be produced for all the different consonants. Each major type of consonant (such as plosives like p, t and k, fricatives like s and z and nasals like m and n) obstructs the airflow in a different way, and these are classed as different **manners of articulation**.

Notes on problems and further reading

4.1, 4.2 If you need to know more about the larynx and about respiration in relation to speech, see Borden and Harris (1984), pp. 58–9; Ladefoged (1967), pp. 1–20; Hardcastle (1976), chapters 3 and 4.

4.3 The outline of the stages in the production of plosives is based on Arnold (1967). In classifying consonants it is possible to go to a very high level of complexity if one wishes to account for all the possibilities. See for example Pike (1945), pp. 85–156 and Catford (1968).

4.4 It has been pointed out that the transcription sb, sd, sg could be used quite appropriately instead of sp, st, sk; see Davidsen-Nielsen (1969).

The vowel length difference before final voiceless consonants is apparently found in many (possibly all) languages, but in English this difference, which is very slight in most languages, has become exaggerated so that it has become the most important factor in distinguishing between final p, t, k and b, d, g (see Chen, 1970). Some phonetics books wrongly state that b, d, g lengthen preceding vowels, rather than that p, t, k shorten them. The conclusive evidence on this point is that if we take the pair 'right' raɪt and 'ride' raɪd, and then compare 'rye' raɪ, the length of the aɪ diphthong when no consonant follows is practically the same as in 'ride'; the aɪ in 'right' is much shorter than the aɪ in 'ride' and 'rye'.

4.5 The "fortis/lenis" distinction is a very complicated question. It is necessary to consider how one could measure "force of articulation"; many different laboratory techniques have been tried to see if the articulators are moved more energetically for fortis consonants, but all have proved inconclusive; the only difference that seems reasonably reliable is that fortis consonants have higher air pressure in the vocal tract, but Lisker (1970) has argued convincingly that this is not conclusive evidence for "force of articulation". It is possible to ask phonetically untrained speakers whether they feel more energy is used in pronouncing **p, t, k** than in **b, d, g**, but (as pointed out in Ashby, 1979) there are many difficulties in doing this. A useful review of the "force of articulation" question is in Catford (1977), pp. 199–208. I feel the best conclusion is that any term one uses to deal with this distinction (whether "fortis"/"lenis" or "voiceless"/"voiced") is to be looked on as a **cover term** (similar to the notion of a "cover feature' in Ladefoged, 1965) – a term which has no simple physical meaning but which may stand for a large and complex set of phonetic characteristics.

Written exercises

1. Try to write brief descriptions of the actions of the articulators and the respiratory system in the words given below. Here as an example is a description of the pronunciation of the word 'be' **bi**:

    "Starting from the position for normal breathing, the lips are closed and the lungs are compressed to create air pressure in the vocal tract. The tongue moves to the position for a close front vowel, with the front of the tongue raised close to the palate. The vocal folds are brought close together and voicing begins; the lips then open, releasing the compressed air. Voicing continues for the duration of an i: vowel. Then the lung pressure is lowered, voicing ceases and the articulators return to the normal breathing position."

    Words to describe: (a) goat (b) ape

2. Indicate with a ˘ mark which of the following vowels and diphthongs are shortened as a result of a following fortis consonant:

a)	tea ti:	*d)*	dark **dɑːk**	*g)*	egg **eg**
b)	meat **miːt**	*e)*	card **kɑːd**	*h)*	oak **əʊk**
c)	toad **təʊd**	*f)*	lip **lɪp**	*i)*	kite **kaɪt**

3. Transcribe the following words:

a)	bake	*d)*	bought	*g)*	bored
b)	goat	*e)*	tick	*h)*	guard
c)	doubt	*f)*	bough	*i)*	peak

5 The phoneme

5.1 The phoneme

In Chapters 2–4 we have been studying some of the sounds of English. It is now necessary to consider some fundamental theoretical questions. What do we *mean* when we use the word "sound"? How do we establish what are the sounds of English, and how do we decide how many there are of them?

When we speak, we produce a continuous stream of sounds. In studying speech we divide this stream into small pieces that we call **segments**. The word 'man' is pronounced with a first segment m, a second segment æ and a third segment n. It is not always easy to decide on the number of segments. To give a simple example, in the word 'mine' the first segment is m and the last is n, as in the word 'man' discussed above. But should we regard the aɪ in the middle as one segment or two? We will return to this question.

As well as the question of how we divide speech up into segments, there is the question of how many different sounds (or segment types) there are in English. Chapters 2 and 3 introduced the set of vowels found in English. Each of these can be pronounced in many slightly different ways, so that the total range of sounds actually produced by speakers is practically infinite. Yet we feel quite confident in saying that the number of English vowels is not more than twenty. Why is this? The answer is that if we put one of those twenty in the place of one of the others, we can change the meaning of a word. For example, if we substitute æ for e in the word 'bed' we get a different word: 'bad'. But in the case of two slightly different ways of pronouncing what we regard as "the same sound", we usually find that, if we substitute one for the other, a change in the meaning of a word does not result. For example, if we substitute a more open vowel (cardinal vowel no. 4 [a]) for the æ in the word 'bad', the word is still heard as 'bad'.

The principles involved here may be easier to understand if we look at a similar situation related to the letters of the alphabet that we use in writing English. The letter of the alphabet in writing is a unit which corresponds fairly well to the unit of speech we have been talking about earlier in this chapter – the segment. In the alphabet we have five letters that are called vowels: 'a', 'e', 'i', 'o', 'u'. If we choose the right context we can show how substituting one letter for another will change meaning. Thus with a letter 'p' before and a letter 't' after the vowel letter, we get the five words spelt 'pat', 'pet', 'pit', 'pot', 'put', each of which has a different meaning. We can do the same with sounds. If we look at the short vowels ɪ, e, æ, ʌ, ɒ, ʊ, for example, we can see how substituting one for another in between the plosives p and t gives us six different words as follows (given in spelling on the left):

'pit'   pɪt
'pet'   pet
'pat'   pæt
'putt' pʌt*
'pot'   pɒt
'put'   pʊt

Let us return to the example of letters of the alphabet. If people who knew nothing about the alphabet saw these four characters:

A   a   ɑ   u

they would not know that to users of the alphabet three of these characters all represent the same letter, while the fourth is a different letter. Of course, they would quickly discover, through noticing differences in meaning, that u is a different letter from the first three. What would our illiterate observers discover about these three? They would probably eventually come to the conclusion about the written characters a and ɑ that the former occurs most often in printed and typed writing while the latter is more common in handwriting, but that if you substitute one for the other it will not cause a difference in meaning. If our observers then examined a lot of typed and printed material they would eventually establish that a word that began with a when it occurred in the middle of a sentence would begin with A, and *never* with a, at the beginning of a sentence. They would also find that names could begin with A but *never* with a; they would conclude that A and a were different ways of writing the same letter and that a context in which one of them *could* occur was always a context in which the other could not. As will be explained below, we find similar situations in speech.

If you have not thought about such things before, you may find some difficulty in understanding the ideas that you have just read about. The principal difficulty lies in the fact that what is being talked about in our example of letters is at the same time something *abstract* (the alphabet, which you cannot see or touch) and something *real and concrete* (marks on paper). The alphabet is something that its users *know*; they also

---

* A rather uncommon word, except to those who play golf.

know that it has twenty-six letters. But when the alphabet is used to write with, these letters appear on the page in a practically infinite number of different shapes and sizes.

Now we will leave the discussion of letters and the alphabet; these have only been introduced in this chapter in order to help explain some important general principles. Let us now go back to the sounds of speech and see how these principles can be explained. As was said earlier in this chapter, we can divide speech up into segments, and we can find great variety in the way these segments are made. But just as there is an abstract alphabet as the basis of our writing, so there is an abstract set of units as the basis of our speech. These units are called **phonemes**, and the complete set of these units is called the **phonemic system** of the language. The phonemes themselves are abstract, but there are many slightly different ways in which we make the sounds that represent these phonemes, just as there are many ways in which we may make a mark on a piece of paper to represent a particular (abstract) letter of the alphabet.

We find cases where it makes little difference which of two possible ways we choose to pronounce a sound. For example, the **b** at the beginning of a word such as 'bad' will usually be pronounced with practically no voicing. Sometimes, though, a speaker may produce the **b** with full voicing, perhaps in speaking very emphatically. If this is done, the sound is still identified as the phoneme **b**, even though we can hear that it is different in some way. We have in this example two different ways of making **b** – two different **realisations** of the phoneme. One can be substituted for the other without changing the meaning; the two realisations are said to be in **free variation**.

We also find cases in speech similar to the writing example of capital A and little a (where one can only occur where the other cannot). For example, we find that the realisation of t in the word 'tea' is aspirated (as are all voiceless plosives when they occur before stressed vowels at the beginning of syllables). In the word 'eat', the realisation of t is unaspirated (as are all voiceless plosives when they occur at the end of a syllable and are not followed by a vowel). The aspirated and unaspirated realisations are both recognised as t by English speakers despite their differences. But the aspirated realisation will never be found in the place where the unaspirated realisation is appropriate, and vice versa. When we find this strict separation of places where particular realisations can occur, we say that the realisations are in **complementary distribution**. One more technical term needs to be introduced: when we talk about different realisations of phonemes, we sometimes call these realisations **allophones**. In the last example, we were studying the aspirated and unaspirated allophones of the phoneme t. Usually we do not indicate different allophones when we write symbols to represent sounds.

5.2 Symbols and transcription

You have now seen a number of symbols of several different sorts. Basically the symbols are for one of two purposes: either they are symbols for phonemes (**phonemic** or **phoneme symbols**) or they are **phonetic symbols** (which is what the symbols were first introduced as).

We will look first at phonemic symbols. The most important point to remember is the rather obvious-seeming fact that the number of phonemic symbols must be exactly the same as the number of phonemes we decide exist in the language. It is rather like writing with a typewriter – there is a fixed number of keys that you can press. However, some of our phoneme symbols consist of two characters; for example, we usually treat tʃ (as in 'chip' tʃɪp) as one phoneme, so tʃ is a phoneme *symbol* consisting of two *characters* (t and ʃ).

One of the traditional exercises in pronunciation teaching by phonetic methods is that of **phonemic transcription**, where every speech sound must be identified as one of the phonemes and written with the appropriate symbol. (There are two different kinds of transcription exercise: in one, **transcription from dictation**, the student must listen to a person – or a tape-recording – and write down what they hear; in the other, **transcription from a written text**, the student is given a passage of dialogue written in orthography and must use phonemic symbols to represent how he or she thinks it would be pronounced by a speaker of RP). In a phonemic transcription, then, only the phonemic symbols may be used; this has the advantage that it is comparatively quick and easy to learn to use it. The disadvantage is that as you continue to learn more about phonetics you become able to hear a lot of sound differences that you were not aware of before, and students at this stage find it frustrating not to be able to write down more detailed information.

The phonemic system described for RP contains forty-four phonemes. We can display the complete set of these phonemes by the usual classificatory methods used by most phoneticians; the vowels and diphthongs can be located in the vowel quadrilateral, as was done in Chapters 2 and 3, and the consonants can be placed in a chart or table according to place of articulation, manner of articulation and voicing. Obviously, human beings can make many more sounds than these, and phoneticians use a much larger set of symbols when they are trying to represent sounds more accurately. The best-known set of symbols is that of the International Phonetic Association's alphabet (the letters IPA are used to refer to the Association and also to its alphabet). The vowel symbols of the cardinal vowel system (plus a few others) are usually included on the chart of this alphabet, which is reproduced here (Table 1). It is important to note that in addition to the many symbols

Table 1. The International Phonetic Alphabet (revised to 1989)

CONSONANTS

	Bilabial	Labiodental	Dental	Alveolar	Postalveolar	Retroflex	Palatal	Velar	Uvular	Pharyngeal	Glottal
Plosive	p b			t d		ʈ ɖ	c ɟ	k ɡ	q ɢ		ʔ
Nasal	m	ɱ		n		ɳ	ɲ	ŋ	ɴ		
Trill	ʙ			r					ʀ		
Tap or Flap				ɾ		ɽ					
Fricative	ɸ β	f v	θ ð	s z	ʃ ʒ	ʂ ʐ	ç ʝ	x ɣ	χ ʁ	ħ ʕ	h ɦ
Lateral fricative				ɬ ɮ							
Approximant		ʋ		ɹ		ɻ	j	ɰ			
Lateral approximant				l		ɭ	ʎ	ʟ			
Ejective stop	pʼ			tʼ		ʈʼ	cʼ	kʼ	qʼ		
Implosive	ɓ			ɗ			ʄ	ɠ	ʛ		

Where symbols appear in pairs, the one to the right represents a voiced consonant. Shaded areas denote articulations judged impossible.

DIACRITICS

◌̥	Voiceless	n̥ d̥	◌̹	More rounded	ɔ̹	ʷ Labialized	tʷ dʷ	◌̃ Nasalized	ẽ
◌̬	Voiced	s̬ t̬	◌̜	Less rounded	ɔ̜	ʲ Palatalized	tʲ dʲ	ⁿ Nasal release	dⁿ
ʰ	Aspirated	tʰ dʰ	◌̟	Advanced	u̟	ˠ Velarized	tˠ dˠ	ˡ Lateral release	dˡ
◌̤	Breathy voiced	b̤ a̤	◌̠	Retracted	i̠	ˤ Pharyngealized	tˤ dˤ	◌̚ No audible release	d̚
◌̰	Creaky voiced	b̰ a̰	◌̈	Centralized	ë	~ Velarized or pharyngealized	ɫ		
◌̼	Linguolabial	t̼ d̼	◌̽	Mid-centralized	e̽	◌̝ Raised	e̝ (ɹ̝ = voiced alveolar fricative)		
◌̪	Dental	t̪ d̪	◌̩	Syllabic	n̩	◌̞ Lowered	e̞ (β̞ = voiced bilabial approximant)		
◌̺	Apical	t̺ d̺	◌̯	Non-syllabic	e̯	◌̘ Advanced Tongue Root	e̘		
◌̻	Laminal	t̻ d̻	◌˞	Rhoticity	e˞	◌̙ Retracted Tongue Root	e̙		

VOWELS

Where symbols appear in pairs, the one to the right represents a rounded vowel.

OTHER SYMBOLS

ʍ Voiceless labial-velar fricative	ʘ Bilabial click
w Voiced labial-velar approximant	ǀ Dental click
ɥ Voiced labial-palatal approximant	ǃ (Post)alveolar click
ʜ Voiceless epiglottal fricative	ǂ Palatoalveolar click
ʢ Voiced epiglottal fricative	ǁ Alveolar lateral click
ʡ Epiglottal plosive	ɺ Alveolar lateral flap
ɕ ʑ Alveolo-palatal fricatives	ɧ Simultaneous ʃ and x
ɝ Additional mid central vowel	

Affricates and double articulations can be represented by two symbols joined by a bar if necessary.

k͡p t͡s

SUPRASEGMENTALS

ˈ	Primary stress	ˌfoʊnəˈtɪʃən
ˌ	Secondary stress	
ː	Long	eː
ˑ	Half-long	eˑ
◌̆	Extra-short	ĕ
.	Syllable break	ɹi.ækt
|	Minor (foot) group	
‖	Major (intonation) group	
‿	Linking (absence of a break)	

TONES & WORD ACCENTS

LEVEL		CONTOUR	
e̋ or ˥	Extra high	ě or ˩˥	Rising
é ˦	High	ê ˥˩	Falling
ē ˧	Mid	e᷄ ˧˥	High rising
è ˨	Low	e᷅ ˩˧	Low rising
ȅ ˩	Extra low	e᷈ ˧˩˧	Rising-falling
ꜜ Downstep		↗ Global rise	etc.
ꜛ Upstep		↘ Global fall	

41

on the chart there are a lot of **diacritics**, marks which modify the symbol in some way; for example, the symbol for cardinal vowel no. 4 [a] may be modified by putting two dots above it. This **centralisation** diacritic then gives us the symbol [ä] for a vowel which is nearer to central than [a]. It would not be possible in this course to teach you to use all these symbols and diacritics, but someone who did know them all could write a transcription that was much more accurate in phonetic detail, and contained much more information, than a phonemic transcription. Such a transcription would be called a **phonetic transcription**; a phonetic transcription containing a lot of information about the exact quality of the sounds would be called a **narrow** phonetic transcription, while one which only included a little more information than a phonemic transcription would be called a **broad** phonetic transcription. In this course, phonetic symbols are used occasionally when it is necessary to give an accurate label to an allophone of some English phoneme, but we do not do any phonetic transcription of continuous speech. That is a rather specialised exercise. When symbols are used to represent precise phonetic values, not just to represent phonemes, we enclose them in square brackets [ ], as we have done already with cardinal vowels. In many phonetics books, phoneme symbols are enclosed within slant brackets / /, but this seems unnecessary for our purposes.

It should now be clear that there is a difference between phonemic symbols and phonetic symbols. Since the phonemic symbols do not have to indicate precise phonetic quality, it is possible to choose among several possible symbols to represent a particular phoneme; this has had the unfortunate result that different books on RP have used different symbols, causing quite a lot of confusion to students. In this course we are using the symbols now most frequently used in English publishing. It would be too long a task to examine other writers' symbols in detail, but it is worth considering some of the reasons for the differences. One factor is the complication and expense of using special symbols which create problems in typing and printing; it could for example be argued that a is a symbol that is found in practically all type-faces whereas æ is unusual, and that the a symbol should be used for the vowel in 'cat' instead of æ. Some writers have concentrated on producing a set of phoneme symbols that need the minimum number of special or non-standard symbols. Other writers have thought it important that the symbols should be as close as possible to the symbols that a phonetician would choose to give a precise indication of sound quality. To use the same example again, referring to the vowel in 'cat', it would be argued that if the vowel is noticeably closer than cardinal vowel no. 4 [a], it is more suitable to use the symbol æ, which is usually used to represent a vowel between open-mid and open. There can be disagreements about the most important characteristics of a sound that a symbol should indicate; one example is the vowels of the words 'bit' and 'beat'. Some writers have claimed that the most important difference between them is that the former is short and the latter long, and transcribed the former with i and the latter with iː (the difference being entirely in the length mark); other writers have said that the length (or **quantity**) difference is less important than the **quality** difference, and transcribe the vowel of 'bit' with the symbol ɪ and that of 'beat' with i. Yet another point of view is that quality and quantity are both important and should both be indicated; this point of view results in a transcription using ɪ for 'bit' and iː, a symbol different from ɪ both in shape of symbol (suggesting quality difference) and in length mark (indicating quantity difference), for 'beat'. This is the approach taken in this course.

5.3   **Phonology**

Chapters 2, 3 and 4 were mainly concerned with matters of **phonetics** – the comparatively straightforward business of describing the sounds that we use in speaking. When we talk about how phonemes function in language, and the relationships among the different phonemes – when, in other words, we study the *abstract* side of the sounds of language – we are studying a related but different subject that we call **phonology**. Only by studying both the phonetics and the phonology of English is it possible to acquire a full understanding of the use of sounds in English speech. Let us look briefly at some areas that come within the subject of phonology; all these areas of study will be met frequently in the rest of the course.

Study of the phonemic system

It is sometimes helpful to think of the phonemic system as similar to the set of cards used in a card game, or the set of pieces used in a game of chess. In chess, for example, the exact shape and colour of the pieces are not important to the game as long as they can be reliably distinguished. But the number of pieces, the moves they can make and their relationship to all the other pieces are very important; we would say that if any of these were to be changed, the game would no longer be what we call chess. Similarly, playing-cards can be printed in many different styles and sizes; but while changing these things does not affect the game played with them, if we were to remove one card from the pack or add one card to it before the start of a game, nobody would accept that we were playing the game correctly. In a similar way, we have a more or less fixed set of "pieces" (phonemes) with which to play the game of speaking English. There may be many slightly different realisations of the various phonemes, but the most important thing for communication is that we should be able to make use of the full set of phonemes.

Phoneme sequences and syllable structure

In every language we find that there are restrictions on the sequences of phonemes that are used. For example, no English word begins with the consonant sequence zbf and no words end with the sequence æh. In phonology we must try to analyse what the restrictions and regularities are in a particular language, and it is usually found helpful to do this by studying the **syllables** of the language.

Suprasegmental phonology

Many significant sound contrasts are not the result of differences between phonemes. For example, **stress** is important: when the word 'import' is pronounced with the first syllable sounding stronger than the second, English speakers hear it as a noun, whereas when the second syllable is stronger the word is heard as a verb. **Intonation** is also important: if the word 'right' is said with the pitch of the voice rising, it is likely to be heard as a question or as an invitation to a speaker to continue, while falling pitch is more likely to be heard as confirmation or agreement. These examples show sound contrasts that extend over several segments (phonemes), and such contrasts are called **suprasegmental**. We will look at many other aspects of suprasegmental phonology later in the course.

Notes on problems and further reading

This chapter is theoretical rather than practical. There is no shortage of material to read on the subject of the phoneme, but much of it is rather difficult and assumes a lot of background knowledge. For basic reading I would suggest Katamba (1989), chapter 2; Hawkins (1984), chapter 1, or Gimson (1989), chapter 5, section 3. There are many classic works: Jones (1976, first published in 1950) is widely regarded as such, though it is often criticised nowadays for being superficial or even naive. Another classic is Pike's *Phonemics* (1947), subtitled "A Technique for

Reducing Languages to Writing": this is essentially a practical handbook for people who need to analyse the phonemes of unknown languages, and contains many examples and exercises. A third classic work is Trubetzkoy (1939, English translation by Baltaxe, 1969), while Bloomfield (1933) is also a historic work – see especially chapter 5. A modern book for more advanced reading is Lass (1984).

The subject of symbols is a large one: there is a very good survey in Abercrombie (1967), chapter 7. For a very brief outline of the field, see Roach (1991). The International Phonetic Association has tried as far as possible to keep to Roman-style symbols, though it is inevitable that these symbols have to be supplemented with diacritics. In 1989 the IPA held a special conference in Kiel, Germany, and papers were produced both before the meeting (to raise issues for discussion) and after it (to present the decisions made). Most of the former appeared in the *Journal of the International Phonetic Association*, vol. 19 no. 2 (1989); see also Roach (1987). Those interested in the history of the IPA's way of classifying sounds should read Albright (1958). Some phoneticians working at the end of the last century tried to develop non-alphabetic sets of symbols whose shape would indicate all essential phonetic characteristics; if you are interested in this you could, in addition to reading the chapter of Abercrombie referred to above, read a little of Sweet's writing on the subject in Henderson (1971), section 4.

It is obvious that one must choose between, on the one hand, symbols that are very informative but slow to write and, on the other, symbols that are not very precise but are quick and convenient to use. Pike (1943) presents at the end of his book an "analphabetic notation" designed to permit the coding of sounds with great precision on the basis of their articulation; an indication of the complexity of the system is the fact that the full specification of the vowel [o] requires eighty-eight characters. On the opposite side, many American writers have avoided the IPA symbols as too complex and have tried to use as far as possible symbols and diacritics which are already in existence for various special alphabetic requirements of European languages and which are available on typewriters. For example where the IPA has ʃ and ʒ, symbols not usually found outside phonetics, Americans use š and ž, the mark above the symbols being widely used for those Slavonic languages that do not use the Cyrillic alphabet. This American approach has many practical advantages, but is not capable of as much detail as the IPA set; part 1 of Trager and Smith (1951) illustrates the problems that are encountered when trying to symbolise a lot of phonetic detail with these conventions. In recent years there has been an important change due to the introduction of computer printers: dot-matrix and laser printers allow users to design their own symbols and print them alongside normal alphabetic characters. For recommendations on computer printing of phonetic symbols, see Wells (1987).

Note for teachers

It should be made clear to students that the treatment of the phoneme in this chapter is only an introduction. It is difficult to go into detailed examples since very few symbols have been introduced at this stage, so further consideration of phonological issues is given in later chapters and it would not be advisable to go beyond the fundamental points at this stage.

Written exercises

The words in the following list should be transcribed first *phonemically*, then (in square brackets) *phonetically*. In your phonetic transcription you can use the following diacritics:

b, d, g pronounced without voicing are transcribed [b̥, d̥, g̊]

p, t, k pronounced with aspiration are transcribed [pʰ, tʰ, kʰ]

iː, aː, oː, ɜː, uː when shortened by a following fortis consonant should be transcribed iˑ, aˑ, oˑ, ɜˑ, uˑ

ɪ, e, æ, ʌ, ɒ, ʊ, ə when shortened by a following fortis consonant should be transcribed ɪ̆, ĕ, æ̆, ʌ̆, ɒ̆, ʊ̆, ə̆. Use the same mark for diphthongs.

Example spelling: 'peat' phonemic: piːt phonetic: [pʰiˑt]

Words for transcription

a) speed   c) book   e) car   g) appeared   i) stalk
b) partake   d) goat   f) bad   h) toast

6 Fricatives and affricates

6.1 Production of fricatives and affricates

Fricatives are consonants with the characteristic that when they are produced, air escapes through a small passage and makes a hissing sound. All languages have fricatives, probably always including something like s. Fricatives are **continuant** consonants, which means that you can continue making them without interruption as long as you have enough air in your lungs. (Plosives, which were described in Chapter 4, are not continuants.) You can demonstrate the importance of the narrow passage for the air in the following ways:

i) Make a long, hissing s sound and gradually lower your tongue so that it is no longer close to the roof of the mouth. The hissing sound will stop as the air passage gets larger.

ii) Make a long f sound, and while you are producing this sound use your fingers to pull the lower lip away from the upper teeth. Notice how the hissing sound of the air escaping between teeth and lip suddenly stops.

Affricates are rather complex consonants. They begin as plosives and end as fricatives. A familiar example is the affricate heard at the beginning and end of the word 'church'. It begins with an articulation practically the same as the closure and hold phases of t, but instead of a rapid release with plosion and aspiration, as we would find in the word 'turn', the tongue moves to the position for the fricative ʃ that we find at the beginning of the word 'ship'. So the plosive is followed immediately by fricative noise. Since phonetically this affricate is composed of t and ʃ we represent it as tʃ, so that the word 'church' is transcribed as tʃɜːtʃ.

However, the definition of an affricate must be a little more restricted than what has been said so far. We would not class *all* sequences of plosive plus fricative as affricates; for example, we find in the middle of the word 'breakfast' the plosive k followed by the fricative f. English speakers would generally not accept that kf forms a consonantal unit in the way that tʃ seems to. It is usually said that the plosive and the following fricative must be made with the same articulators – to use a technical term, the plosive and fricative must be **homorganic**. k and f are not homorganic, but t and ʃ, both being made with the tongue blade against the alveolar ridge, *are* homorganic. This still leaves the possibility of quite a large number of affricates, since for example t is homorganic not only with ʃ but also with s, so ts would also count as an affricate.

Although the affricates can be said to be composed of a plosive and a fricative, it is usual to regard them as being single, independent phonemes of English. In this way, t is one phoneme, ʃ is another and tʃ yet another. We would say that the pronunciation of the word 'church' tʃɜːtʃ is composed of three phonemes, tʃ, ɜː and tʃ. We will look at this question of "two sounds = one phoneme" from the theoretical point of view in a later chapter.

6.2 The fricatives of English

English has quite a complex system of fricative phonemes. They can be seen in the table below:

	PLACE OF ARTICULATION					
	labiodental	dental	alveolar	palato-alveolar		glottal
FORTIS ("voice-less")	f	θ	s	ʃ		
						h
LENIS ("voiced")	v	ð	z	ʒ		

With the exception of glottal, each place of articulation has a pair of phonemes, one fortis and one lenis. This is similar to what was seen with the plosives. The fortis fricatives are said to be articulated with greater force than the lenis, and their friction noise is louder. The lenis fricatives have very little or no voicing in initial and final positions, but may be voiced when they occur between voiced sounds. The fortis fricatives have the effect of shortening a preceding vowel, as do fortis plosives. Thus in a pair of words like 'ice' and 'eyes' (aɪs, aɪz), the aɪ diphthong in the first word is considerably shorter than in the second. Since there is only one fricative with glottal place of articulation, the fortis–lenis distinction does not apply in that case. It would be rather misleading to call it fortis or lenis (which is why there is a line on the chart above dividing h from the other fricatives).

We will now look at the fricatives separately, according to their place of articulation.

TU 6,
Exs 1–3

f, v (example words: 'fan', 'van'; 'safer', 'saver'; 'half', 'halve')

These are labiodental, that is, the lower lip is in contact with the upper teeth as shown in Fig. 14a. The fricative noise is never very strong and is scarcely audible in the case of v.

θ, ð (example words: 'thumb', 'thus'; 'ether', 'father'; 'breath', 'breathe')

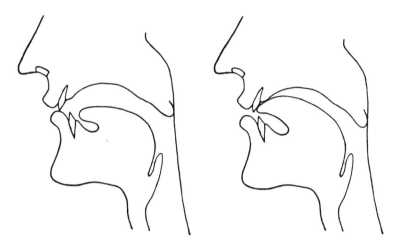

Fig. 14a Labiodental fricative   b Dental fricative

The dental fricatives have sometimes been described as if the tongue was actually placed between the teeth, and it is common for teachers to make their students do this when they are trying to teach them to make this sound. In fact, however, the tongue is normally placed *inside* the teeth, as shown in Fig. 14b, with the tip touching the inside of the lower front teeth and the blade touching the inside of the upper teeth. The air escapes through the gaps between the tongue and the teeth. As with f and v, the fricative noise is weak.

s, z (example words: 'sip', 'zip'; 'facing', 'phasing'; 'rice', 'rise')
These are alveolar fricatives, with the same place of articulation as t and d. The air escapes through a narrow passage along the centre of the tongue, and the sound produced is comparatively intense. The tongue position is shown in Fig. 12 in Chapter 4.

ʃ, ʒ (example words: 'ship' (initial ʒ is very rare in English); 'Russia', 'measure'; 'Irish', 'garage')
These fricatives are called palato-alveolar, which can be taken to mean that their place of articulation is partly palatal, partly alveolar. The tongue is in contact with an area slightly further back than that for s, z (see Fig. 14c). If you make s, then ʃ, you should be able to feel your

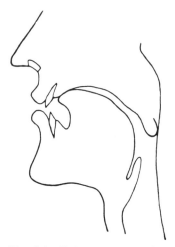

Fig. 14c Palato-alveolar fricative

tongue move backwards. The air escapes through a passage along the centre of the tongue, as in s and z, but the passage is a little wider. Most speakers of RP have rounded lips for ʃ and ʒ, and this is an important difference between these consonants and s and z.

ʃ is a common and widely-distributed phoneme, but ʒ is not. All the fricatives described so far (f, v, θ, ð, s, z) can be found in initial, medial and final positions, as shown in the example words. In the case of ʒ, however, the distribution is much more limited. Very few English words begin with ʒ (most of them have come into the language comparatively recently from French) and not many end with this consonant. Only medially, in words such as 'measure', 'usual' (meʒə, juːʒʊəl) is it found at all commonly.

h (example words: 'head', 'ahead', 'playhouse')
The place of articulation of this consonant is glottal. This means that the narrowing that produces the friction noise is between the vocal folds, as described in Chapter 4. If you breathe out silently, then produce h, you are moving your vocal folds from wide apart to close together. However, this is not producing speech. When we produce h in speaking English, many different things happen in different contexts. In the word 'hat', the h must be followed by an æ vowel. The tongue, jaw and lip positions for the vowel are all produced simultaneously with the h consonant, so that the glottal fricative has an æ quality. The same is found for all vowels following h; it always has the quality of the vowel it precedes, so that in theory if you could listen to a tape-recording of h-sounds cut off from the beginnings of different vowels in words like 'hit', 'hat', 'hot', 'hut', etc., you should be able to identify which vowel would have followed the h. One way of stating the above facts is to say

that *phonetically* h is a voiceless vowel with the quality of the voiced vowel that follows it.

Phonologically, h is a consonant. It is usually found before vowels. As well as being found in initial position it is found medially in words such as: 'ahead' əhed, 'greenhouse' griːnhaʊs, 'boathook' bəʊthʊk. It is noticeable that when h occurs between voiced sounds (as in the words 'ahead' and 'greenhouse'), it is pronounced with voicing – not the normal voicing of vowels but a weak, slightly fricative sound called **breathy voice**. It is not necessary for foreign learners to attempt to copy this voicing, though it *is* important to pronounce h where it should occur in RP. Many English speakers are surprisingly sensitive about this consonant; they tend to judge as sub-standard a pronunciation in which h is missing, though in fact practically all English speakers, however carefully they speak, omit the h in unstressed pronunciations of the words 'her', 'he', 'him', 'his' and the auxiliary 'have', 'has', 'had', though few of them are aware that they do this.

There are two rather uncommon sounds that need to be introduced; since they are said to have some association with h, they will be mentioned here. The first is the sound produced by some speakers in words which begin orthographically (that is, in their spelling form) with 'wh'; most RP speakers pronounce the initial sound in such words (e.g. 'which', 'why', 'whip', 'whale') as w, but there are some (particularly when they are speaking clearly or emphatically) who pronounce the sound used by most American and Scottish speakers, a *voiceless* fricative with the same lip, tongue and jaw position as w. The phonetic symbol for this voiceless fricative is ʍ. We can find pairs of words showing the difference between this sound and the voiced sound w (which is introduced in the next chapter):

'witch' wɪtʃ		'which' ʍɪtʃ	
'wail' weɪl		'whale' ʍeɪl	
'Wye' waɪ		'why' ʍaɪ	
'wear' weə		'where' ʍeə	

The obvious conclusion to draw from this is that, since substituting one sound for the other causes a difference in meaning, the two sounds are two different phonemes. It is therefore rather surprising to find that practically all writers on the subject of the phonemes of English decide that this answer is not correct, and that the sound ʍ in 'which', 'why', etc., is *not* a phoneme of English but is a realisation of a sequence of two phonemes, h and w. Fortunately we do not need to worry about this problem in RP; we can make the decision to exclude this sound altogether from the accent we are describing. However, it should be noted that in the analysis of the many accents of English that do have a "voiceless w" there is not much more theoretical justification in treating the sound as h plus w than there is for treating p as h plus b.

Whether the question of this sound is approached phonetically or phonologically, there is no h sound in the "voiceless w".

A very similar case is the sound found at the beginning of words such as 'huge', 'human', 'hue'. Phonetically this sound is a voiceless palatal fricative (for which the phonetic symbol is ç); there is no glottal fricative at the beginning of 'huge', etc. However, it is usual to treat this sound as h plus j (the latter is another consonant that is to be introduced in the next chapter – it is the sound at the beginning of 'yes', 'yet'). Again we can see that a phonemic analysis does not necessarily have to be exactly in line with phonetic facts. If we were to say that these two sounds ʍ and ç were phonemes of English, we would have two extra phonemes that do not occur very frequently. We will follow the usual practice of transcribing the sound at the beginning of 'huge', etc., as hj just because it is convenient and common practice.

6.3 The affricates

TU 6, Exs 4 & 5

tʃ, dʒ are the only two affricate phonemes in English. As with the plosives and most of the fricatives, we have a fortis/lenis pair, and the voicing characteristics are the same as for these other consonants. tʃ is slightly aspirated in the positions where p, t, k are aspirated, but not strongly enough for it to be necessary for foreign learners to give much attention to it. The place of articulation is the same as for ʃ, ʒ, that is, palato-alveolar. This means that the t component of tʃ has a place of articulation rather further back in the mouth than the t plosive usually has. When tʃ is final in the syllable it has the effect of shortening a preceding vowel, as do other fortis consonants. tʃ and dʒ often have rounded lips.

6.4 Fortis consonants

All the consonants described so far, with the exception of h, belong to pairs distinguished by the difference between fortis and lenis. Since the remaining consonants to be described are not paired in this way, a few points that still have to be made about fortis consonants are included in this chapter.

The first point concerns the shortening of a preceding vowel by a syllable-final fortis consonant. As was said in Chapter 4, the effect is most noticeable in the case of long vowels and diphthongs, though it does also affect short vowels.

What happens if something other than a vowel precedes a fortis consonant? This arises in syllables ending with l, m, n or ŋ, followed by a fortis consonant such as p, t, k, as in 'belt' belt, 'bump' bʌmp, 'bent' bent, 'bank' bæŋk. The effect on those continuant consonants is the same as on a vowel – they are considerably shortened.

A similar question arises with *initial* fortis consonants. When p, t, k come at the beginning of a syllable and are followed by a vowel, they are aspirated, as was explained in Chapter 4. This means that the beginning of a vowel is voiceless in this context. However, p, t, k may be followed not by a vowel but by one of l, r, w, j. These voiced continuant consonants undergo a similar process – they lose their voicing. So words like 'play' pleɪ, 'tray' treɪ, 'quick' kwɪk contain *devoiced* l, r, w, whereas 'lay', 'ray', 'wick' contain *voiced* l, r, w. Consequently, if for example 'tray' were to be pronounced without devoicing of the r (i.e. with fully voiced r) English speakers would hear the word 'dray'

Voiceless consonants are usually articulated with open glottis, i.e. with the vocal folds separated. This is always the case with fricatives, where airflow is essential for successful production. However, with plosives an alternative possibility is to produce the consonant with completely *closed* glottis. This type of articulation is found quite widely in English pronunciation, including that of younger speakers of RP. This **glottalised** pronunciation, in which a glottal stop occurs just before p, t, k or tʃ, is only found in certain contexts, and foreign learners usually find the rules too difficult to learn, from the practical point of view; it is therefore simpler to keep to the more conservative pronunciation and not try to use glottalisation. However, it is worth pointing out the fact that this occurs, since many learners notice the glottal stops and want to know what it is that they are hearing. A few examples are given below.

The most widespread glottalisation is that of tʃ at the end of a stressed syllable (I leave defining what "stressed syllable" means until Chapter 8). If we use the symbol ʔ to represent a glottal closure, the phonetic transcription for various words containing tʃ can be given as follows:

	With glottalisation	*Without glottalisation*
'nature'	neɪʔtʃə	neɪtʃə
'catching'	kæʔtʃɪŋ	kætʃɪŋ
'riches'	rɪʔtʃɪz	rɪtʃɪz

There is similar glottalisation of p, t, k, though this is not found so regularly. It normally happens when the plosive is followed by another consonant or a pause; for example:

	With glottalisation	*Without glottalisation*
'actor'	æʔktə	æktə
'petrol'	peʔtrəl	petrəl
'mat'	mæʔt	mæt
'football'	fʊʔtbɔːl	fʊtbɔːl

Foreign learners do not need to learn this type of pronunciation, but many seem to acquire it unintentionally through speaking to English people. It is undoubtedly becoming more widely used within RP.

Notes on problems and further reading

The description of fricatives is in general quite straightforward. However, something that is mentioned only briefly in section 6.2 is the difference between fricatives in terms of the width and depth of the air passage. The terms **slit** and **groove** are sometimes used: the air passage in s and z is said to be grooved and that in ʃ and ʒ slit; see Gimson (1989), 8.4.4, and 8.4.5; O'Connor (1973), pp. 48 and 142.

The dental fricative ð is something of a problem: although there are not many English words in which this sound appears, those words are ones which occur very frequently – words like 'the', 'this', 'there', 'that', and so on. In my experience this consonant often shows so little friction noise that on purely phonetic grounds it seems incorrect to class it as a fricative. It is more like a weak (lenis) dental plosive. This matter is discussed again in Chapter 14, section 14.2.

On the phonological side, I have brought in a discussion of the phonemic analysis of two "marginal" fricatives which present a problem (though not a particularly important or fundamental one): I feel that this is worth discussing in that it gives a good idea of the sort of problem that can arise in analysing the phonemic system of a language. The other problem area is the glottalisation described at the end of the chapter. There is, I think, now a growing awareness of how frequently this is to be found in the speech of younger RP speakers; however, it is not at all easy to formulate rules stating the contexts in which this occurs. There is discussion in Brown (1990), pp. 28–30, in Gimson (1989), 8.2.3 (3) and 8.2.7 and in Wells (1982), 3.4.5. I have tried to analyse the very complex distribution of glottalisation myself (Roach, 1973)* and to measure the timing of articulatory events in glottalised consonants (Roach, 1979).

---

* If you do read this paper, please note that the two rules given on p. 13 were printed in the wrong order.

Notes for teachers

Although it is important to be aware of the ways in which fricatives differ from each other, I have never found it helpful to teach learners to aim consciously at slit and groove articulations – it is not something that most people feel they have control over, so simple imitation works better.

Although I do not recommend teaching learners to produce glottalis-ation of p, t, k, tʃ, I have sometimes found advanced learners have been able to "get the hang of it", and I find the increase in naturalness in their accent very striking.

Written exercises

1. Transcribe the following words phonemically:
    a) fishes   *e)* achieves
    b) shaver   *f)* others
    c) sixth   *g)* measure
    d) these   *h)* ahead
2. Following the style introduced in Exercise 1 for Chapter 4, describe the movements of the articulators in the first word of the above list.

C

7 Nasals and other consonants

So far we have studied two major groups of consonants, the plosives and fricatives, and also the affricates, tʃ and dʒ, a total of seventeen. There remain the nasals m, n, ŋ and four others, l, r, w and j, which are not easy to fit into groups. All of these consonants are continuants and usually have no friction noise, but in other ways they are very different from each other.

7.1 Nasals

The basic characteristic of a nasal consonant is that the air escapes through the nose. For this to happen, the soft palate must be lowered; in the case of all the other consonants and vowels, the soft palate is raised and air cannot pass through the nose. In nasal consonants, however, the air does not pass through the mouth; it is prevented by a complete closure in the mouth at some point. If you produce a long sequence dndndndndndndn without moving your tongue from the position for alveolar closure, you will feel your soft palate moving up and down. The three types of closure are: bilabial (lips), alveolar (tongue blade against alveolar ridge) and velar (back of tongue against the soft palate). This set of places produces three nasal consonants, m, n, ŋ, which correspond to the three places of articulation for the pairs of plosives p b, t d, k g.

m and n are simple, straightforward consonants with distributions like those of the plosives. There is in fact little to describe. However, ŋ is a different matter. It is a sound that gives considerable problems to foreign learners, and one that is so unusual in its phonological aspect that some people argue that it is not one of the phonemes of English at all. The place of articulation of ŋ is the same as that of k, g; it is a useful exercise to practise making a continuous ŋ sound. If you do this, it is very important not to produce a k or g at the end – pronounce the ŋ just like m or n.

We will now look at some ways in which the distribution of ŋ is unusual.

i) In initial position we find m and n occurring freely, but ŋ never occurs in this position. With the possible exception of ʒ, this makes ŋ the only English consonant that cannot occur initially.

ii) Medially, ŋ occurs quite frequently, but there is in RP a rather complex and quite interesting rule concerning the question of when ŋ may be pronounced without a following plosive. When we find the letters 'nk' in the middle of a word in its orthographic form, a k will always be pronounced; however, some words with orthographic 'ng' in the middle will have a pronunciation containing ŋg and others will have ŋ without g. For example, in RP we find the following:

A	B
'finger' fɪŋgə	'singer' sɪŋə
'anger' æŋgə	'hanger' hæŋə

In the words of column A the ŋ is followed by g, while the words of column B have no g. What is the difference between A and B? The important difference is in the way the words are constructed – their **morphology**. The words of column B can be divided into two grammatical pieces: 'sing' + '-er', 'hang' + '-er'. These pieces are called **morphemes**, and we say that column B words are **morphologically** different from column A words, since these can *not* be divided into two morphemes. 'Finger' and 'anger' consist of just one morpheme each.

We can summarise the position so far by saying that (within a word containing the letters 'ng' in the spelling) ŋ occurs without a following g if it occurs at the end of a morpheme; if it occurs in the middle of a morpheme it has a following g.

Let us now look at the ends of words *ending* orthographically with 'ng'. We find that these always end with ŋ; this ŋ is never followed by a g. Thus we find that the words 'sing' and 'hang' are pronounced as sɪŋ and hæŋ; to give a few more examples, 'song' is sɒŋ, 'bang' is bæŋ and 'long' is lɒŋ. We do not need a separate explanation for this: the rule given above, the g is not pronounced after ŋ at the end of a morpheme, works in these cases too, since the end of a word must also be the end of a morpheme. (If this point seems difficult, think of the comparable case of words and sentences: a sound that comes at the end of a sentence must necessarily also come at the end of a word, so that the final k of 'This is a book' is also the final k of the word 'book'.)

Unfortunately, rules tend to have exceptions. The main exception to the above morpheme-based rule concerns the comparative and superlative suffixes '-er' and '-est'. According to the rule given above, the adjective 'long' will be pronounced lɒŋ, which is correct. It would also predict correctly that if we add another morpheme to 'long', such as the suffix '-ish', the pronunciation of ŋ would again be without a following g. However, it would additionally predict that the comparative and superlative forms 'longer' and 'longest' would be pronounced with no g following the ŋ, while in fact the correct pronunciation of the words is:

'longer' lɒŋgə   'longest' lɒŋgəst (or lɒŋgɪst)

As a result of this, the rule must be modified; it must state that comparative and superlative forms of adjectives are to be treated as single-morpheme words for the purposes of this rule. The resulting rule is, of course, difficult to understand. It is important to remember that English speakers in general (apart from those trained in phonetics) are quite ignorant of this rule, and yet if a foreigner uses the wrong pronunciation (that is, pronounces ŋg where ŋ should occur, or ŋ where ŋg should be used), they notice that a mispronunciation has occurred.

iii) A third way in which the distribution of ŋ is unusual is the small number of vowels it is found to follow. It never occurs after a diphthong or long vowel, and in fact there are only five vowels ever found preceding this consonant: ɪ, e, æ, ʌ and ɒ.

The velar nasal consonant ŋ is, in summary, phonetically simple (it is no more difficult to produce than m or n) but phonologically complex (it is, as we have shown, not easy to describe the contexts in which it occurs).

7.2 l

TU 7,
Ex 3

A **lateral** consonant is one in which the passage of air through the mouth does not go in the usual way along the centre of the tongue; instead, there is complete closure between the centre of the tongue and the part of the roof of the mouth where contact is to be made (the alveolar ridge in the case of l). Because of this complete closure along the centre, the only way for the air to escape is along the sides of the tongue. If you make a long l sound you may be able to feel that the sides of your tongue are pulled in and down while the centre is raised, but it is not easy to become consciously aware of this; what is more revealing (if you can do it) is to produce a long sequence of alternations between d and l without any intervening vowel. If you produce dldldldldldldl *without moving the middle of the tongue*, you will be able to feel the movement of the sides of the tongue that is necessary for the production of a lateral. It is also possible to *see* this movement in a mirror if you open your lips wide as you produce it. Finally, it is also helpful to see if you can *feel* the movement of air past the sides of the tongue; this is not really possible in a voiced sound (the obstruction caused by the vibrating vocal folds reduces the airflow), but if you try to make a very loud *whispered* l, you should be able to feel the air rushing along the sides of your tongue.

We find l initially, medially and finally, and its distribution is therefore not particularly limited. In RP, the consonant has one unusual characteristic: the realisation of l found before vowels sounds quite different from that found in other contexts. For example, the realisation of l in the word 'lea' liː is quite different from that in 'eel' iːl. The sound in iːl is what we call a "dark l"; it has a quality rather similar to an [u] vowel, with the back of the tongue raised. The sound in liː is what is called a "clear l"; it resembles an [i] vowel, with the front of the tongue raised. The "dark l" is also found when it precedes a consonant, as in 'eels' iːlz. We can therefore predict which realisation of l (clear or dark) will occur in a particular context: clear l will never occur before consonants or before a pause, but only before vowels; dark l never occurs before vowels. We can say, using terminology introduced in Chapter 5, that clear l and dark ɫ are allophones of the phoneme l in complementary distribution. Most English speakers do not consciously know about the difference between clear and dark l, yet they are quick to detect the difference when they hear English speakers with different accents or foreign learners who have not learned the correct pronunciation.

Another allophone of l is found when it follows p or k at the beginning of a stressed syllable. The l is then **devoiced**, i.e. produced without the voicing found in most realisations of this phoneme. The situation is (as explained in Chapter 4) similar to aspiration when a vowel follows p, t or k in a stressed syllable; the first part of the vowel is devoiced.

7.3 r

TU 7,
Ex 4

This consonant is important in that considerable differences in its articulation and its distribution are found in different accents of English. As far as the articulation of the sound is concerned, there is really only one pronunciation that can be recommended to the foreign learner of RP, and that is what is called a **post-alveolar approximant**. An **approximant**, as a type of consonant, is rather difficult to describe; informally, we can say that it is an articulation in which the articulators approach each other but do not get sufficiently close to each other to produce a "complete" consonant such as a plosive, nasal or fricative.

The difficulty with this is that articulators are always in *some* positional relationship with each other, and any vowel articulation could also be classed as an approximant – but the term "approximant" is usually used only for consonants.

The important thing about the articulation of r is that the tip of the tongue approaches the alveolar area in approximately the way it would for a t or d, but never actually makes contact with any part of the roof of the mouth. You should be able to make a long r sound and feel that no part of the tongue is in contact with the roof of the mouth at any time. (This is, of course, very different from the "r-sounds" of many other languages where some kind of tongue–palate contact is made.) The tongue is in fact usually slightly curled backwards with the tip raised; consonants with this tongue shape are usually called **retroflex**. If you pronounce an alternating sequence of d and r (drdrdrdrdrdr) while looking in a mirror you should be able to see more of the underside of the tongue in the r than in the d, where the tongue tip is not raised and the tongue is not curled back. The "curling-back" process usually carries the tip of the tongue to a position slightly further back in the mouth than that for alveolar consonants such as t and d, which is why this approximant is called "post-alveolar". A rather different r sound is found at the beginning of a syllable if it is preceded by p, t or k; it is then voiceless and slightly fricative. This pronunciation is found in words such as 'press', 'tress', 'cress'.

One final characteristic of the articulation of r is that it is usual for the lips to be slightly rounded; foreign learners should do this but should be careful not to exaggerate it. If the lip-rounding is too strong the consonant will sound too much like w, which is the sound that most English children produce until they have learned to pronounce r in the adult way.

The distributional peculiarity of r in RP is very easy to state: this phoneme only occurs before vowels. No one has any difficulty in remembering this rule, but foreign learners (most of whom, quite reasonably, expect that if there is a letter 'r' in the spelling then a r should be pronounced) find it difficult to apply the rule to their own pronunciation. There is no problem with words like the following:

i) 'red' red   'arrive' əraɪv   'hearing' hɪərɪŋ

In these words r is followed by a vowel. But in the following words there is no r in the pronunciation:

ii) 'car' kɑ: 'ever' evə   'here' hɪə
iii) 'hard' hɑ:d   'verse' vɜ:s   'cares' keəz

Many accents of English *do* pronounce r in words like those of (ii) and (iii) (for example, most American, Scots and West of England accents); accents which have r in final position (before a pause) and before a consonant are called **rhotic** accents, while accents in which r only occurs before vowels (such as RP) are called **non-rhotic**.

7.4 j and w

TU 7, Ex 5

These are the consonants found at the beginning of words such as 'yet' and 'wet'. They have been called **semivowels** by many writers, but we will use the more modern term "approximant" (introduced in 7.3 above). The most important thing to remember about these phonemes is that they are *phonetically* like vowels but *phonologically* like consonants. From the phonetic point of view the articulation of j is practically the same as that of a front close vowel such as iː, but is very short. In the same way w is closely similar to uː. If you make the initial sound of 'wet' or 'yet' very long, you will be able to hear this. But despite this vowel-like character, we use them like consonants. For example, they only occur before vowel phonemes; this is a typically consonantal distribution. We can show that a word beginning with w or j is regarded as beginning with a consonant in the following way: the indefinite article is 'a' before a consonant (as in 'a cat', 'a dog'), and 'an' before a vowel (as in 'an apple', 'an orange'). If a word beginning with w or j is preceded by the indefinite article, it is the 'a' form that is found (as in 'a way', 'a year'). Another example is that of the definite article. Here the rule is that 'the' is pronounced as ðə before consonants (as in ðə kæt, ðə dɒg) and as ðɪ before vowels (as in ðɪ æpl, ðɪ ɒrɪndʒ). This evidence illustrates why it is said that j and w are phonologically consonants. However, it is important to remember that to pronounce them as fricatives (as many foreign learners do), or even affricates, is a mispronunciation. Only in special contexts do we hear friction noise in j or w; this is when they are preceded by p, t or k at the beginning of a syllable, as in these words:

'pure' pjʊə	(no words begin with pw)
'tune' tjuːn	'twin' twɪn
'queue' kjuː	'quin' kwɪn

The j and w sounds are devoiced (that is, become voiceless) and are slightly fricative in these contexts. For place of articulation, we regard j as palatal and w as bilabial.

This completes our examination of the consonant phonemes of English. It is useful to place them on a consonant chart, and this is done in Table 2. On this chart, the different places of articulation are arranged from left to right and the manners of articulation are arranged from top to bottom. When there is a pair of phonemes with the same

Table 2. *Chart of English consonant phonemes*

| | Place of articulation | | | | | | | |
Manner of articulation	Bilabial	Labiodental	Dental	Alveolar	Palato-alveolar (Post-alveolar)	Palatal	Velar	Glottal
Plosive	p b			t d			k g	
Fricative		f v	θ ð	s z	ʃ ʒ			h
Affricate					tʃ dʒ			
Nasal	m			n			ŋ	
Lateral				l				
Approximant	w				r	j		

place and manner of articulation but differing in whether they are fortis or lenis (voiceless or voiced), the symbol for the fortis consonant is placed to the left of the symbol for the lenis consonant.

Notes on problems and further reading

The notes for this chapter are devoted to giving further detail on a particularly difficult theoretical problem. The argument that ŋ is an allophone of n, not a phoneme in its own right, is so widely accepted by contemporary phonological theorists that few seem to feel it worth-while to explain it fully. Since the velar nasal is introduced in this chapter, I have chosen to attempt this here. However, it is a rather complex theoretical matter, and you may prefer to leave consideration of it until after the discussion of problems of phonemic analysis in Chapter 13.

A quite interesting examination of the question was written by Vachek (1964). There are brief discussions of the phonemic status of ŋ in Chomsky and Halle (1968), p. 85, Hyman (1975), pp. 74–6 and Ladefoged (1982), p. 60; the fullest treatment in recent years is Wells (1982), pp. 60–4.

Everyone agrees that English has at least two contrasting nasal phonemes, m and n. However, there is disagreement about whether there is a third nasal phoneme in RP. In favour of accepting ŋ as a phoneme is the fact that traditional phoneme theory more or less demands its acceptance despite the general tendency to make phoneme inventories as small as possible. Consider minimal pairs like these: 'sin' sɪn – 'sing' sɪŋ; 'sinner' sɪnə – 'singer' sɪŋə.

There are three main arguments *against* accepting ŋ as a phoneme:

i)   In some English accents it can easily be shown that ŋ is an allophone of n, which suggests that something similar might be true of RP too.

ii) If ŋ is a phoneme, its distribution is very different from that of m and n, being restricted to syllable-final position (phonologically) and to morpheme-final position (morphologically) unless it is followed by k or g.

iii) English speakers with no phonetic training are said to feel that ŋ is not a 'single sound' like m and n. Sapir (1925) said that 'no native speaker of English could be made to feel in his bones' that ŋ formed part of a series with m and n. This is, of course, very hard to establish, if not impossible.

We need to look at point (i) in more detail and go on to see how this leads to the argument against having ŋ as a phoneme. Please note that I am not trying to argue that this proposal is correct; my aim is just to explain the argument. The whole question may seem of little or no practical consequence, but we ought to be interested in any phonological problem if it appears that conventional phoneme theory is not able to deal satisfactorily with it.

In some English accents, particularly those of the Midlands, ŋ is only found in front of k and g. For example:

| 'sink' | sɪŋk | 'singer' | sɪŋgə |
| 'sing' | sɪŋg | 'singing' | sɪŋgɪŋg |

(This was my own pronunciation as a boy, living in the West Midlands, but I now usually have RP sɪŋk, sɪŋ, sɪŋə, sɪŋɪŋ.)

In the case of an accent like this, it can be shown that within the morpheme the only nasal that occurs before k and g is ŋ. Neither m nor n can occur in this environment. Thus within the morpheme ŋ is in complementary distribution with m and n. Since m and n are already established as distinct English phonemes in other contexts (mæp, næp, etc.), it is clear that for such non-RP accents ŋ must be an allophone of one of the other nasal consonant phonemes. We choose n because when a morpheme-final n is followed by a morpheme-initial k or g it is usual for that n to change to ŋ; however, a morpheme-final m followed by a morpheme-initial k or g usually *doesn't* change to ŋ. Thus:

'rain-coat' reɪŋkəʊt BUT 'tram-car' træmkɑː

So in an analysis which contains no ŋ phoneme, we would transcribe 'rain-coat' phonemically as reɪnkəʊt and 'sing', 'singer', 'singing' as sɪŋg, sɪŋgə, sɪŋgɪŋg. The phonetic realisation of the n phoneme as a velar nasal will be accounted for by a general rule that we will call Rule 1:

Rule 1: n is realised as [ŋ] when it occurs in an environment in which it precedes either k or g.

Let us now look at RP. When we see words like sɪŋ, sɪŋə, sɪŋɪŋ, we can see no k or g that could have caused the above rule to apply. However, we must look at one important fact: the word 'finger' is pronounced in RP as fɪŋgə. What is the reason for the difference between 'singer' sɪŋə and 'finger' fɪŋgə? The crucial difference is that 'finger' is a single, indivisible morpheme whereas 'singer' is composed of two morphemes, 'sing' and '-er'. When ŋ occurs without a following k or g it is *always* immediately before a morpheme boundary. Consequently, the sound ŋ and the sequence ŋg are in complementary distribution in RP. But within the morpheme there is no contrast between the sequence ŋg and the sequence ng, which makes it possible to say that ŋ is also in complementary distribution with the sequence ng.

After establishing these 'background facts', we can go on to state the argument as follows:

i)   English has only m and n as nasal phonemes.

ii) The sound ŋ is an allophone of the phoneme n.

iii) The words 'finger', 'sing', 'singer', 'singing' should be represented phonemically as fɪŋgə, sɪŋg, sɪŋgə, sɪŋgɪŋg.

iv) Rule 1 (see above) applies to all these phonemic representations to give these phonetic forms: fɪŋgə, sɪŋg, sɪŋgə, sɪŋgɪŋg.

v) A further rule (Rule 2) must now be introduced:

Rule 2: g is deleted when it occurs after ŋ and before a morpheme boundary.

It should be clear that Rule 2 will not apply to 'finger' because the ŋ is not immediately followed by a morpheme boundary, but the rule does apply to all the others, hence the final phonetic forms: fɪŋgə, sɪŋ, sɪŋə, sɪŋɪŋ.

vi) Now we have to deal with an exception: comparative and superlative forms of adjectives ending in ŋ contain the sequence ŋg, e.g. 'long' lɒŋ, 'longer' (comparative) lɒŋgə, 'longest' (superlative) lɒŋgɪst. In fact there is a minimal pair in RP comprising 'longer' (= a person who longs) lɒŋə and 'longer' (comparative of 'long') lɒŋgə. Most generative phonologists would 'solve' this problem by saying that there is a *different* morpheme boundary found in the comparative and superlative forms, and that Rule 2 would have to be altered so as to exclude this particular type of morpheme boundary from its influence. An alternative is to say that the words 'longer', 'longest', 'stronger', 'strongest', etc. are specifically exempted from Rule 2. Both solutions are, of course, very '*ad hoc*' – that is, thought up just to explain away one particular problem.

The argument against treating ŋ as a phoneme may not appeal to you very much. The important point, however, is that if one is prepared to use the kind of complexity and abstractness illustrated above, one can produce quite far-reaching changes in the phonemic analysis of a language.

The other consonants, l, r, w and j do not, I think, need further explanation, except to mention that the question of whether j, w are consonants or vowels is discussed in O'Connor and Trim (1953).

Written exercises

1. List all the consonant phonemes of RP, grouped according to manner of articulation.

2. Transcribe the following words phonemically:

a)	sofa	e)	square
b)	verse	f)	anger
c)	steering	g)	bought
d)	breadcrumb	h)	nineteen

3. When the vocal tract is in its resting position for normal breathing, the soft palate is usually lowered. Describe what movements are carried out by the soft palate in the pronunciation of the following items:

    a) banner   b) mid   c) angle

8 The syllable

The syllable is a very important unit. Most people seem to believe that, even if they cannot define what a syllable *is*, they can count how many syllables there are in a given word or sentence. If they are asked to do this they often tap their finger as they count, which illustrates the syllable's importance in the rhythm of speech. As a matter of fact, if one tries the experiment of asking English speakers to count the syllables in, say, a tape-recorded sentence, there is often a considerable amount of disagreement.

The nature of the syllable

When we looked at the nature of vowels and consonants in Chapter 1 it was shown that one could decide whether a particular sound was a vowel or a consonant on phonetic grounds (in relation to how much they obstructed the airflow) or on phonological grounds (vowels and consonants having different distributions). We find a similar situation with the syllable, in that it may be defined both phonetically and phonologically. Phonetically (that is, in relation to the way we produce them and the way they sound), syllables are usually described as consisting of a centre which has little or no obstruction to airflow and which sounds comparatively loud; before and after this centre (that is, at the beginning and end of the syllable), there will be greater obstruction to airflow and/or less loud sound. We will now look at some examples:

i) What we might call a **minimum syllable** would be a single vowel in isolation, e.g. the words 'are' ɑː, 'or' ɔː, 'err' ɜː. These are preceded and followed by silence. Isolated sounds such as m, which we sometimes produce to indicate agreement, or ʃ, to ask for silence, must also be regarded as syllables.

ii) Some syllables have an **onset** (that is, they have more than just silence preceding the centre of the syllable):

'bar' bɑː   'key' kiː   'more' mɔː

iii) Syllables may have no onset but have a **coda**:

'am' æm   'ought' ɔːt   'ease' iːz

iv) Some syllables have onset and coda:

'run' rʌn   'sat' sæt   'fill' fɪl

There are still problems with this phonetic description of the syllable, particularly in the matter of deciding on the division between syllables. We will look at two words that are good examples of this difficulty. Most English speakers feel that the word 'going' gəʊɪŋ consists of two syllables; presumably we can decide that the ʊ in the middle is the dividing point between the two syllables, since the articulation is slightly closer to obstructing airflow than the vowels next to it. This still leaves unanswered the question of whether the ʊ belongs to the first or to the second syllable; of course, we know that the ʊ is part of the əʊ diphthong phoneme, but this is a fact of phonology, not of the phonetic structure of the syllable. Another difficult case is the word 'extra' ekstrə. One problem is that by some definitions the s in the middle, between k and t, would be counted as a syllable, which most English speakers would reject. They feel that the word has two syllables. However, opinions usually differ as to where the two syllables are to be divided; the possibilities are (using the symbol + to signify a syllable boundary):

e + kstrə   ek + strə   eks + trə   ekst + rə   ekstr + ə

Usually the second or third possibilities are chosen; it is not possible to say which of these is the correct choice.

Looking at syllables in this way, which at first seems the obvious thing to do, turns out not to be very useful. Looking at them from the phonological point of view is quite different. What this involves is looking at the possible combinations of English phonemes. It is simplest to start by looking at what can occur in initial position – in other words, what can occur at the beginning of the first word when we begin to speak after a pause. We find that the word can begin with a vowel, or with one, two or three consonants. No word begins with more than three consonants. In the same way, we can look at how a word ends when it is the last word spoken before a pause; it can end with a vowel, or with one, two, three or (in a small number of cases) four consonants. No word ends with more than four consonants.

The structure of the English syllable

Let us now look in more detail at syllable onsets. If the first syllable of the word in question begins with a vowel (any vowel may occur, though ʊ is rare) we say that this initial syllable has a **zero onset**. If the syllable begins with one consonant, that **initial** consonant may be any consonant phoneme except ŋ; ʒ is rare. We now look at syllables beginning with two consonants. When we have two or more consonants together we call them a **consonant cluster**.

Table 3. *Two-consonant clusters with pre-initial* s

PRE-s+									INITIAL								
p	t	k	b	d	g	f	θ	s	ʃ	h	v	ð	z	ʒ	m	n	ŋ
spɪn	stɪk	skɪn	—	—	—	sfɪə	—	—	—	—	—	—	—	—	smel	snəʊ	—

Note: Two-consonant clusters of s plus l, w, j are also possible (e.g. slɪp, swɪŋ, sjuː), and even perhaps sr in 'syringe' srɪndʒ for some speakers. These clusters can be analysed *either* as pre-initial s plus initial l, w, j, r or as initial s plus post-initial l, w, j, r. There is no clear answer to the question of which analysis is better; here they are treated in the latter way, and appear on Table 4.

69

Table 4. *Two-consonant clusters with post-initial* l, r, w, j

POST-INITIAL	p	t	k	b	d	g	f	θ	s	ʃ	h	v	ð	z	ʒ	m	n	ŋ	l	r	w	j
INITIAL																						
l	pleɪ	—	kleɪ	blæk	—	gluː	flaɪ	—	slɪp	—	—	—	—	—	—	—	—	—	—	—	—	—
r	preɪ	treɪ	kraɪ	brɪŋ	drɪp	grɪn	fraɪ	θrəʊ	?¹	ʃruː	—	—	—	—	—	—	—	—	—	—	—	—
w	—	twɪn	kwɪk	—	dwel	?²	—	θwɔːt	swɪm	?³	—	—	—	—	—	—	—	—	—	—	—	—
j	pjʊə	tjuːn	kjuː	bjuːti	djuː	?⁴	fjuː	?⁵	sjuː	—	hjuːdʒ	vjuː	—	—	—	mjuːz	njuːz	—	ljuːd	—	—	—

Notes on doubtful cases:

1 Some people pronounce the word 'syringe' as srɪndʒ; there are no other cases of sr, unless one counts foreign place names (Sri Lanka).

2 Many Welsh names (including some well-known outside Wales), such as girls' names like Gwen and place names like the county of Gwent, have initial gw and English speakers seem to find them perfectly easy to pronounce.

3 Two cases make ʃw seem familiar: the vowel name 'schwa', and the name of the soft drinks firm Schweppes. This is, however, a very infrequent consonant cluster for English.

4 The only possible occurrence of gj would be in the archaic (heraldic) word 'gules', which is in very few people's vocabulary.

5 θj occurs in the archaic word 'thew' only.

TU 8,
Exs 1 & 2

Initial two-consonant clusters are of two sorts in English. One sort is composed of s followed by one of a small set of consonants; examples of such clusters are found in words such as 'sting' stɪŋ, 'sway' sweɪ, 'smoke' sməʊk. The s in these clusters is called the **pre-initial** consonant and the other consonant (t, w, m in the above examples) the **initial** consonant. These clusters are shown in Table 3. The other sort begins with one of a set of about fifteen consonants, followed by one of the set l, r, w, j, as in, for example, 'play' pleɪ, 'try' traɪ, 'quick' kwɪk, 'few' fju:. We call the first consonant of these clusters the **initial** consonant and the second the **post-initial**.

There are some restrictions on which consonants can occur together. This can best be shown in table form (see Table 4).

TU 8,
Ex 2

When we look at three-consonant clusters we can recognise a clear relationship between them and the two sorts of two-consonant cluster described above; examples of three-consonant initial clusters are: 'split' splɪt, 'stream' stri:m, 'square' skweə. The s is the pre-initial consonant, the p, t and k that follow s in the three example words are the initial consonant and the l, r and w are post-initial. In fact, the number of possible initial three-consonant clusters is quite small and they can be set out in full (words given in spelling form):

		POST-INITIAL		
		l	r	w	j
	p	'splay'	'spray'	—	'spew'
S PLUS INITIAL	t	—	'string'	—	'stew'
	k	'sclerosis'	'screen'	'squeak'	'skewer'

TU 8,
Exs 3 & 4

We now have a similar task to do in studying **final** consonant clusters. Here we find the possibility of up to four consonants at the end of a word. If there is no final consonant we say that there is a **zero coda**. When there is one consonant only, this is called the **final** consonant. Any consonant may be a final consonant except h, r, w, j. There are two sorts of two-consonant final cluster, one being a final consonant preceded by a **pre-final** consonant and the other a final consonant followed by a **post-final** consonant. The pre-final consonants form a small set: m, n, ŋ, l, s. We can see these in 'bump' bʌmp, 'bent' bent, 'bank' bæŋk, 'belt' belt, 'ask' ɑ:sk. The post-final consonants also form a small set: s, z, t, d, θ; example words are: 'bets' bets, 'beds' bedz, 'backed' bækt, 'bagged' bægd, 'eighth' eɪtθ. These post-final consonants can often be identified as separate morphemes (though not always, e.g. 'axe' æks is a single morpheme and its final s has no separate meaning). A point of pronunciation can be pointed out here: the release of the first plosive of a plosive-plus-plosive cluster such as the g (of gd) in bægd or the k (of kt) in bækt is usually without plosion and is therefore practically inaudible.

TU 8, Ex 5

There are two types of final three-consonant cluster; the first is pre-final plus final plus post-final, as set out in the following table:

		PRE-FINAL	FINAL	POST-FINAL
'helped'	he	l	p	t
'banks'	bæ	ŋ	k	s
'bonds'	bɒ	n	d	z
'twelfth'	twe	l	f	θ

The second type shows that more than one post-final consonant can occur in a final cluster: final plus post-final 1 plus post-final 2. Post-final 2 is again one of s, z, t, d, θ.

		PRE-FINAL	FINAL	POST-FINAL 1	POST-FINAL 2
'fifths'	fɪ	—	f	θ	s
'next'	ne	—	k	s	t
'lapsed'	læ	—	p	s	t

Most four-consonant clusters can be analysed as consisting of a final consonant preceded by a pre-final and followed by post-final 1 and post-final 2, as shown below:

		PRE-FINAL	FINAL	POST-FINAL 1	POST-FINAL 2
'twelfths'	twe	l	f	θ	s
'prompts'	prɒ	m	p	t	s

A small number of cases seem to require different analysis, as consisting of a final consonant with no pre-final but *three* post-finals:

		PRE-FINAL	FINAL	POST-FINAL 1	POST-FINAL 2	POST-FINAL 3
'sixths'	sɪ	—	k	s	θ	s
'texts'	te	—	k	s	t	s

To sum up, we may describe the English syllable as having the following maximum phonological structure:

pre-initial	initial	post-initial	VOWEL	pre-final	final	post-final 1	post-final 2	post-final 3
ONSET				CODA				

It will be noticed that there must be a vowel in the centre of the syllable. There is a special case, that of **syllabic consonants** (which are introduced in the next chapter); we do *not*, for example, analyse the word 'students' stju:dn̩ts as consisting of one syllable with the three-consonant cluster stj for its onset and ending with a four-consonant cluster dnts. To fit in with what English speakers feel, we say that the word contains two syllables, with the consonant d dividing them and the second syllable ending with the cluster n̩ts; in other words, we treat the word as though there was a vowel between d and n, though a vowel only occurs here in very slow, careful pronunciation. This phonological problem of interpretation will be discussed in Chapter 13.

Recent work in phonology makes use of a rather more refined analysis of the syllable in which the vowel and the coda (if there is one) are known as the **rhyme**; if you think of rhyming English verse you will see that this works by matching just that part of the last syllable of a line. The rhyme is divided into the **peak** (normally the vowel) and the coda (but note that this is *optional* – the rhyme may have no coda, as in a word like 'me'). As we have seen, the syllable may also have an onset, but this is not obligatory. The structure is thus the following:

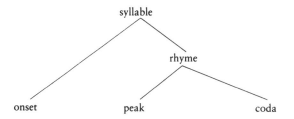

Analysing syllable structure, as we have been doing in this chapter, can be useful to foreign learners of English. Obviously there are many more limitations on possible combinations of vowels and consonants, but an understanding of the basic structures described above will help learners to become aware of precisely what type of consonant cluster presents pronunciation problems – most learners find *some* English clusters difficult, but few find *all* of them difficult.

Notes on problems and further reading

After rather a long period of neglect, the study of syllable structure has become a subject of considerable interest to phonologists. A paper that had a lot of influence on more recent work was Fudge (1969): this is not easy to read. Gimson (1989), section 9.8, gives a thorough coverage without much difficult theory, and presents useful tables of combinations of onsets with vowels and vowels with codas. Among more theoretical works, Kahn (1976) is an important monograph; you could read Hogg and McCully (1987), chapter 2, Katamba (1989), chapter 9, or Goldsmith (1990), chapter 3, for a modern review of the field.

The paper by Fudge brings up two ideas first discussed by earlier writers. The first is that **sp, st, sk** could be treated as individual phonemes, removing the pre-initial position from the syllable onset altogether and removing **s** from the pre-final set of consonants; the second is that since post-initial j only occurs before ʊ, uː and ʊə (which in his analysis all begin with the same vowel), one could postulate a diphthong ju and remove j from post-initial position. These are interesting proposals, but there is not enough space here to examine the arguments in full.

Note for teachers

The last paragraph of Chapter 8 explains why the study of syllable structure is relevant to the learner of English. English has a more complex syllable structure than most languages, and it follows from what is said in this chapter that it is advisable to discover exactly which types of consonant cluster are difficult for learners of a particular native-language background and construct exercises to give practice in them. There is practice material on consonant clusters in Mortimer (1984).

Written exercises

Using the analysis of the word 'cramped' given below as a model, analyse the structure of the following one-syllable English words:

	POST-INITIAL	INITIAL		PRE-FINAL	FINAL	POST-FINAL
'cramped'	k	r	æ	m	p	t
	ONSET		PEAK	CODA		

a)   squealed
b)   eighths
c)   splash
d)   texts

9 Strong and weak syllables

9.1 Strong and weak

One of the most noticeable features of English is that many syllables are **weak**; this is true of many other languages, but it is necessary to study how these weak syllables are pronounced and where they occur in English. The distribution of strong and weak syllables is a subject that will be met in several later chapters. For example, we will look later at **stress**, which is a major factor in determining whether a syllable will be strong or weak. **Elision** is a closely related subject, and in considering **intonation** the difference between strong and weak syllables is also important. Finally, words with "strong" and "weak" forms are clearly a related matter. In this chapter we look at the general nature of weak syllables.

What do we mean by "strong" and "weak"? In the present context, we are using these terms to refer to phonetic characteristics of syllables. We could describe them partly in terms of stress (by saying, for example, that strong syllables are stressed and weak syllables unstressed), but until we describe what "stress" *means* such a description would not be very useful. The most important thing to note at present is that any strong syllable will have as its peak one of the vowel phonemes (or possibly a triphthong) listed in Chapter 3, but not ə. Weak syllables, on the other hand, as they are being defined here, can only have four types of peak:

i)   the vowel ə ("schwa")
ii) a close front unrounded vowel in the general area of iː and ɪ
iii) a close back rounded vowel in the general area of uː and ʊ
iv) a syllabic consonant.

When we compare weak syllables containing vowels with strong syllables, we find the vowel in a weak syllable tends to be shorter, of lower intensity and different in quality. For example, in the word 'father' fɑːðə the second syllable, which is weak, is shorter than the first, is less loud and has a vowel that cannot occur in strong syllables. In a word like 'bottle' bɒtl̩ the weak second syllable contains no vowel at all, but consists entirely of the consonant l̩. We call this a **syllabic consonant**. In the rest of this chapter we will look at the different types of weak syllable in more detail.

9.2 The ə vowel ("schwa")

TU 9,
Ex 1 The most frequently occurring vowel in English is ə, which is always associated with weak syllables. In quality it is mid (that is, half-way between close and open) and central (that is, half-way between front and back). It is generally described as lax, that is, not articulated with much energy. Of course, the quality of this vowel is not always the same, but the variation is not important.

Not all weak syllables contain ə, though many do. Learners of English need to learn where ə is appropriate and where it is not. To do this we often have to use information that traditional phonemic theory would not accept as relevant – we must consider spelling. The question to ask is: if the speaker were to pronounce a particular weak syllable as strong instead, which vowel would it be most likely to have, according to the usual rules of English spelling? Of course, knowing this will not tell us which syllables in a word or utterance should be weak – that is something we look at in later chapters – but it will give us a rough guide to the correct pronunciation of weak syllables. Let us look at some examples:

i) Spelt with 'a'; strong pronunciation would have æ
      'attend' ətend   'character' kærəktə
      'barracks' bærəks

ii) Spelt with 'ar'; strong pronunciation would have ɑː
      'particular' pətɪkjələ   'molar' məʊlə
      'monarchy' mɒnəkɪ

iii) Adjectival endings spelt 'ate'; strong pronunciation would have eɪ
      'intimate' ɪntɪmət   'accurate' ækjərət
      'desolate' desələt (though there are exceptions to this: 'private' is usually praɪvɪt)

iv) Spelt with 'o'; strong pronunciation would have ɒ
      'tomorrow' təmɒrəʊ   'potato' pəteɪtəʊ
      'carrot' kærət

v) Spelt with 'or'; strong pronunciation would have ɔː
      'forget' fəget   'ambassador' æmbæsədə
      'opportunity' ɒpətjuːnɪtɪ

vi) Spelt with 'e'; strong pronunciation would have e
      'settlement' set|mənt   'violet' vaɪələt
      'postmen' pəʊstmən

vii) Spelt with 'er'; strong pronunciation would have ɜː
      'perhaps' pəhæps   'stronger' strɒŋgə
      'superman' suːpəmæn

viii) Spelt with 'u'; strong pronunciation would have ʌ
      'Autumn' ɔːtəm   'support' səpɔːt
      'halibut' hælɪbət

ix) Spelt with 'ough' (there are, of course, many other pronunciations for the letter-sequence 'ough')

'thor*ough*' θʌrə   'bor*ough*' bʌrə

x) Spelt with 'ous'

'graci*ous*' greɪʃəs   'call*ous*' kæləs

9.3   Close front and close back vowels

Two other vowels are commonly found in weak syllables, one close front (in the general region of iː and ɪ) and the other close back rounded (in the general region of uː and ʊ). In strong syllables it is comparatively easy to distinguish iː from ɪ, uː from ʊ, but in weak syllables the difference is not so clear. For example, although it is easy enough to decide which vowel one hears in 'beat' or 'bit', it is much less easy to decide which vowel one hears in the second syllable of words such as, for example, 'easy' or 'busy'. There are accents of English (for example Welsh accents) in which the second syllable sounds most like the iː in the first syllable of 'easy', and others (for example Yorkshire accents) in which it sounds more like the ɪ in the first syllable of 'busy'. In present-day RP, however, the matter is not so clear. There is uncertainty, too, about the corresponding close back rounded vowels. If we look at the words 'good to eat' and 'food to eat', we must ask if the word 'to' is pronounced with the ʊ vowel phoneme of 'good' or the uː phoneme of 'food'. Again, which vowel comes in 'to' in 'I want to'?

One common feature is that the vowels in question are more like iː or uː when they precede another vowel, less so when they precede a consonant or pause. You should notice one further thing: with the exception of one or two very artificial examples, there is really no possibility in these contexts of contrast between iː and ɪ, or between uː and ʊ. Effectively, then, the two distinctions, which undoubtedly exist within strong syllables, are **neutralised** in RP. How should we transcribe the words 'easy' and 'busy' as pronounced in RP? We will use the close front unrounded case as an example, since it is more straightforward. The possibilities, using our phoneme symbols, are the following:

    'easy'   'busy'
i) iːziː   bɪziː
ii) iːzɪ   bɪzɪ

Few speakers of RP seem to feel satisfied with any of these transcriptions. There is a possible solution to this problem, but it goes against standard phoneme theory. We can symbolise this weak vowel as i, that is, using the symbol for the vowel in 'beat' but without the length-mark. Thus:

iːzi   bɪzi

The i vowel is neither the iː of 'beat' nor the ɪ of 'bit', and is not in contrast with them. We can set up a corresponding vowel u that is neither the uː of 'shoe' nor the ʊ of 'book' but a weak vowel that shares the characteristics of both. If we use i and u in our transcription as well as iː, ɪ, uː and ʊ, it is no longer a true phonemic transcription in the traditional sense. However, this need not be too serious an objection, and the fact that native speakers seem to think that this transcription fits better with their feelings about the language is a good argument in its favour.

Let us now look at where these vowels are found, beginning with close front unrounded ones. We find i occurring:

i) In word-final position in words spelt with final 'y' or 'ey' (after one or more consonant letters), e.g. 'happy' hæpi, 'valley' væli, and in morpheme-final position when such words have suffixes beginning with vowels, e.g. 'happier' hæpiə, 'easiest' iːziəst, 'hurrying' hʌriiŋ.

ii) In a prefix such as those spelt 're', 'pre', 'de' if it precedes a vowel and is unstressed, for example in 'react' riækt, 'preoccupied' priɒkjʊpaɪd, 'deactivate' diæktɪveɪt.

iii) In the suffixes spelt 'iate', 'ious' when they have two syllables, for example in 'appreciate' əpriːʃieɪt, 'hilarious' hɪleəriəs.

iv) In the following words when unstressed: 'he', 'she', 'we', 'me', 'be' and the word 'the' when it precedes a vowel.

In most other cases of weak syllables containing a close front unrounded vowel we can assign the vowel to the ɪ phoneme, as in the first syllable of 'resist' rɪzɪst, 'inane' ɪneɪn, 'enough' ɪnʌf, the middle syllable of 'incident' ɪnsɪdn̩t, 'orchestra' ɔːkɪstrə, 'artichoke' ɑːtɪtʃəʊk, and the final syllable of 'swimming' swɪmɪŋ, 'liquid' lɪkwɪd, 'optic' ɒptɪk. It can be seen that this vowel is most often represented in spelling by the letters 'i' and 'e'.

Weak syllables with close back rounded vowels are not so commonly found. We find u most frequently in the words 'you', 'to', 'into', 'do', when they are unstressed and are not immediately preceding a consonant, and 'through' and 'who' in all positions when they are unstressed. This vowel is also found before another vowel within a word, as in 'evacuation' ɪvækjueɪʃn̩, 'influenza' ɪnfluenzə.

9.4 Syllabic consonants

In the above sections we have looked at vowels in weak syllables. We must also consider syllables in which no vowel is found. In this case, a consonant, either l, r or a nasal, stands as the centre of the syllable instead of the vowel. It is usual to indicate that a consonant is syllabic by means of a small vertical mark ˌ, for example 'cattle' kætl̩.

l

TU 9,
Ex 3

Syllabic l̩ is perhaps the most noticeable example of the English syllabic consonant, though it would be wrong to expect to find it in all accents. It occurs after another consonant, and the way it is produced depends to some extent on the nature of that consonant. If the preceding consonant is alveolar, as in 'bottle' bɒtl̩, 'muddle' mʌdl̩, 'tunnel' tʌnl̩, the articulatory movement from the preceding consonant to the syllabic l is quite simple. The sides of the tongue, which are raised for the preceding consonant, are lowered to allow air to escape over them (this is called **lateral release**). The tip and blade of the tongue do not move until the articulatory contact for the l̩ is released. The l̩ is a "dark l" (as explained in Chapter 7). In some accents – particularly London ones – we often find a close back rounded vowel instead.

Where do we find syllabic l̩ in RP? It is useful to look at the spelling as a guide. The most obvious case is where we have a word ending with one or more consonant letters followed by 'le' (or, in the case of noun plurals or third person singular verb forms, 'les'). Examples are:

i) with alveolar consonant preceding

'cattle' kætl̩   'bottle' bɒtl̩
'wrestle' resl̩   'muddle' mʌdl̩

ii) with non-alveolar consonant preceding

'couple' kʌpl̩   'trouble' trʌbl̩
'struggle' strʌgl̩   'knuckle' nʌkl̩

Such words usually lose their final letter 'e' when a suffix beginning with a vowel is attached, but the l usually remains syllabic. Thus:

'bottle' – 'bottling'   bɒtl̩ – bɒtl̩ɪŋ
'muddle' – 'muddling'   mʌdl̩ – mʌdl̩ɪŋ
'struggle' – 'struggling'   strʌgl̩ – strʌgl̩ɪŋ

Similar words not derived in this way do not have the syllabic l̩ – it has been pointed out that the two words 'coddling' (derived from the verb 'coddle') and 'codling' (meaning "small cod", derived by adding the diminutive suffix '-ling' to 'cod') show a contrast between syllabic and non-syllabic l: 'coddling' kɒdl̩ɪŋ and 'codling' kɒdlɪŋ. In the case of words such as 'bottle', 'muddle', 'struggle', which are quite common, it would be a mispronunciation to insert a vowel between the l and the preceding consonant. There are a few accents of English which may do this, so that, for example, 'cattle' is pronounced kætəl, but this is not the case in RP.

We also find syllabic l̩ in words spelt with, at the end, one or more consonant letters followed by 'al' or 'el', for example:

'panel' pænl̩	'papal' peɪpl̩
'petal' petl̩	'parcel' pɑːsl̩
'kernel' kɜːnl̩	'Babel' beɪbl̩
'pedal' pedl̩	'ducal' djuːkl̩

In some less common or more technical words, it is not obligatory to pronounce syllabic l̩ and the sequence əl may be used instead, though it is less likely: 'missal' mɪsl̩ or mɪsəl; 'acquittal' əkwɪtl̩ or əkwɪtəl.

n

TU 9,
Ex 4

Of the syllabic nasals, the most frequently found and the most important is n̩. When should it be pronounced? A general rule could be made that weak syllables which are phonologically composed of a plosive or fricative consonant plus ən are uncommon except in initial position in the words. So we can find words like 'tonight' tənaɪt, 'canary' kəneəri with an ə before n, but medially and finally, as in words like 'threaten', 'threatening', we find much more commonly a syllabic n̩: θretn̩, θretn̩ɪŋ. To pronounce a vowel before the nasal consonant would sound strange (or at best overcareful) in RP. Syllabic n̩ is most common after alveolar plosives and fricatives; in the case of t and d followed by n̩ the plosive is **nasally released** by lowering the soft palate, so that in the word 'eaten' iːtn̩, for example, the tongue does not move in the tn̩ sequence but the soft palate is lowered at the end of t so that compressed air escapes through the nose. We do not find n̩ after l or tʃ, dʒ, so that for example 'sullen' must be pronounced sʌlən, 'Christian' as krɪstʃən (though this word may be pronounced with t plus i or j instead of tʃ) and 'pigeon' as pɪdʒən.

Syllabic n̩ after non-alveolar consonants is not so widespread. In words where the syllable following a velar consonant is spelt 'an' or 'on' (for example, 'toboggan', 'wagon') it is rarely heard, the more usual pronunciation being təbɒgən, wægən. After bilabial consonants, in words like 'happen', 'happening', 'ribbon' we can consider it equally acceptable to pronounce them with syllabic n̩ (hæpn̩, hæpn̩ɪŋ, rɪbn̩) or with ən (hæpən, hæpənɪŋ, rɪbən). As we will see, syllabic m̩ is also possible in this context. In a similar way, after velar consonants in words like 'thicken', 'waken', syllabic n̩ is possible but ən is also acceptable. Syllabic velar nasal ŋ̍ is also possible in this context.

After f or v, syllabic n̩ is more common than ən (except, as with the other cases described, in word-initial syllables). Thus 'seven', 'heaven', 'often' are more usually sevn̩, hevn̩, ɒfn̩ than sevən, hevən, ɒfən.

In all the examples given so far the syllabic n̩ has been following another consonant; sometimes it is possible for another consonant to precede that consonant, but in this case a syllabic consonant is less likely to occur. If l is followed by a plosive, as in 'Wilton', the pronunciation wɪltn̩ is possible, but wɪltən is also found regularly. If s precedes, as in 'Boston', a final syllabic nasal is less frequent, while clusters formed by nasal + plosive + syllabic nasal are very unusual: thus 'Minton', 'lantern', 'London', 'abandon' will normally have ə in the last syllable and be pronounced mɪntən, læntən, lʌndən, əbændən. Other nasals also discourage a following plosive plus syllabic nasal, so that for example 'Camden' is normally pronounced kæmdən.

m, ŋ

We will not spend much time on the syllabic pronunciation of these consonants. Both c̩·n occur as syllabic, but only as a result of processes such as assimilation and elision that I have not yet described. We find them sometimes in words like 'happen', which can be pronounced hæpm̩, though hæpn̩ and hæpən are equally acceptable, and 'uppermost', which could be pronounced as ʌpm̃aʊst though ʌpəməʊst would be more usual. Examples of possible syllabic velar nasals would be 'thicken' θɪkŋ̩ (where θɪkən and θɪkn̩ are also possible), and 'broken key' brəʊkŋ̩ kiː, where the nasal consonant occurs between velar consonants (again, n̩ or ən could be substituted for ŋ).

A note about symbols: the usual convention for the syllabic mark is that it should be placed below symbols that do not come below the line, for example m̩, n̩ but above a symbol that does come below the line, for example ŋ̇. In this course, however, it is felt preferable to put the mark underneath the symbol in all cases of syllabic consonants.

r

In many accents of the type called "rhotic" (as explained in Chapter 7), such as most American accents, syllabic r̩ is very common. The word 'particular', for example, would probably be pronounced pr̩tɪkjəlr̩ by most Americans, while RP speakers would pronounce this word pətɪkjələ. Syllabic r̩ is less common in RP and in most cases where it occurs there are perfectly acceptable alternative pronunciations without the syllabic consonant. Here are some examples:

a) where non-syllabic r is also acceptable
     'history' hɪstr̩i or hɪstri (not usually hɪstəri)
     'wanderer' wɒndr̩ə or wɒndrə (not usually wɒndərə)

b) where ər is also acceptable

    'buttering' bʌtrɪŋ or bʌtərɪŋ (not usually bʌtrɪŋ)

    'flattery' flætrɪ or flætəri (not usually flætri)

It seems that type (a) concerns cases where more than one consonant precedes the weak syllable in question, and type (b) where there is only one consonant preceding. There are a few pairs of words (**minimal pairs**) in which a difference in meaning appears to depend on whether a particular r is syllabic or not, for example:

    'Hungary' hʌŋgrɪ   'hungry' hʌŋgri

    'adulterous' ədʌltrəs   'adultress' ədʌltrəs

But we find no case of syllabic r̩ where it would not be possible to substitute either non-syllabic r (type a) or ər (type b); in the examples above, 'Hungary' could equally well be pronounced hʌŋgəri and 'adulterous' as ədʌltərəs.

Combinations of syllabic consonants

It is not unusual to find two syllabic consonants together. Examples are: 'national' næʃn̩l̩ 'literal' lɪtr̩l̩ 'visionary' vɪʒn̩ri 'veteran' vetrn̩. It is important to remember that it is often not possible to say with certainty whether a speaker has pronounced a syllabic consonant, a non-syllabic consonant or a non-syllabic consonant plus ə. For example, the word 'veteran' given above could be pronounced in other ways than vetrn̩. An RP speaker might instead say vetrən, vetərn̩ or vetərən. The transcription makes it look as if the difference between these words was clear; it is not. In examining colloquial English it is often more or less a matter of arbitrary choice how one transcribes such a word. Transcription has the unfortunate tendency to make things seem simpler and more clear-cut than they really are.

Notes on problems and further reading

9.1   I have at this point tried to bring in some preliminary notions of stress and prominence without giving a full explanation; by this stage in the course it is important to be getting familiar with the difference between stressed and unstressed syllables, and the nature of "schwa", but the subject of stress is such a large one that I have felt it best to leave its main treatment until later.

9.2   On the subject of schwa, see Jones (1975), sections 355–72; Gimson (1989), 7.9.12.

9.3 The introduction of i and u is an idea that not everyone agrees with, but its acceptance as a convention in two influential dictionaries (the *Longman Dictionary of Contemporary English* and the *Longman Pronunciation Dictionary*) gives substantial support. Since I mention native speakers' feelings in this connection, and since I am elsewhere rather sceptical about appeals to native speakers' feelings, I had better explain that in this case my evidence comes from the native speakers of English I have taught in practical classes on transcription over many years. A substantial number of these students have either been speakers of RP or had accents only slightly different from it, and their usual reaction to being told to use ɪ for the vowel at the end of 'easy', 'busy' has been one of puzzlement and frustration; like them, I cannot equate this vowel with the vowel of 'bit'. I am, however, reluctant to use iː, which suggests a stronger vowel than should be pronounced (like the final vowel in 'evacuee', 'Tennessee'). For some time, I told students that since ɪ and iː were equally unsuitable for this vowel in the context in question, I would accept either in a transcription. This, not unnaturally, led to further confusion on the students' part, and the treatment suggested here was adopted as the solution that fitted best with what the students felt they wanted to write. I must emphasise that the vowels i and u are *not* included in the set of English phonemes but are simply additional symbols to make the writing and reading of transcription easier.

9.4 I feel that the subject of syllabic consonants is an area that we need to know more about, and that there has not yet been enough discussion of the problems found in their analysis. See Wells (1965).

Notes for teachers

Introduction of the "schwa" vowel has been deliberately delayed until this chapter, since I wanted it to be presented in the context of weak syllables in general. Since students should by now be comparatively well-informed about basic segmental phonetics, it is very important that their production and recognition of this vowel should be good before moving on to the following chapters.

This chapter is in a sense a crucial point in the course: although the segmental material of the preceding chapters is important as a foundation, the relationship between strong and weak syllables and the overall prosodic characteristics of words and sentences are essential to intelligibility, and most of the remaining chapters of the course are concerned with such matters.

Written exercises

The following sentences have been partially transcribed, but the vowels have been left blank. Fill in the vowels, taking care to identify which vowels are weak; put no vowel at all if you think a syllabic consonant is appropriate, but put a syllabic mark beneath the syllabic consonant.

1. A particular problem of the boat was a leak
   p   t kjl   pr bl m   v ð   b   t w z   l   k
2. Opening the bottle presented no difficulty
   p n ŋ   ð   b tl   pr z nt d n   d f k|t
3. There is no alternative to the Government's proposal
   ð   r   z n   lt n t v   t   ð   g v nm nt s pr p z|
4. We ought to make a collection to cover the expenses
   w   t t   m   k l kʃ   n t   k v   ð   k sp ns z
5. Finally they arrived at a harbour at the edge of the mountains
   f n l   ð   r vd   t   h   b   r t ð   dʒ v   m   nt nz

10 Stress in simple words

10.1 The nature of stress

TU 10,
Ex 1

Stress has been mentioned several times already in this course without any attempt to define what the word means. The nature of stress is simple enough – practically everyone would agree that the first syllable of words like 'father', 'open', 'camera' is stressed, that the middle syllable is stressed in 'potato', 'apartment', 'relation' and that the final syllable is stressed in 'about', 'receive', 'perhaps', and most people feel they have some sort of idea of what the difference is between stressed and unstressed syllables, though they might explain it in many different ways. We will mark a stressed syllable in transcription by placing a small vertical line ' high up, just before the syllable it relates to; the words quoted above will thus be transcribed as follows:

'fɑːðə	pə'teɪtəʊ	ə'baʊt
'əʊpən	ə'pɑːtmənt	rɪ'siːv
'kæmrə	rɪ'leɪʃn̩	pə'hæps

What are the characteristics of stressed syllables that enable us to identify them? It is important to understand that there are two different ways of approaching this question, one being to consider what the speaker does in producing stressed syllables and the other being to consider what characteristics of sound make a syllable seem to a listener to be stressed. In other words we can study stress from the point of view of **production** and of **perception**; the two are obviously closely related, but are not identical. The production of stress is generally believed to depend on the speaker using more muscular energy than is used for unstressed syllables. Measuring muscular effort is difficult, but it seems possible, according to experimental studies, that when we produce stressed syllables, the muscles that we use to expel air from the lungs are more active, producing higher subglottal pressure. It seems probable that similar things happen with muscles in other parts of our speech apparatus.

Many experiments have been carried out on the perception of stress, and it is clear that many different sound characteristics are important in making a syllable recognisably stressed. From the perceptual point of view, all stressed syllables have one characteristic in common, and that is

prominence; stressed syllables are recognised as stressed because they are more **prominent** than unstressed syllables. What makes a syllable prominent? At least four different factors are important.

i) Most people seem to feel that stressed syllables are **louder** than unstressed; in other words, loudness is a component of prominence. In a sequence of identical syllables (e.g. **ba:ba:ba:ba:**), if one syllable is made louder than the others, it will be heard as stressed. However, it is important to realise that it is very difficult for a speaker to make a syllable louder without changing other characteristics of the syllable such as those explained below (ii–iv); if one literally changes *only* the loudness, the perceptual effect is not very strong.

ii) The **length** of syllables has an important part to play in prominence. If one of the syllables in our "nonsense word" **ba:ba:ba:ba:** is made longer than the others, there is quite a strong tendency for that syllable to be heard as stressed.

iii) Every syllable is said on some **pitch**; pitch in speech is closely related to the frequency of vibration of the vocal folds and to the musical notion of low- and high-pitched notes. It is essentially a *perceptual* characteristic of speech. If one syllable of our "nonsense word" is said with a pitch that is noticeably different from that of the others, this will have a strong tendency to produce the effect of prominence. For example, if all syllables are said with low pitch except for one said with high pitch, then the high-pitched syllable will be heard as stressed and the others as unstressed. To place some *movement* of pitch (e.g. rising or falling) on a syllable is even more effective.

iv) A syllable will tend to be prominent if it contains a vowel that is different in **quality** from neighbouring vowels. If we change one of the vowels in our "nonsense word" (e.g. **ba:bi:ba:ba:**) the "odd" syllable **bi:** will tend to be heard as stressed. This effect is not very powerful nor very important, but there is one particular way in which it is relevant in English: the previous chapter explained how the most frequently encountered vowels in weak syllables are ɪ, ʊ and ə (syllabic consonants are also quite common). We can look on stressed syllables as occurring against a "background" of these weak syllables, so that their prominence is increased by contrast with these background qualities.

Prominence, then, is produced by four main factors: (i) loudness, (ii) length, (iii) pitch and (iv) quality. Generally these four factors work together in combination, though syllables may sometimes be made prominent by means of only one or two of them. Experimental work has shown that these factors are not equally important; the strongest effect is produced by pitch, and length is also a powerful factor. Loudness and quality have much less effect.

10.2 **Levels of stress**

Up to this point we have talked about stress as though there was a simple distinction between "stressed" and "unstressed" syllables with no intermediate levels; such a treatment would be a **two-level** analysis of stress. Usually, however, we have to recognise one or more intermediate levels. It should be remembered that in this chapter we are dealing only with stress *within the word*; this means that we are looking at words as they are said in isolation, which is a rather artificial situation – we do not often say words in isolation, except for a few such as 'yes', 'no', 'possibly', 'please' and interrogative words such as 'what', 'who', etc., but looking at words in isolation does help us to see stress placement and stress levels more clearly than studying them in the context of continuous speech.

Let us begin by looking at the word 'around' əˈraʊnd, where the stress always falls clearly on the last syllable and the first syllable is weak. From the point of view of stress, the most important fact about the way we pronounce this word is that on the second syllable the pitch of the voice does not remain level, but usually falls from a higher to a lower pitch. We might diagram the pitch movement as shown below, where the two parallel lines represent the speaker's high and low pitch level:

The prominence that results from this pitch movement, or **tone**, gives the strongest type of stress; this is called **primary stress**.

In some words, we can observe a type of stress that is weaker than primary stress but stronger than that of the first syllable of 'around', for example in the first syllables of the words 'photographic' fəʊtəgræfɪk, 'anthropology' ænθrəpɒlədʒi. The stress in these words is called **secondary stress**. It is sometimes represented in transcription with a low mark ˌ so that the examples could be transcribed as ˌfəʊtəˈgræfɪk, ˌænθrəˈpɒlədʒi. This convention will only be used where necessary in this course.

We have now identified two levels of stress: primary and secondary, as well as a third level which can be called unstressed and regarded as being the absence of any recognisable amount of prominence. These are the three levels that we will use in describing English stress. However, it is worth noting that unstressed syllables containing ə, ɪ, ʊ or a syllabic

87

D

consonant will sound less prominent than an unstressed syllable containing some other vowel. For example, the first syllable of 'poetic' pəʊˈetɪk is more prominent than the first syllable of 'pathetic' pəˈθetɪk. This *could* be used as a basis for a further division of stress levels, giving us a third and fourth level, but it seems unnecessarily complex to do so.

10.3 Placement of stress within the word

We now come to a question that causes a great deal of difficulty, particularly to foreign learners (who cannot simply dismiss it as an academic question): how can one select the correct syllable or syllables to stress in an English word? As is well known, English is not one of those languages where word stress can be decided simply in relation to the syllables of the word, as can be done in French (where the last syllable is usually stressed), Polish (where the syllable before the last – the penultimate syllable – is stressed) or Czech (where the first syllable is stressed). Many writers have said that English word stress is so difficult to predict that it is best to treat stress placement as a property of the individual word, to be learned when the word itself is learned. Certainly anyone who tries to analyse English stress placement has to recognise that it is a highly complex matter. However, it must also be recognised that in most cases when English speakers come across an unfamiliar word, they can pronounce it with the correct stress (there are exceptions to this, of course); in principle, it should be possible to discover what it is that the English speaker knows and to write in the form of rules. The following summary of ideas on stress placement in nouns, verbs and adjectives is an attempt to present a few rules in the simplest possible form. Nevertheless, practically all the rules have exceptions and readers may feel that the rules are so complex that it would be easier to go back to the idea of learning the stress for each word individually.

In order to decide on stress placement, it is necessary to make use of some or all of the following information:

i)   Whether the word is morphologically **simple**, or whether it is **complex** as a result either of containing one or more affixes (that is, prefixes or suffixes) or of being a compound word.

ii) The grammatical category to which the word belongs (noun, verb, adjective, etc.).

iii) The number of syllables in the word.

iv) The phonological structure of those syllables.

It is sometimes difficult to make the decision referred to in (i). The rules

[handwritten: Single syllables]

for complex words are different from those for simple words and these will be dealt with in Chapter 11. Obviously, single-syllable words present no problems – if they are pronounced in isolation they are said with primary stress.

Two-syllable words

[handwritten: on 2 syllable words only 1 syl will be stressed]

Here the *choice* is still simple: either the first or the second syllable will be stressed – not both. We will look first at verbs. The basic rule is that if the second syllable of the verb contains a long vowel or diphthong, or if it ends with more than one consonant, that second syllable is stressed. Thus:

TU 10,
Ex 3

'apply' ə'plaɪ	'attract' ə'trækt
'arrive' ə'raɪv	'assist' ə'sɪst

If the final syllable contains a short vowel and one (or no) final consonant, the first syllable is stressed. Thus:

'enter' 'entə	'open' 'əʊpən
'envy' 'envi	'equal' 'iːkwəl

A final syllable is also unstressed if it contains əʊ (e.g. 'follow' 'fɒləʊ, 'borrow' 'bɒrəʊ). Most two-syllable verbs that seem to be exceptions to the above might be interpreted as being morphologically complex (e.g. 'permit' pə'mɪt = 'per' + 'mit'), or we could simply list all such verbs as exceptions.

TU 10,
Ex 3

Two-syllable simple adjectives are stressed according to the same rule, giving:

'lovely' 'lʌvli	'divine' dɪ'vaɪn
'even' 'iːvn̩	'correct' kə'rekt
'hollow' 'hɒləʊ	'alive' ə'laɪv

As with most stress rules, there are exceptions, for example 'honest' 'ɒnɪst, 'perfect' 'pɜːfɪkt or 'pɜːfekt, both of which end with two consonants but are stressed on the first syllable.

Nouns require a different rule: if the second syllable contains a short vowel the stress will usually come on the first syllable. Otherwise it will be on the second syllable.

'money' 'mʌni	'estate' ɪ'steɪt
'product' 'prɒdʌkt	'balloon' bə'luːn
'larynx' 'lærɪŋks	'design' dɪ'zaɪn

Other two-syllable words such as adverbs and prepositions seem to behave like verbs and adjectives.

Three-syllable words

Here we find a more complicated picture. In verbs, if the last syllable contains a short vowel and ends with not more than one consonant, that syllable will be unstressed, and stress will be placed on the preceding (penultimate) syllable. Thus:

'encounter' ɪŋˈkaʊntə   'determine' dɪˈtɜːmɪn

If the final syllable contains a long vowel or diphthong, or ends with more than one consonant, that final syllable will be stressed. Thus:

'entertain' entəˈteɪn   'resurrect' rezəˈrekt

Nouns require a different rule. Here, if the final syllable contains a short vowel or əʊ, it is unstressed; if the syllable preceding this final syllable contains a long vowel or diphthong, or if it ends with more than one consonant, that middle syllable will be stressed. Thus:

'mimosa' mɪˈməʊzə   'disaster' dɪˈzɑːstə
'potato' pəˈteɪtəʊ   'synopsis' sɪˈnɒpsɪs

If the final syllable contains a short vowel and the middle syllable contains a short vowel and ends with not more than one consonant, both final and middle syllables are unstressed and the first syllable is stressed:

'quantity' ˈkwɒntɪti   'emperor' ˈempr̩ə
'cinema' ˈsɪnəmə   'custody' ˈkʌstədi

Most of the above rules show stress tending to go on syllables containing a long vowel or diphthong and/or ending with more than one consonant. However, three-syllable simple nouns are different. If the final syllable is of this type, the stress will usually be placed on the *first* syllable. The last syllable is usually quite prominent so that in some cases it could be said to have secondary stress.

'intellect' ˈɪntəlekt   'marigold' ˈmærɪɡəʊld
'alkali' ˈælkəlaɪ   'stalactite' ˈstæləktaɪt
  (or ˈælkḷaɪ)

Adjectives seem to need the same rule, to produce stress patterns such as:

'opportune' ˈɒpətjuːn   'insolent' ˈɪnsl̩ənt
'derelict' ˈderəlɪkt   'anthropoid' ˈænθrəpɔɪd

The above rules do not, of course, cover all English words. They apply only to major categories of **lexical** words (nouns, verbs and adjectives in this chapter), not to **function** words such as articles and prepositions. There is not enough space in this course to deal with simple words of more than three syllables, nor with special cases of **loan words** (words brought into the language from other languages comparatively recently). Complex and compound words are dealt with in the next chapter. One problem that we must also leave until the next chapter is the fact that there are many cases of English words with alternative possible stress patterns (e.g. 'controversy', either 'kɒntrəvɜːsi or kən'trɒvəsi). Other words, which we will look at in studying connected speech, change their stress pattern according to the context they occur in. Above all, there is not space to discuss the many exceptions to the above rules. Despite the exceptions, it seems better in many ways to attempt to produce some stress rules (even if they are rather crude and inaccurate) than to claim that there is no rule or regularity in English word stress.

Notes on problems and further reading

The subject of English stress has received a large amount of attention, and the references given here are only a small selection from an enormous number. As I implied in the notes on the previous chapter, incorrect stress placement is the major cause of intelligibility problems for foreign learners, and is therefore a subject that needs to be treated very seriously.

10.1 I have deliberately avoided using the term **accent**, which is found widely in the literature on stress. This is for three main reasons:

(i)   it increases the complexity of the description without, in my view, contributing much to its value.

(ii) different writers do not agree with each other about the way the term should be used.

(iii) the word 'accent' is used elsewhere to refer to different varieties of pronunciation (e.g. "a foreign accent"); it is confusing to use it for a quite different purpose – to a lesser extent we also have this problem with 'stress', which can be used to refer to psychological tension.

There is a good discussion of the confusing nature of the terms 'stress' and 'accent' in Clark and Yallop (1990), pp. 288–9; see also Kreidler (1989), pp. 75–6 and Gimson (1989), sections, 9.1–9.7, 10.1–10.4.

An important study of muscular effort and air-pressure in stressed syllables is that reported in Ladefoged (1967), pp. 1–49. Although many experimental studies have been carried out since then, this remains the clearest and best-known work. On the perception of stress, the pioneering work is by Fry (e.g. 1958).

10.2   Many studies of stress have tried to deal with the question of the numbers of different levels. Arnold (1957) presents a well-reasoned approach; most writers conclude that three levels (primary, secondary and unstressed) are required, as outlined in this chapter.

10.3   It is said above that one must take one of two positions: one is that stress is *not* predictable by rule and must be learned word by word (see for example Jones (1975), sections 920–1). The second (which I prefer) is to say that, difficult though the task is, one must try to find a way of writing rules that express what native speakers naturally tend to do in placing stress (while acknowledging that there will always be a substantial residue of cases which appear to follow no regular rules). Kingdon (1958b) produced a detailed survey of stress tendencies in a corpus of many thousands of words; the analysis is based not only on phonological structure but also on etymology and morphology. The result is that it is very complex; in addition, I must note that quite a few words are given stress patterns that I do not feel are acceptable in present-day English. A more modern, and very thorough treatment is Fudge (1984), which is an extremely valuable work on the subject and in many ways takes over the place of Kingdon's earlier work.

The other well-known approach to English stress rules is radically different, being based on **generative phonology**. This is the analysis which was presented in Chomsky and Halle (1968) and has been followed by an enormous number of works exploring the same field. To anyone not familiar with this type of treatment, the presentation will seem difficult or even unintelligible; within the generative approach, many different theories, all with different names, tend to come and go with changes in fashion, which is very confusing. The following paragraph is an attempt to summarise the main characteristics of basic generative phonology, and recommends some further reading for those interested in learning about it properly.

The level of phonology is very abstract in this theory. An old-fashioned view of speech communication would be that what the speaker intends to say is coded, or *represented*, as a string of phonemes just like a phonemic transcription, and what a hearer hears is also converted by the brain from sound waves into a similar string of phonemes. But a generative phonologist would say that this phonemic representation is irrelevant; the representation in the brain of the speaker or hearer is much more complex and is often quite different from the 'real' sounds recognisable in the sound wave. You may *hear* the word 'football' pronounced as fʊpbɔːl, but your brain recognises the word as made up of 'foot' and 'ball' and interprets it phonologically as fʊtbɔːl. You may hear ə in the first syllable of 'photography', in the second syllable of 'photograph' and in the third syllable of 'photographer', but the brain recognises links between these ə vowels and əʊ, ɒ and æ respectively, and supplies *underlying* vowels which change into the appropriate sound as the stress pattern changes. These vowel changes are brought about by *rules* – not the sort of rules that one might teach to language learners, but more like the instructions that one might build into a machine or write into a computer program. According to Chomsky and Halle, at the abstract phonological level there is no stress; stress (of many different levels) is the result of the application of phonological rules, which are simple enough in theory but highly complex in practice. The principles of these rules are explained first in pp. 15–43 of their book, and in greater detail in pp. 69–162.

There is a clear and thorough introductory account of generative phonology in Clark and Yallop (1990), chapter 6, and they present a brief account of the generative treatment of stress on pp. 300–3. A brief review that covers more modern forms of generative treatment is in Katamba (1989), chapter 11, section 1.

Notes for teachers

It should be clear from what is said above that from the purely practical classroom point of view, generative phonology has little to offer and could well create confusion. Producing practice and testing material for word stress is very simple: any modern English dictionary will show word stress patterns as part of word entries, and lists of these can be made either with stress marks for student to read from (as in Exercise 2 of Tape Unit 10), or without stress marks for students to put their own marks on (as in Exercise 1 of the same Tape Unit).

Written exercises
(mainly for foreign learners)

Mark the stress on the following words:

1. verbs
a)	protect	*e)*	bellow
b)	clamber	*f)*	menace
c)	festoon	*g)*	disconnect
d)	detest	*h)*	entering

2. nouns
   a)   language   *e)*   event
   b)   captain   *f)*   jonquil
   e)   career   *g)*   injury
   d)   paper   *h)*   connection

(Native speakers of English should transcribe the words phonemically as well as marking stress.)

11 Complex word stress

11.1 Complex words

In the last chapter the nature of stress was explained and some broad general rules were given for deciding which syllable in a word should receive primary stress. The words that were described were called "simple" words; "simple" in this context means "not composed of more than one grammatical unit", so that, for example, the word 'care' is simple while 'careful' and 'careless' (being composed of two grammatical units each) are complex; 'carefully' and 'carelessness' are also complex, and are composed of three grammatical units each. Unfortunately, as was suggested in the last chapter, it is often difficult to decide on whether a word should be treated as complex or simple. The majority of English words of more than one syllable (**polysyllabic words**) have come from other languages whose way of constructing words is easily recognisable; for example, we can see how combining 'mit' with the prefixes 'per-', 'sub-', 'com-' produced 'permit', 'submit', 'commit', words which have come into English from Latin. Similarly, Greek has given us 'catalogue', 'analogue', 'dialogue', 'monologue', in which the prefixes 'cata-', 'ana-', 'dia-', 'mono-' are recognisable. But we cannot automatically treat the separate grammatical units of other languages as separate grammatical units of English; if we did, we would not be able to study English morphology without first studying the morphology of five or six other languages, and we would be forced into ridiculous analyses such as that the English word 'parallelepiped' was composed of four or five grammatical units (which is the case in Ancient Greek). We must accept, then, that the distinction between "simple" and "complex" words is difficult to draw, and is therefore not always useful.

Complex words are of two major types: words made from a basic **stem** word with the addition of an **affix**, and **compound words**, which are made of two (or occasionally more) independent English words (e.g. 'ice-cream', 'armchair'). We will look first at the words made with affixes; these will be called **affix words**. Affixes are of two sorts in English: **prefixes**, which come before the stem (e.g. prefix 'un-' + stem 'pleasant' → 'unpleasant') and **suffixes**, which come after the stem (e.g. stem 'good' + suffix '-ness' → 'goodness').

Affixes will have one of three possible effects on word stress:

i)   The affix itself receives the primary stress (e.g. 'semi-' + 'circle' 'sɜːkl̩ → 'semicircle' 'semɪsɜːkl̩; '-ality' + 'person' 'pɜːsn̩ → 'personality' pɜːsn̩'ælɪti).

ii) The word is stressed just as if the affix was not there (e.g. 'pleasant' 'pleznt̩, 'unpleasant' ʌn'pleznt̩; 'market' 'mɑːkɪt, 'marketing' 'mɑːkɪtɪŋ).

iii) The stress remains on the stem, not the affix, but is shifted to a different syllable (e.g. 'magnet' 'mægnət, 'magnetic' mæg'netɪk).

11.2 Suffixes

There are so many suffixes that it will only be possible here to examine a small proportion of them; we will concentrate on those which are common and **productive** (that is, are applied to a considerable number of stems and could be applied to more to make new English words). In the case of the others, foreign learners would probably be better advised to learn the stem + affix combination as an individual item.

One of the problems that will be encountered is that we may find words which are obviously complex but which, when we divide them into stem + affix, turn out to have a stem that it is difficult to imagine is an English word. For example, the word 'audacity' seems to be a complex word – but what is its stem? Another problem is that it is difficult in some cases to know whether a word has one, or more than one, suffix (e.g. should we analyse 'personality', from the point of view of stress assignment, as pɜːsn̩ + ælɪti or as pɜːsn̩ + æl + ɪti?). We will not spend more time here on looking at the problems, but go on to look at some generalisations about suffixes and stress. The suffixes are referred to in their spelling form.

Suffixes carrying primary stress themselves

TU 11,
Ex 1

In the examples given, which seem to be the most common, the primary stress is on the first syllable of the suffix. If the stem consists of more than one syllable there will be a secondary stress on one of the syllables of the stem. This cannot fall on the last syllable of the stem, and is, if necessary, moved to an earlier syllable. For example, in 'Japan' dʒə'pæn the primary stress is on the last syllable, but when we add the stress-carrying suffix '-ese' the primary stress is on the suffix and the secondary stress is placed not on the second syllable but on the first: 'Japanese' ˌdʒæpə'niːz.

'-ain' (for verbs only)
'entertain' ˌentəˈteɪn   'ascertain' ˌæsəˈteɪn
'-ee'
'refugee' ˌrefjʊˈdʒiː   'evacuee' ɪˌvækjuˈiː
'-eer'
'mountaineer' ˌmaʊntɪˈnɪə   'volunteer' ˌvɒlənˈtɪə
'-ese'
'Portuguese' ˌpɔːtʃəˈgiːz   'journalese' ˌdʒɜːnlˈiːz
'-ette'
'cigarette' sɪgˌret   'launderette' ˌlɔːndˌret
'-esque', '-ique'
'picturesque' ˌpɪktʃəˈresk   'unique' ˌjuːˈniːk

TU 11,
Ex 2

Suffixes that do not affect stress placement

'-able': 'comfort' ˈkʌmfət; 'comfortable' ˈkʌmftəbl̩
'-age': 'anchor' ˈæŋkə; 'anchorage' ˈæŋkrɪdʒ
'-al': 'refuse' (verb) rɪˈfjuːz; 'refusal' rɪˈfjuːzl̩
'-en': 'wide' waɪd; 'widen' ˈwaɪdn̩
'-ful': 'wonder' ˈwʌndə; 'wonderful' ˈwʌndəfl̩
'-ing': 'amaze' əˈmeɪz; 'amazing' əˈmeɪzɪŋ
'-ish': 'devil' ˈdevl̩; 'devilish' ˈdevl̩ɪʃ

(This is the rule for adjectives; verbs with stems of more than one syllable always have the stress on the syllable immediately preceding 'ish', e.g. 'replenish' rɪˈplenɪʃ, 'demolish' dɪˈmɒlɪʃ.)

'-like': 'bird' bɜːd; 'birdlike' ˈbɜːdlaɪk
'-less': 'power' ˈpaʊə; 'powerless' ˈpaʊələs
'-ly': 'hurried' ˈhʌrɪd; 'hurriedly' ˈhʌrɪdli
'-ment' (noun): 'punish' ˈpʌnɪʃ; 'punishment' ˈpʌnɪʃmənt
'-ness': 'yellow' ˈjeləʊ; 'yellowness' ˈjeləʊnəs
'-ous': 'poison' ˈpɔɪzn̩; 'poisonous' ˈpɔɪznəs
'-fy': 'glory' ˈglɔːri; 'glorify' ˈglɔːrɪfaɪ
'-wise': 'other' ˈʌðə; 'otherwise' ˈʌðəwaɪz
'-y' (adjective or noun): 'fun' fʌn; 'funny' ˈfʌni

Suffixes that influence stress in the stem

TU 11,
Ex 3

PRIMARY STRESS ON THE LAST SYLLABLE OF THE STEM

'-eous': 'advantage' ədˈvɑːntɪdʒ; 'advantageous' ˌædvənˈteɪdʒəs
'-graphy': 'photo' ˈfəʊtəʊ; 'photography' fəˈtɒgrəfi

'-ial': 'proverb' 'prɒvɜːb; 'proverbial' prə'vɜːbiəl
'-ic': 'climate' 'klaɪmɪt; 'climatic' klaɪ'mætɪk
'-ion': 'perfect' 'pɜːfɪkt; 'perfection' pə'fekʃn̩
'-ious': 'injure' 'ɪndʒə; 'injurious' ɪn'dʒʊəriəs
'-ty': 'tranquil' 'træŋkwɪl; 'tranquillity' træŋ'kwɪlɪti
'-ive': 'reflex' 'riːfleks; 'reflexive' rɪ'fleksɪv

THE SUFFIXES '-ANCE', '-ANT' AND '-ARY'

When these suffixes are attached to single-syllable stems, the stress is almost always placed on the stem. When the stem has two syllables the stress is sometimes on the first, sometimes on the second syllable of the stem. To explain this we need to use a rule based on syllable-structure, as was done for simple words in the previous chapter. If the final syllable of the stem contains a long vowel or diphthong, or if it ends with more than one consonant, that syllable receives the stress. For example: 'importance' ɪm'pɔːtns; 'centenary' sen'tiːnɾi. Otherwise the syllable *before* the last one receives the stress: 'consonant' 'kɒnsn̩ənt; 'military' 'mɪlɪtɾi. We will not consider words with stems of more than two syllables. Such words are, from the point of view of this course, too complex and uncommon for it to be worth attempting to write rules.

11.3 Prefixes

We will only deal briefly with prefixes. Their effect on stress does not have the comparative regularity, independence and predictability of suffixes, and there is no prefix of one or two syllables that always carries primary stress. Consequently, the best treatment seems to be to say that stress in words with prefixes is governed by the same rules as those for words without prefixes.

11.4 Compound words

TU 11,
Ex 4
The words discussed so far in this chapter have all consisted of a stem plus an affix. We now pass on to another type of word. This will be called **compound**, and its main characteristic is that it can be analysed into two words, both of which can exist independently as English words. (Some compounds are made of more than two words, but we will not consider these.) As with many of the distinctions being made in connection with stress, there are areas of uncertainty. For example, it

could be argued that 'photograph' may be divided into two independent words, 'photo' and 'graph'; yet we usually do not regard it as a compound, but as an affix word. (If someone drew a graph displaying numerical information about photos, this would perhaps be called a 'photo-graph' and the word *would* be regarded as a compound). Compounds are written in different ways; sometimes they are written as one word, e.g. 'armchair', 'sunflower', sometimes with the words separated by a hyphen, e.g. 'gear-change', 'fruit-cake', and sometimes with two words separated by a space, e.g. 'desk lamp', 'battery charger'. In this last case there would, of course be no indication to the foreign learner that the pair of words was to be treated as a compound. There is no clear dividing line between two-word compounds and pairs of words that simply happen to occur together quite frequently.

As far as stress is concerned, the question is quite simple. When is primary stress placed on the first word of the compound and when on the second? Both patterns are found. A few rules can be given, though these are not completely reliable. Words which do not receive primary stress normally have secondary stress, though for the sake of simplicity this is not marked here. Perhaps the most familiar type of compound is the one which combines two nouns, and normally has the stress on the first element, as in:

'typewriter'	'taɪpraɪtə	'suitcase'	'sjuːtkeɪs
'car-ferry'	'kɑːferi	'tea-cup'	'tiːkʌp
'sunrise'	'sʌnraɪz		

It is probably safest for foreign learners to assume that stress will normally fall in this way on other compounds; however, a variety of compounds receive stress instead on the second element. For example, compounds with an adjectival first element and the *-ed* morpheme at the end have this pattern (given in spelling only):

bad-'tempered
half-'timbered
heavy-'handed

Compounds in which the first element is a number in some form also tend to have final stress:

three-'wheeler
second-'class
five-'finger

Compounds functioning as adverbs are usually final-stressed:

head-'first
North-'East
down'stream

Finally, compounds which function as verbs and have an adverbial first element take final stress:

down-'grade
back-'pedal
ill-'treat

11.5 Variable stress

It would be wrong to imagine that the stress pattern is always fixed and unchanging in English words. Stress position may vary for one of two reasons: either as a result of the stress on other words occurring next to the word in question, or because not all speakers of RP agree on the placement of stress in some words. The former case is an aspect of connected speech that will be encountered again in Chapter 14: the main effect is that the stress on a final-stressed compound tends to move to the preceding syllable if the following word begins with a strongly stressed syllable. Thus (using some examples from the previous section):

bad-'tempered	*but*	a 'bad-tempered 'teacher
half-'timbered	*but*	a 'half-timbered 'house
heavy-'handed	*but*	a 'heavy-handed 'sentence

The second is not a serious problem, but one that foreign learners should be aware of. A well-known example is 'controversy', which is pronounced by some speakers as 'kɒntrəvɜːsi and by others as kən'trɒvəsi; it would be quite wrong to say that one version was correct and one incorrect. Other examples of different possibilities are 'ice-cream', 'kilometer' (either 'kɪləmiːtə or kɪ'lɒmɪtə) and 'formidable' ('fɔːmɪdəbl̩ or fə'mɪdəbl̩).

11.6 Word-class pairs

TU 11,
Ex 5

One aspect of word stress is best treated as a separate issue. There are several dozen pairs of two-syllable words with identical spelling which differ from each other in stress placement, apparently according to word class (noun, verb or adjective). All appear to consist of prefix + stem. We shall treat them as a special type of word and give them the following rule: when a pair of prefix-plus-stem words exists, both members of which are spelt identically, one of which is a verb and

the other is either a noun or an adjective, the stress will be placed on the
second syllable of the verb but on the first syllable of the noun or
adjective. Some common examples are given below (V = verb,
A = adjective, N = noun):

'abstract' 'æbstrækt (A), æb'strækt (V)
'conduct' 'kɒndʌkt (N), kən'dʌkt (V)
'contract' 'kɒntrækt (N), kən'trækt (V)
'contrast' 'kɒntrɑːst (N), kən'trɑːst (V)
'desert' 'dezət (N), dɪ'zɜːt (V)
'escort' 'eskɔːt (N), ɪ'skɔːt (V)
'export' 'ekspɔːt (N), ɪk'spɔːt (V)
'import' 'ɪmpɔːt (N), ɪm'pɔːt (V)
'insult' 'ɪnsʌlt (N), ɪn'sʌlt (V)
'object' 'ɒbdʒɪkt (N), əb'dʒekt (V)
'perfect' 'pɜːfɪkt (A), pə'fekt (V)
'permit' 'pɜːmɪt (N), pə'mɪt (V)
'present' 'prezn̩t (N, A), prɪ'zent (V)
'produce' 'prɒdjuːs (N), prə'djuːs (V)
'protest' 'prəʊtest (N), prə'test (V)
'rebel' 'rebl̩ (N), rɪ'bel (V)
'record' 'rekɔːd (N), rɪ'kɔːd (V)
'subject' 'sʌbdʒɪkt (N), səb'dʒekt (V)

Notes on problems and further reading

Most of the reading recommended in the notes for the previous chapter
is relevant for this one too. Looking specifically at compounds, it is
worth reading Fudge (1984), chapter 5.

If you wish to go more deeply into compound word stress, you
should first study English word formation. Recommended reading for
this is Bauer (1983).

Written exercises

1 Put stress marks on the following words (try to put secondary stress
marks on as well).

a)	shop-fitter	b)	open-ended	c)	Javanese
d)	birth-mark	e)	anti-clockwise	f)	confirmation
g)	eight-sided	h)	fruit-cake	i)	defective
j)	roof-timber				

2 Write the words in phonemic transcription, including the stress marks.

12 Weak forms

Chapter 9 discussed the difference between strong and weak syllables in English. We have now moved on from looking at syllables to looking at words, and we will consider certain well-known English words that can be pronounced in two different ways, which are called **strong forms** and **weak forms**. As an example, the word 'that' can be pronounced ðæt (strong form) or ðət (weak form). The sentence 'I like that' is pronounced aɪ laɪk ðæt (strong form); the sentence 'I hope that she will' is pronounced aɪ həʊp ðət ʃi wɪl (weak form). There are roughly forty such words in English. It *is* possible to use only strong forms in speaking, and some foreigners do this. Usually they can still be understood by other speakers of English, so why is it important to learn how weak forms are used? There are two main reasons; firstly, most native speakers of English find an "all-strong-form" pronunciation unnatural and foreign-sounding, something that most learners would wish to avoid. Secondly, and more importantly, speakers who are not familiar with the use of weak forms are likely to have difficulty understanding speakers who do use weak forms; since practically all native speakers of British English use them, learners of the language need to learn about these weak forms to help them to understand what they hear.

We must distinguish between **weak forms** and **contracted forms**. Certain English words are shortened so severely (usually to a single phoneme) and so consistently that they are represented differently in informal writing, e.g. 'it is' – 'it's'; 'we have' – 'we've'; 'do not' – 'don't'. These contracted forms are discussed in a later chapter, and are not included here.

Almost all the words which have both a strong and weak form belong to a category that may be called **function words** – words that do not have a dictionary meaning in the way that we normally expect nouns, verbs, adjectives and adverbs to have. These function words are words such as auxiliary verbs, prepositions, conjunctions, etc., all of which are in certain circumstances pronounced in their strong forms but which are more frequently pronounced in their weak forms. It is important to remember that there are certain contexts where only the strong form is acceptable, and others where the weak form is the normal pronunciation. There are some fairly simple rules; we can say that the strong form is used in the following cases:

i) For many weak-form words, when they occur at the end of a sentence. For example, the word 'of' has the weak form əv in the following sentence:

'I'm fond of chips' aɪm 'fɒnd əv 'tʃɪps

but when it comes at the end of the sentence, as in the following example, it has the strong form ɒv:

'Chips are what I'm fond of' 'tʃɪps ə 'wɒt aɪm 'fɒnd ɒv

Many of the words given below (particularly the first nine) never occur at the end of a sentence, e.g. 'the', 'your'. Some words (particularly the pronouns numbered 10–14 below) *do* occur in their weak forms in final position.

ii) When a weak-form word is being *contrasted* with another word, e.g.:

'The letter's *from* him, not *to* him' ðə 'letəz 'frɒm ɪm nɒt 'tu: ɪm

A similar case is what we might call a **co-ordinated** use of prepositions:

'I travel to and from London a lot' aɪ 'trævl̩ 'tu: ən 'frɒm 'lʌndən ə 'lɒt

'A work of and about literature' ə 'wɜ:k 'ɒv ən ə'baʊt 'lɪtrɪtʃə

iii) When a weak-form word is given stress for the purpose of emphasis, e.g.:

'You *must* give me more money' ju 'mʌst 'gɪv mi 'mɔ: 'mʌni

iv) When a weak-form word is being "cited" or "quoted", e.g.:

'You shouldn't put "and" at the end of a sentence' ju 'ʃʊdn̩t pʊt 'ænd ət ði 'end əv ə 'sentəns

Another point to remember is that when weak-form words whose spelling begins with 'h' (e.g. 'her', 'have') occur at the beginning of a sentence, the pronunciation is with initial h, even though this is usually omitted in other contexts.

In the rest of this chapter, the most common weak-form words will be introduced.

TU 12, Exs 1–4

1. 'THE'

Weak forms: ðə (before consonants)

'Shut the door' 'ʃʌt ðə 'dɔ:

ði (before vowels)

'Wait for the end' 'weɪt fə ði 'end

2. 'A', 'AN'

Weak forms: ə (before consonants)

'Read a book' 'ri:d ə 'bʊk

ən (before vowels)

'Eat an apple' 'i:t ən 'æpl̩

3. 'AND'
   Weak form: ən (sometimes n̩ after t, d, s, z, ʃ)
        'Come and see' 'kʌm ən 'siː
        'Fish and chips' 'fɪʃ n̩ 'tʃɪps

4. 'BUT'
   Weak form: bət 'It's good but expensive' ɪts 'gʊd bət
       ɪks'pensɪv

5. 'THAT' (This word only has a weak form when used in a
   relative clause; when used with a demonstrative sense it is
   always pronounced in its strong form.)
   Weak form: ðət 'The price is the thing that annoys me' ðə
       'praɪs ɪz ðə 'θɪŋ ðət ə'nɔɪz mi

6. 'THAN'
   Weak form: ðən 'Better than ever' 'betə ðən 'evə

7. 'HIS' (when it occurs before a noun)
   Weak form: ɪz (hɪz at the beginning of a sentence)
        'Take his name' 'teɪk ɪz 'neɪm
   (Another sense of 'his', as in 'it was his', or 'his was late', always
   has the strong form.)

8. 'HER' (When used with possessive sense, preceding a noun; as an
   object pronoun, this can also occur at the end of a sentence.)
   Weak forms: ə (before consonants)
        'Take her home' 'teɪk ə 'həʊm
       ər (before vowels)
        'Take her out' 'teɪk ər 'aʊt

9. 'YOUR'
   Weak forms: jə (before consonants)
        'Take your time' 'teɪk jə 'taɪm
       jər (before vowels)
        'On your own' 'ɒn jər 'əʊn

10. 'SHE', 'HE', 'WE', 'YOU'
    This group of pronouns has weak forms pronounced with weaker
    vowels than the iː and uː of their strong forms. I will use the
    symbols i and u (in preference to ɪ and ʊ) to represent them. There
    is little difference in the pronunciation in different places in the
    sentence, except in the case of 'he'.
    Weak forms:
    'SHE' ʃi
      'Why did she read it?' 'waɪ dɪd ʃi 'riːd ɪt
      'Who is she?' 'huː 'ɪz ʃi
    'HE' i (the weak form is usually pronounced without h except at
    the beginning of a sentence)
      'Which did he choose?' 'wɪtʃ dɪd i 'tʃuːz
      'He was late, wasn't he?' hi wəz 'leɪt 'wɒzn̩t i

'we' wi
    'How can we get there?' 'haʊ kən wi 'get ðeə
    'We need that, don't we?' wi 'niːd ðæt 'dəʊnt wi
'you' ju
    'What do you think?' 'wɒt də ju 'θɪŋk
    'You like it, do you?' ju 'laɪk ɪt 'duː ju

11. 'him'
    Weak form: ɪm
                'Leave him alone' 'liːv ɪm ə'ləʊn
                'I've seen him' aɪv 'siːn ɪm

12. 'her'
    Weak form: ə (hə when sentence-initial)
                'Ask her to come' 'ɑːsk ə tə 'kʌm
                'I've met her' aɪv 'met ə

13. 'them'
    Weak form: ðəm
                'Leave them here' 'liːv ðəm 'hɪə
                'Eat them' 'iːt ðəm

14. 'us'
    Weak form: əs
                'Write us a letter' 'raɪt əs ə 'letə
                'They invited all of us' ðeɪ ɪn'vaɪtɪd
                'ɔːl əv əs

The next group of words (some prepositions and other function words) occur in their strong forms when they are final in a sentence; examples of this are given. (19 is a partial exception.)

15. 'at'
    Weak form: ət
                'I'll see you at lunch' aɪl 'siː ju ət
                'lʌnʃ
    In final position: æt
                'What's he shooting at?' 'wɒts i
                'ʃuːtɪŋ æt

16. 'for'
    Weak form: fə (before consonants)
                'Tea for two' 'tiː fə 'tuː
        fər (before vowels)
                'Thanks for asking' 'θæŋks fər 'ɑːskɪŋ
    In final position: fɔː
                'What's that for?' 'wɒts 'ðæt fɔː

17. 'from'
    Weak form: frəm
                'I'm home from work' aɪm 'həʊm frəm
                'wɜːk

In final position: frɒm

    'Here's where it came from' 'hɪəz
weər ɪt 'keɪm frɒm

18. 'ᴏꜰ'
Weak form: əv

    'Most of all' 'məʊst əv 'ɔːl
In final position: ɒv

    'Someone I've heard of' 'sʌmwʌn aɪv
'hɜːd ɒv

19. 'ᴛᴏ'
Weak forms: tə (before consonants)

    'Try to stop' 'traɪ tə 'stɒp
tu (before vowels)

    'Time to eat' 'taɪm tu 'iːt
In final position: tu (It is not usual to use the strong form tuː, and
        the pre-consonantal weak form tə is never
        used.)

    'I don't want to' aɪ 'dəʊnt 'wɒnt tu

20. 'ᴀꜱ'
Weak form: əz

    'As much as possible' əz 'mʌtʃ əz
'pɒsɪbl̩
In final position: æz

    'That's what it was sold as' 'ðæts
'wɒt ɪt wəz 'səʊld æz

21. 'ꜱᴏᴍᴇ'
This word is used in two different ways. In one sense (typically,
when it occurs before a countable noun, meaning "an unknown
individual") it has the strong form:

    'I think some animal broke it' aɪ 'θɪŋk sʌm 'ænɪml̩
'brəʊk ɪt

It is also used before uncountable nouns (meaning "an unspecified
amount of") and before other nouns in the plural (meaning "an
unspecified number of"), in such uses it has the weak form səm.

    'Have some more tea' 'hæv səm 'mɔː 'tiː
In final position: sʌm

    'I've got some' aɪv 'gɒt sʌm

22. 'ᴛʜᴇʀᴇ'
When this word has a demonstrative function, it always occurs in
its strong form ðeə (ðeər before vowels), e.g.

    'There it is' 'ðeər ɪt 'ɪz
    'Put it there' 'pʊt ɪt 'ðeə
Weak forms: ðə (before consonants)

    'There should be a rule' ðə 'ʃʊd bi
ə 'ruːl

ðər (before vowels)

'There is' ðər 'ız

In final position the pronunciation may be ðə or ðeə.

'There isn't any, is there?' ðər 'ıznt eni 'ız ðə

or ðər 'ıznt eni 'ız ðeə

The remaining weak-form words are all auxiliary verbs, which are always used in conjunction with (or at least implying) another ("full") verb. It is important to remember that in their negative form (i.e. combined with 'not') they never have the weak pronunciation, and some (e.g. 'don't', 'can't') have different vowels from their non-negative strong forms.

23. 'CAN', 'COULD'

Weak forms: kən, kəd

'They can wait' 'ðeı kən 'weıt

'He could do it' 'hiː kəd 'duː ıt

In final position: kæn, kʊd

'I think we can' aı 'θıŋk wi kæn

'Most of them could' 'məʊst əv ðəm kʊd

24. 'HAVE', 'HAS'. 'HAD'

Weak forms: əv, əz, əd (with initial h in initial position)

'Which have you seen?' 'wıtʃ əv ju 'siːn

'Which has been best?' 'wıtʃ əz 'biːn 'best

'Most had gone home' 'məʊst əd 'gɒn 'həʊm

In final position: hæv, hæz, hæd

'Yes, we have' 'jes wi 'hæv

'I think she has' aı 'θıŋk ʃi 'hæz

'I thought we had' aı 'θɔːt wi 'hæd

25. 'SHALL', 'SHOULD'

Weak forms: ʃəl or ʃl̩; ʃəd

'We shall need to hurry' wi ʃl̩ 'niːd tə 'hʌri

'I should forget it' 'aı ʃəd fə'get ıt

In final position: ʃæl, ʃʊd

'I think we shall' aı 'θıŋk wi 'ʃæl

'So you should' 'səʊ ju 'ʃʊd

26. 'MUST'

This word is sometimes used with the sense of forming a conclusion or deduction, e.g. 'she left at 8 o'clock, so she must have arrived by now'; when 'must' is used in this way, it is rather less likely to occur in its weak form than when it is being used in its more familiar sense of "obligation".

Weak forms: məs (before consonants)

    'You must try harder' ju məs 'traɪ 'hɑːdə

məst (before vowels)

    'He must eat more' hi məst 'iːt 'mɔː

In final position: mʌst

    'She certainly must' ʃi 'sɜːtn̩li 'mʌst

27. 'DO', 'DOES'

  Weak forms:

      'DO' də (before consonants)

      'Why do they like it?' 'waɪ də ðeɪ

      'laɪk ɪt

      du (before vowels)

      'Why do all the cars stop?' 'waɪ du

      ɔːl ðə 'kɑːz 'stɒp

      'DOES' dəz

      'When does it arrive?' 'wen dəz ɪt

      ə'raɪv

In final position: duː, dʌz

      'We don't smoke, but some people do'

      'wiː dəʊnt 'sməʊk bət 'sʌm 'piːpl̩ 'duː

      'I think John does' aɪ 'θɪŋk

      'dʒɒn dʌz

28. 'AM', 'ARE', 'WAS', 'WERE'

  Weak forms: əm

      'Why am I here?' 'waɪ əm aɪ 'hɪə

      ə (before consonants)

      'Here are the plates' 'hɪər ə ðə 'pleɪts

      ər (before vowels)

      'The coats are in there' ðə 'kəʊts ər

      ɪn 'ðeə

      wəz 'He was here a minute ago' hi wəz

      'hɪər ə 'mɪnɪt ə'gəʊ

      wə (before consonants)

      'The papers were late' ðə 'peɪpəz

      wə 'leɪt

      wər (before vowels)

      'The questions were easy' ðə 'kwestʃənz

      wər 'iːzi

In final position: æm, ɑː, wɒz, wɜː

      'She's not as old as I am' ʃiz 'nɒt

      əz 'əʊld əz 'aɪ æm

      'I know the Smiths are' aɪ 'nəʊ

      ðə 'smɪθs ɑː

'The last record was' ðə 'lɑːst
'rekɔːd wɒz
'They weren't as cold as we were'
ðeɪ 'wɜːnt əz 'kəʊld əz 'wiː wɜː

Notes on problems and further reading

This chapter is almost entirely practical. All books about English pronunciation devote a lot of attention to these words. Some of them give a great deal of importance to using weak forms, but do not stress the importance of also knowing when to use the strong forms, something which I feel is very important. See Mortimer (1984).

Written exercises

In the following sentences, the transcription for the weak-form words is left blank. Fill in the blanks, taking care to use the appropriate form.

1. I want her to park that car over there.
   aɪ wɒnt   pɑːk   kɑːr əʊvə
2. Of all the proposals, the one that you made is the silliest.
        ɔːl   prəpəʊz|z   wʌn   meɪd   sɪliəst
3. Jane and Bill could have driven them to and from the party.
   dʒeɪn   bɪl   drɪvən   pɑːti
4. To come to the point, what shall we do for the rest of the week?
        kʌm   pɔɪnt wɒt   rest   wiːk
5. Has anyone got an idea where it came from?
        enɪwʌn gɒt   aɪdɪə weər ɪt keɪm
6. Pedestrians must always use the crossings provided for them.
   pədestrɪənz   ɔːlwɪz juːz   krɒsɪŋz prəvaɪdɪd
7. Each one was a perfect example of the art that had been developed there.
   iːtʃ wʌn   pɜːfɪkt ɪgzɑːmp| ɑːt   biːn dɪveləpt

13 Problems in phonemic analysis

The concept of the phoneme was introduced in Chapter 5, and a few theoretical problems connected with phonemic analysis have been mentioned in other chapters. The general assumption (as in most phonetics books) has been that speech is composed of phonemes and that usually whenever a speech sound is produced by a speaker it is possible to identify which phoneme that sound belongs to. While this is often true, we must recognise that there are several quite serious theoretical problems that should be considered. From the comparatively simple point of view of learning pronunciation, these problems are not particularly important; however, from the point of view of learning about the phonology of English they are too important to ignore.

There are two main areas of difficulty. The first will be called the problem of **analysis**: we may accept the principle of the phoneme as a fundamental unit in language, but we find difficulty in deciding what *are* the phonemes of a language (in our case, of English). The result of this is that different writers produce different analyses of the phonemic system of English; it is clear that phonemic analysis is not as clear and simple as studying the letters of the alphabet.

The second area of difficulty will be called the problem of **assignment**. As an example of what is meant by "assignment", we might say that a botanist who discovers an unusual plant will try to assign it to a known species; if this is found impossible, it will be decided that a new species has been discovered, and that future examples of this plant will be assigned to this new species. We find many cases where it is difficult to assign a particular speech sound to a particular phoneme.

13.1 Problems of analysis

The affricates tʃ and dʒ are, phonetically, composed of a plosive followed by a fricative, as explained in Chapter 6. It is possible to treat each of the pair tʃ, dʒ as a single consonant phoneme (we will call this the **one-phoneme analysis** of tʃ, dʒ), and it is also possible to say that they are composed of two phonemes each – either t plus ʃ or d plus ʒ – all of which are already established as independent phonemes of English; this will be called the **two-phoneme analysis** of tʃ and dʒ. If we adopted the two-phoneme analysis, the words 'church' and 'judge' would be composed of five phonemes each, like this:

t·ʃ·ɜ:·t·ʃ   d·ʒ·ʌ·d·ʒ

instead of the three phonemes, resulting from the one-phoneme analysis:

tʃ·ɜ:··tʃ   dʒ·ʌ·dʒ

and there would be no separate tʃ and dʒ phonemes. But how can we decide which analysis is preferable? The two-phoneme analysis has one main advantage: if there are no separate tʃ and dʒ phonemes, then our total set of English consonants is smaller. Many phonologists have claimed that one should prefer the analysis which is the most "economical" in the number of phonemes it results in. The argument for this might be based on the claim that when we speak to someone we are using a "code", and the most efficient codes do not use unnecessary symbols. Further, it could be claimed that a phonological analysis is a type of scientific theory, and a scientific theory should be stated as economically as possible. Both of these points of view have serious weaknesses, but in fact the one-phoneme analysis is generally chosen by phonologists. Why is this? There are several arguments; no single one of them is conclusive, but added together they are felt to make the one-phoneme analysis seem preferable. We will look briefly at some of these arguments.

i)   One argument could be called "phonetic" or "allophonic": if it could be shown that the phonetic quality of the t and ʃ (or d and ʒ) in tʃ, dʒ was clearly different from realisations of t, ʃ, d, ʒ found elsewhere in similar contexts, this would support the analysis of tʃ, dʒ as separate phonemes. As an example, it might be claimed that ʃ in 'hutch' hʌtʃ was different (perhaps in having shorter duration) from ʃ in 'hush' or 'Welsh' hʌʃ, welʃ; or it might be claimed that the place of articulation of t in 'watch apes' wɒtʃ eɪps is different from that of t in 'what shapes' wɒt ʃeɪps. This argument is a weak one: there is no clear evidence that such phonetic differences exist, and even if there *were* such evidence, it would be easy to produce explanations for the differences that did not depend on phonemic analyses (e.g. the position of the word boundary in 'watch apes', 'what shapes'). In fact there is some allophonic evidence that supports the two-phoneme analysis: we find this in the occurrence of glottalisation (which was described at the end of Chapter 6). If we look at glottalisation of p, t, k and then tʃ in RP we find the following pattern of occurrence: (phonetic transcription showing glottalisation is given in square brackets).

- One-consonant phoneme occurring medially; no glottalisation is found:

  'upper' ʌpə   'better' betə   'backer' bækə

- Two-consonant phonemes occurring medially; glottalisation is normal:

  'optic' ɒptɪk [ɒʔptɪk]   'Betsy' betsi [beʔtsi]

  'boxer' bɒksə [bɒʔksə]

- tʃ occurring medially; glottalisation is normal after a stressed syllable:

  'butcher' 'bʊtʃə ['bʊʔtʃə]

  'matches' 'mætʃɪz ['mæʔtʃɪz]

  'watching' 'wɒtʃɪŋ ['wɒʔtʃɪŋ]

This makes the medial occurrence of tʃ look more similar to a medial two-consonant-phoneme cluster.

The phonetic argument is therefore inconclusive.

ii) It could be argued that the proposed phonemes tʃ and dʒ (if one were arguing for the one-phoneme analysis) have distributions similar to other consonants, while other combinations of plosive plus fricative do not. It can easily be shown that tʃ and dʒ are found initially, medially and finally, and that no other combination (e.g. pf, dz, tθ) has such a wide distribution. However, several consonants *are* generally accepted as phonemes of RP despite not being free to occur in all positions (e.g. r, w, j, h, ŋ, ʒ), so this argument, though supporting the one-phoneme analysis, does not actually *prove* that tʃ, dʒ must be classed with other single-consonant phonemes.

iii) If tʃ and dʒ were able to combine quite freely with other consonants to form consonant clusters, this would support the one-phoneme analysis. Initially, however, tʃ and dʒ never occur in clusters with other consonants. In final position in the syllable, we find that tʃ can be followed by t (e.g. 'watched' wɒtʃt) and dʒ by d (e.g. 'wedged' wedʒd). tʃ and dʒ can be preceded by l (e.g. 'squelch' skweltʃ, 'bulge' bʌldʒ); ʒ is never preceded by l, and ʃ is preceded by l only in a few words and names, e.g. 'Welsh', 'Walsh' welʃ, wɒlʃ. A fairly similar situation is found if we ask if n can precede tʃ and dʒ; some RP speakers have ntʃ in 'lunch', 'French', etc., and never pronounce the sequence nʃ within a syllable, while other speakers always have nʃ in these contexts and never ntʃ. It seems, then, that no contrast between syllable-final lʃ and ltʃ exists in RP, and the same appears to be true in relation to nʃ and ntʃ and to nʒ and ndʒ. There are no other possibilities for final consonant clusters containing tʃ and dʒ, except that the pre-initial l or n may occur in combination with post-final t, d as in 'squelched' skweltʃt, 'hinged' hɪndʒd. It could not, then, be said that tʃ and dʒ combine freely with other consonants in forming consonant clusters; this is particularly noticeable in initial position.

How would the two-phoneme analysis affect the syllable-structure framework that was introduced in Chapter 8? Initial tʃ, dʒ would have to be interpreted as initial t, d plus post-initial ʃ, ʒ, with the result that the post-initial set of consonants would have to contain l, r, w, j and also ʃ, ʒ – consonants which are rather different from the other four and which could only combine with t, d. (The only alternative would be to put t, d with s in the pre-initial category, again with very limited possibilities of combining with another consonant.)

iv) Finally, it has been suggested that if native speakers of English who have not been taught phonetics feel that tʃ and dʒ are each "one sound", we should be guided by their "intuitions" and prefer the one-phoneme analysis. The problem with this is that discovering what untrained (or "naive") speakers feel about their own language is not as easy as it might sound. Presumably it would be necessary to ask questions like this: "Would you say that the word 'chip' begins with *one* sound, like 'tip' and 'sip', or with *two* sounds, like 'trip' and 'skip'?" But the results would be distorted by the fact that two consonant letters are used in the spelling; to do the test properly one should use illiterate subjects, which raises many further problems.

This rather long discussion of the phonemic status of tʃ and ʒ shows how difficult it can be to reach a conclusion in phonemic analysis. For the rest of this chapter a number of different problems will be discussed comparatively briefly. I have already mentioned (in Chapter 6) problems of analysis in connection with the sounds usually transcribed hw and hj. The velar nasal ŋ, described in Chapter 7, also raises a lot of analysis problems; some writers have suggested that the correct analysis is one in which there is no ŋ phoneme, and this sound is treated as an allophone of the phoneme n that occurs when it precedes the phoneme g. It was explained in Chapter 7 that in certain contexts no g is pronounced, but the theory mentioned in the last sentence would claim that at an abstract level there *is* a g phoneme, though in certain contexts the g is not actually pronounced. ŋ is therefore, according to this theory, an allophone of n.

The analysis of the English vowel system presented in Chapters 2 and 3 contains a large number of phonemes, and it is not surprising that some phonologists (who believed in the importance of keeping the total number of phonemes small) proposed different analyses which contain less than ten vowel phonemes and treat all long vowels and diphthongs as composed of two phonemes each. There are different ways of doing this: one way is to treat long vowels and diphthongs as composed of two vowel phonemes. If we start with a set of basic or "simple" vowel phonemes ɪ, e, æ, ʌ, ɒ, ʊ, ə it would then be possible to make up long vowels by using vowels twice. Our usual transcription is given in brackets:

ɪɪ (iː)   ææ (ɑː)   ɒɒ (ɔː)   ʊʊ (uː)   əə (ɜː)

This can be made to look less unusual by choosing different symbols for the basic vowels. Diphthongs are made from a simple vowel phoneme followed by one of ɪ, ʊ, ə. Triphthongs are made from a basic vowel plus one of ɪ, ʊ followed by ə, and are therefore composed of three phonemes.

Another way of doing this kind of analysis is to treat long vowels and diphthongs as composed of a vowel plus a consonant; this may seem a less obvious way of proceeding, but it was for many years the choice of most American phonologists. The idea is that long vowels and diphthongs are composed of a basic vowel phoneme followed by one of j, w, h (in the case of RP). Thus the diphthongs could be made up like this (our usual transcription is given in brackets):

ej (eɪ)	əw (əʊ)	ɪh (ɪə)
æj (aɪ)	æw (aʊ)	eh (eə)
ɒj (ɔɪ)		ʊh (ʊə)

Long vowels:

ɪj (iː)   æh (ɑː)   ɒh (ɔː)   əh (ɜː)   ʊw (uː)

Diphthongs and long vowels are now of exactly the same phonological composition. An important point about this analysis is that j, w, h do not otherwise occur finally in the syllable. In this analysis, the inequality of distribution is corrected. There are many other ways of analysing the very complex vowel system of English, some of which are extremely ingenious. Each has its own advantages and disadvantages.

A final analysis problem that we will consider is that mentioned at the end of Chapter 8 – how to deal with syllabic consonants. It has to be recognised that syllabic consonants are a problem – they *are* phonologically different from their non-syllabic counterparts. How do we account for the minimal pairs given in Chapter 9?

syllabic	*non-syllabic*
'coddling' kɒdl̩ɪŋ	'codling' kɒdlɪŋ
'Hungary' hʌŋgr̩i	'hungry' hʌŋgri

One possibility is to add new consonant phonemes to our list. We could invent the phonemes l̩, r̩, n̩ etc. The distribution of these consonants would be rather limited, but the main problem would be fitting them into the pattern of syllable structure. For a word like 'button' bʌtn̩ or 'bottle' bɒtl̩, it would be necessary to add n̩ and l̩ to the first post-final set; the argument would be extended to include the r̩ in 'Hungary'. But if these consonants now form part of a syllable-final consonant cluster, how do we account for the fact that English speakers hear the consonants as extra syllables? The question might be answered by saying that the new phonemes are to be classed as vowels. Another possibility is to set up a phoneme that we might name **syllabicity**, symbolised with the mark ˌ. Then the word 'codling' would consist of the following six phonemes: k·ɒ·d·l·ɪ·ŋ, while the word 'coddling' would consist of the following *seven* phonemes: k·ɒ·d· (l and simultaneously ˌ) ·ɪ·ŋ. This is a superficially attractive theory, but the proposed phoneme is nothing like the other phonemes we have identified up to this point – putting it simply, it doesn't have any sound.

Some phonologists maintain that a syllabic consonant is really a case of a vowel and a consonant that have become combined. Let us suppose that the vowel is ə. We could then say that, for example, 'Hungary' is phonemically hʌngəri while 'hungry' is hʌngri; it would then be necessary to say that the vowel phoneme in the phonemic represent-ation is not pronounced as a vowel, but instead causes the following consonant to become syllabic. This is an example of the abstract view of phonology where the way a word is represented phonemically may be significantly different from the actual sequence of sounds heard, so that the phonetic and the phonemic levels are quite widely separated.

13.2 Problems of assignment

One problem of assignment has already been encountered: in Chapter 9 we saw how, although ɪ and iː are clearly distinct in most contexts, there are other contexts where we find a sound which cannot clearly be said to belong to one or other of these two phonemes. The suggested solution to this problem was to use the symbol i, which does not represent any single phoneme; a similar proposal was made for u. We use the term **neutralisation** for cases where contrasts between phonemes which exist in other places in the language disappear in particular contexts. A clearer case of neutralisation can be found in the case of plosives following s in syllable-initial position. Words like 'spill', 'still', 'skill' are usually represented with the phonemes p, t, k following the s. But, as many writers have pointed out, it would be quite reasonable to transcribe them with b, d, g instead. For example, b, d, g are unaspirated while p, t, k in syllable-initial position are usually aspirated; but in sp, st, sk we find an unaspirated plosive – there could be a strong argument for transcribing them as sb, sd, sg. We do not do this, perhaps because of the spelling, but it is important to remember that the contrasts between p and b, between t and d and between k and g are neutralised in this context.

There are some other cases which are not so clear. It has been suggested that there is not really a contrast between ə and ʌ, since ə only occurs in weak syllables and no minimal pairs can be found to show a clear contrast between ə and ʌ in unstressed syllables (though there have been some ingenious attempts). This has resulted in a proposal that one phoneme symbol (e.g. ə) be used for representing any occurrence of ə or ʌ, so that 'cup' would be transcribed 'kəp and 'upper' as 'əpə. This new ə phoneme would have two allophones, one being [ə] and the other [ʌ]; the stress mark would indicate the [ʌ] allophone and in syllables not marked for stress it would be unimportant whether [ə] or [ʌ] was used.

Other phonologists have suggested that ə is an allophone of several other vowels; for example, compare the middle two syllables in the words 'economy' ɪˈkɒnəmi and 'economic' ˌiːkəˈnɒmɪk – it appears that when the stress moves away from the syllable containing ɒ the vowel becomes ə. Similarly, compare 'Germanic' dʒɜːmænɪk with 'German' ˈdʒɜːmən – when the stress is taken away from the syllable mæn, the vowel weakens to ə. Many similar examples could be constructed with other vowels; some possibilities may be suggested by the list of words given in 9.2 to show the different spellings that can be pronounced with ə. The conclusion that could be drawn from this argument is that ə is not a phoneme of English, but is an allophone of several different vowel phonemes when those phonemes occur in an unstressed syllable. The argument is in some ways quite an attractive one, but since it leads to a rather complex and abstract phonemic analysis it is not adopted for this course.

This chapter was intended to show that there are many ways of analysing the English phonemic system, each with its own advantages and disadvantages. We need to consider the practical goal of teaching or learning about English pronunciation, and for this purpose a very abstract analysis would be unsuitable. This is one criterion for judging the value of an analysis; unless one believes in carrying out phonological analysis for purely aesthetic reasons, the only other important criterion is whether the analysis corresponds to the representation of sounds in the human brain. We do not yet know much about this but the brain is so powerful and complex that it is very unlikely that any of the analyses proposed so far bear much resemblance to this reality; they are too heavily influenced by the theoretician's preoccupation with economy, elegance and simplicity.

Notes on problems and further reading

13.1 The analysis of tʃ and dʒ is one of the most intractable problems. The general principles in traditional phoneme theory have been set out by Trubetzkoy (1939); the German original has been translated into English (1969), and the relevant section of this translation was reprinted in Fudge (1973), pp. 65–70. The problem is also discussed in Gimson (1980), pp. 172–4. The phonemic analysis of the velar nasal has already been discussed above (notes on Chapter 7).

The 'double vowel' interpretation of English long vowels was put forward by MacCarthy (1952) and is used by Kreidler (1989).

The 'vowel-plus-semivowel' interpretation of long vowels and diphthongs was almost universally accepted by American (and some British) writers from the 1940s to the 1960s, and still pervades contemporary descriptions. It has the advantage of being economical on phonemes and very 'neat and tidy'. The analysis in this form is presented in Trager and Smith (1951). This work was claimed to provide an analysis that could produce a phonologically distinct representation for all English short vowels, long vowels and diphthongs. An early attack on this view was made by Sledd (1955), pp. 316–24. Kreidler (1989) reviews this approach and others (pp. 293–304), but his treatment of Gimson's vowel analysis is inaccurate.

In generative phonology, the claim is that, at the abstract level, vowels are simply tense or lax. If they are lax they are realised as short vowels, if tense as diphthongs (this category including what I have been calling long vowels). The quality of the first element of the diphthongs/long vowels is modified by some phonological rules, while other rules supply the second element automatically. This is set out in Chomsky and Halle (1968), pp. 178–87.

13.2 The 'problems of assignment' have all been mentioned briefly in earlier chapters. On the interpretation of sp, st, sk, see Davidsen-Nielsen (1969). There is an interesting discussion of the ə – ʌ contrast in Wells (1970), pp. 233–5. The idea that ə is an allophone of many English vowels is not a new one – for example, it was discussed in Bloomfield (1933), though unfortunately this is left out of the edition sold in Britain. In generative phonology, ə results from *vowel reduction* in vowels which have never received stress in the process of the application of stress rules. This is explained – in rather difficult terms – in Chomsky and Halle (1968), pp. 110–26.

Note for teachers

Since this is a theoretical chapter it is difficult to come up with practical work. I do not feel that it is helpful for students to do exercises on using different ways of transcribing phonemes – just learning one set of conventions is difficult enough. Some books on phonology give exercises on the phonemic analysis of other languages (e.g. Katamba, 1989; Hawkins, 1984), but though these are useful, I do not feel that it would be appropriate in this book to divert attention from English. The exercises given below therefore concentrate on bits of *phonetically* transcribed English which involve problems when a phonemic representation is required.

Written exercises

The following are all exercises in which you must look at phonetically transcribed material from different English accents, and decide on the best way to transcribe them phonemically. Information is given where necessary about the meaning of the phonetic symbols.

1.   *a)* 'thing'   [θɪŋg]
     b) 'think'   [θɪŋk]
     c) 'thinking'   [θɪŋkɪŋg]
     d) 'finger'   [fɪŋgə]
     e) 'singer'   [sɪŋgə]
     f) 'singing'   [sɪŋgɪŋg]

2. It often happens in rapid speech that a nasal consonant disappears when it comes between a vowel and another consonant (for example, this may happen to the n in 'front': when this happens the preceding vowel becomes nasalised (some of the air escapes through the nose). We symbolise a nasalised vowel in phonetic transcription by putting the ˜ diacritic above it; for example, the word 'front' may be pronounced [frʌ̃t]. Nasalised vowels are found in the words given in phonetic transcription below. Transcribe them phonemically.
     a) [sã ʊ̃d]
     b) [æ̃gə]
     c) [kã:t]
     d) [kæ̃pə]
     e) [bõd]

3. When the t phoneme occurs between vowels it is sometimes pronounced as a "tap" (the tongue blade strikes the alveolar ridge sharply,

producing a very brief voiced plosive: the phonetic symbol is ɾ); this is very common in American English, and is also found in a number of accents in England: think of a typical American pronunciation of "getting better" [gerɪŋ berə].

Look at the transcriptions of a number of words given below and see if you can work out (for the accent in question) the environment in which [ɾ] is found.

a) 'betting' [berɪŋ]   d) 'attitude' [ærɪtʃuːd]
b) 'bedding' [bedɪŋ]   e) 'time'   [tʰaɪm]
c) 'attend'   [ətʰend]   f) 'tight'   [tʰaɪt]

E

14 Aspects of connected speech

Many years ago scientists tried to develop machines that produced speech from a vocabulary of pre-recorded words; the machines were designed to join these words together to form sentences. For very limited messages, such as those of a "talking clock", this technique was usable, but for other purposes the quality of the speech was so unnatural that it was practically unintelligible. The failure of this "mechanical speech" approach (which eventually led to the development of **speech synthesis by rule**) has many lessons to teach us about pronunciation teaching and learning, and it will be useful, in looking at connected speech, to bear in mind the difference between the way humans speak and what would be found in "mechanical speech".

14.1 Rhythm

The notion of **rhythm** involves some noticeable event happening at regular intervals of time; one can detect the rhythm of a heart-beat, of a flashing light or of a piece of music. It has often been claimed that English speech is rhythmical, and that the rhythm is detectable in the regular occurrence of stressed syllables; of course, it is not suggested that the timing is as regular as a clock – the regularity of occurrence is only relative. The theory that English has **stress-timed rhythm** implies that stressed syllables will tend to occur at relatively regular intervals whether they are separated by unstressed syllables or not; this would not be the case in "mechanical speech". An example is given below. In this sentence, the stressed syllables are given numbers: syllables 1 and 2 are not separated by any unstressed syllables, 2 and 3 are separated by one unstressed syllable, 3 and 4 by two and 4 and 5 by three.

```
 1     2        3          4            5
'Walk 'down the 'path to the 'end of the ca'nal
```

The stress-timed rhythm theory states that the times from each stressed syllable to the next will tend to be the same, irrespective of the number of intervening unstressed syllables. The theory also claims that while some languages (e.g. Russian and Arabic) have stress-timed rhythm similar to that of English, others (such as French, Telugu and Yoruba) have a different rhythmical structure called **syllable-timed rhythm**; in these languages, all syllables, whether stressed or unstressed, tend to occur at regular time-intervals and the time between stressed syllables will be shorter or longer in proportion to the number of unstressed syllables. Some writers have developed theories of English rhythm in which a unit of rhythm, the **foot**, is used (with an obvious parallel in the metrical analysis of verse); the foot begins with a stressed syllable and includes all following unstressed syllables up to (but not including) the following stressed syllable. The example sentence given above would be divided into feet as follows:

1	2	3	4	5
'Walk	'down the	'path to the	'end of the ca	'nal

Some theories of rhythm go further than this, and point to the fact that some feet are stronger than others, producing strong-weak patterns in larger pieces of speech above the level of the foot. To understand how this could be done, let's start with a simple example: the word 'twenty' has one strong and one weak syllable, forming one foot. A diagram of its rhythmical structure can be made, where **s** stands for "strong" and **w** stands for "weak".

The word 'places' has the same form:

Now consider the phrase 'twenty places', where 'places' will normally carry stronger stress than 'twenty', i.e. will be rhythmically stronger. We can make our "tree diagram" grow to look like this:

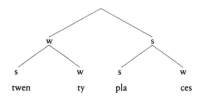

If we then look at this phrase in the context of a longer phrase 'twenty places further back', and build up the 'further back' part in a similar way, we would end up with an even more elaborate structure:

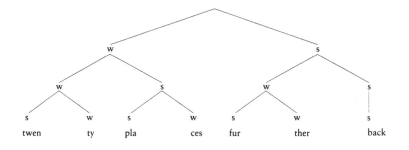

By analysing speech in this way we are able to show the relationships between strong and weak elements, and the different levels of stress that we find. The strength of any particular syllable can be measured by counting up the number of times an **s** symbol occurs above it; the levels in the sentence shown above can be diagrammed like this (leaving out syllables that have never received stress at any level):

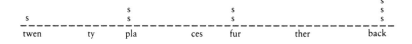

The above pattern may be correct for very slow speech, but we must now look at what happens to the rhythm in normal speech: many English speakers would feel that, although in 'twenty places' the right-hand foot is the stronger, the word 'twenty' is stronger than 'places' in 'twenty places further back' when spoken in conversational style. It is widely claimed that English speech tends towards a regular alternation between stronger and weaker, and tends to adjust stress levels to bring this about. The effect is particularly noticeable in cases such as the following:

> compact (adjective) kəm'pækt *but* compact disc 'kɒmpækt 'dɪsk
> thirteen θɜː'tiːn *but* thirteenth place 'θɜːtiːnθ 'pleɪs Westminster
> west'mɪnstə *but* Westminster Abbey 'westmɪnstər 'æbi

In brief, it seems that stresses are altered according to context: we need to be able to explain how and why this happens, but this is a difficult question and one for which we have only partial answers.

An additional factor is that in speaking English we vary in how rhythmically we speak: sometimes we speak very rhythmically (this is typical of some styles of public speaking) while at other times we speak arhythmically (that is, without rhythm) – for example, when we are hesitant or nervous. Stress-timed rhythm is thus perhaps characteristic of one *style* of speaking, not of English speech as a whole; one always speaks with *some* degree of rhythmicality, but the degree will vary between a minimum value (arhythmical) and a maximum (completely stress-timed rhythm).

It follows from what was said earlier that in a stress-timed language all the feet are supposed to be of roughly the same duration. Many foreign learners of English are made to practise speaking English with a regular rhythm, often with the teacher beating time or clapping hands on the stressed syllables. It must be pointed out, however, that the evidence for the existence of stress-timed rhythm is not strong. There are many laboratory techniques for measuring time in speech, and measurement of the time intervals between stressed syllables in connected English speech has not shown the expected regularity; moreover, using the same measuring techniques on different languages, it has not been possible to show a real difference between "stress-timed" and "syllable-timed" languages. Experiments have shown that we tend to hear speech as more rhythmical than it actually is, and one suspects that this is what the proponents of the stress-timed rhythm theory have been led to do in their auditory analysis of English rhythm. However, one ought to keep an open mind on the subject, remembering that the large-scale, objective study of suprasegmental aspects of real speech is only just beginning, and there is much research that needs to be done.

What, then, is the practical value of the traditional "rhythm exercise" for foreign learners? The argument about rhythm should not make us forget the very important difference in English between strong and weak syllables; some languages do not have such a noticeable difference (which may, perhaps, explain the subjective impression of "syllable-timing"), and for native speakers of such languages learning English it can be helpful to practise repeating strongly rhythmical utterances since this forces the speaker to concentrate on making unstressed syllables weak. Speakers of languages like Japanese, Hungarian and Spanish, which do not have weak syllables to anything like the same extent as English does, may well find such exercises of some value (as long as they are not overdone to the point where learners feel they have to speak English as though they were reciting verse).

14.2 Assimilation

The device mentioned earlier that produces "mechanical speech" would contain all the words of English, each having been recorded in isolation. A significant difference in natural connected speech is the way that sounds belonging to one word can cause changes in sounds belonging to neighbouring words. Assuming that we know how the phonemes of a particular word would be realised when the word was pronounced in isolation, when we find a phoneme realised differently as a result of being near some other phoneme belonging to a neighbouring word we call this an instance of **assimilation**. Assimilation is something which varies in extent according to speaking rate and style; it is more likely to be found in rapid, casual speech and less likely in slow, careful speech. Sometimes the difference caused by assimilation is very noticeable, and sometimes it is very slight. Generally speaking, the cases that have most often been described are assimilations affecting consonants.

As an example, consider a case where two words are combined, the first of which ends with a single final consonant (which we will call C^f) and the second of which starts with a single initial consonant (which we will call C^i); we can construct a diagram like this:

$$- - - - C^f \ \Big| \ C^i - - - -$$
$$\text{word}$$
$$\text{boundary}$$

If C^f changes to become like C^i in some way, the assimilation is called **regressive** (the phoneme that comes first is affected by the one that comes after it); if C^i changes to become like C^f in some way, the assimilation is called **progressive**. In what ways can a consonant change? We have seen that the main differences between consonants are of three types:

i)   differences in place of articulation
ii) differences in manner of articulation
iii) differences in voicing.

In parallel with this, we can identify assimilation of place, of manner and of voicing in consonants. Assimilation of place is most clearly observable in some cases where a final consonant (C^f) with alveolar place of articulation is followed by an initial consonant (C^i) with a place of articulation that is *not* alveolar. For example, the final consonant in 'that' ðæt is alveolar t. In rapid, casual speech the t will become p before a bilabial consonant, as in: 'that person' ðæp pɜːsn̩; 'light blue' laɪp bluː; 'meat pie' miːp paɪ. Before a dental consonant, t will change to a dental plosive, for which the symbol is t̪, as in: 'that thing' ðæt̪ θɪŋ; 'get those' get̪ ðəʊz; 'cut through' kʌt̪ θruː. Before a velar consonant, the t will become k, as in: 'that case' ðæk keɪs; 'bright colour' braɪk kʌlə; 'quite good' kwaɪk gʊd. In similar contexts d would become b, d̪ and g, respectively, and n would become m, n̪ and ŋ. However, the same is not true of the other alveolar consonants: s and z behave differently, the only noticeable change being that s becomes ʃ, and z becomes ʒ when followed by ʃ or j, as in: 'this shoe' ðɪʃ ʃuː; 'those years' ðəʊʒ jɪəz. It is important to note that the consonants that have undergone assimilation have *not* disappeared; in the above examples, the duration of the consonants remains more or less what one would expect for a two-consonant cluster. Assimilation of place is only noticeable in this regressive assimilation of alveolar consonants; it is not something that foreign learners need to learn to do.

Assimilation of manner is much less noticeable, and is only found in the most rapid and casual speech; generally speaking, the tendency is again for regressive assimilation and the change in manner is most likely to be towards an "easier" consonant – one which makes less obstruction to the airflow. It is thus possible to find cases where a final plosive becomes a fricative or nasal (e.g. 'that side' ðæs saɪd, 'good night' gʊn naɪt), but most unlikely that a final fricative or nasal would become a plosive. In one particular case we find progressive assimilation of manner, when a word-initial ð follows a plosive or nasal at the end of a preceding word: it is very common to find that the C^i becomes identical in manner to the C^f but with dental place of articulation. For example (the arrow symbol means "becomes"):

'in the'	ɪn ðə → ɪn̪n̪ə
'get them'	get ðəm → get̪t̪əm
'read these'	riːd ðiːz → riːd̪d̪iːz

It seems that the ð phoneme frequently occurs with no discernible friction noise.

Assimilation of voice is also found, but again only in a limited way. Only *regressive* assimilation of voice is found across word boundaries, and then only of one type; since this matter is important for foreign learners we will look at it in some detail. If C^f is a lenis (i.e. "voiced") consonant and C^i is fortis ("voiceless") we often find that the lenis consonant has no voicing; this is not a very noticeable case of assimilation, since, as was explained in Chapter 4, initial and final lenis consonants usually have little or no voicing anyway. When C^f is fortis ("voiceless") and C^i lenis ("voiced"), a context in which in many languages C^f would become voiced, assimilation of voice *never* takes place; consider the following example: 'I like that black dog' aɪ laɪk ðæt blæk dɒg. It is typical of many foreign learners of English to allow regressive assimilation of voicing to change the final k of 'like' to g, the final t of 'that' to d and the final k of 'black' to g. This creates a very strong impression of a foreign accent, and is something that should obviously be avoided.

Up to this point we have been looking at some fairly clear cases of assimilation across word boundaries. However, similar effects are also observable across morpheme boundaries and to some extent also within the morpheme. Sometimes in the latter case it seems that the assimilation is rather different from the word-boundary examples; for example, if in a syllable-final consonant cluster a nasal consonant precedes a plosive or a fricative in the same morpheme, the place of articulation of the nasal is always determined by the place of articulation of the other consonant; thus: 'bump' bʌmp; 'tenth' tenθ; 'hunt' hʌnt; 'bank' bæŋk. It could be said that this assimilation had become "fixed" as part of the phonological structure of English syllables, since exceptions are almost non-existent. A similar example of a type of assimilation that has become fixed is the *progressive* assimilation of voice with the suffixes s and z; when a verb carries a third person singular '-s' suffix, or a noun carries an '-s' plural suffix or an '-'s' possessive suffix, that suffix will be pronounced as s if the preceding consonant is fortis ("voiceless") and as z if the preceding consonant is lenis ("voiced"), thus:

'cats' kæts	'dogs' dɒgz
'jumps' dʒʌmps	'runs' rʌnz
'Pat's' pæts	'Pam's' pæmz

Much more could be said about assimilation, but from the point of view of learning or teaching English pronunciation, to do so would not be very useful. It is essentially a natural phenomenon that can be seen in any sort of complex physical activity, and the only important matter is to remember the restriction, specific to English, on voicing assimilation mentioned above.

Assimilation creates something of a problem for phoneme theory; when, for example, d in 'good' gʊd becomes g in the context '... girl' (gʊg gɜ:l) or b in the context '... boy' (gʊb bɔɪ), should we say that one phoneme has been substituted for another? If we do this, how do we describe the assimilation in 'good thing', where d becomes dental d̪ before the θ of 'thing', or in 'good food', where d becomes a labiodental plosive before the f in 'food'? English has no dental or labiodental plosive phonemes, so in these cases, although there is clearly assimilation, there could not be said to be a substitution of one phoneme for another. The alternative is to say that assimilation causes a phoneme to be realised by a different allophone; this would mean that, in the case of gʊg gɜ:l and gʊb bɔɪ, the phoneme d of 'good' has velar and bilabial allophones. Traditionally, phonemes were supposed not to overlap in their allophones, so that the only plosives that could have allophones with bilabial place of articulation were p and b; this restriction is no longer looked on as so important.

14.3 **Elision**

TU 14

The nature of **elision** may be stated quite simply: under certain circumstances sounds disappear; one might express this in more technical language by saying that in certain circumstances a phoneme may be realised as **zero**, or have **zero realisation** or be **deleted**. As with assimilation, elision is typical of rapid, casual speech; the process of change in phoneme realisations produced by changing the speed and casualness of speech is sometimes called **gradation**. Producing elisions is something which foreign learners do not need to learn to do, but it is important for them to be aware that when native speakers of English talk to each other, quite a number of phonemes that the foreigner might expect to hear are not actually pronounced. We will look at some examples, though only a small number of the many possibilities can be given here.

i) Loss of weak vowel after p, t, k.
    In words like 'potato', 'tomato', 'canary', 'perhaps', 'today', the vowel in the first syllable may disappear; the aspiration of the initial plosive takes up the whole of the middle portion of the syllable, resulting in these pronunciations (where ᴴ indicates aspiration): pʰˈteɪtəʊ; tʰˈmɑːtəʊ; kʰˈneəri; pʰˈhæps; tʰˈdeɪ

ii) Weak vowel + n, l or r becomes syllabic consonant. (Syllabic consonants were introduced in Chapter 9.)
     Examples: 'tonight' tn̩aɪt; 'police' pl̩iːs; 'correct' kr̩ekt.

iii) Avoidance of complex consonant clusters.
      It has been said that no normal English speaker would ever pronounce all the consonants between the last two words of the following:
      'George the Sixth's throne' dʒɔːdʒ ðə sɪksθs θrəʊn
      Though this is not impossible to pronounce, something like … sɪksθrəʊn is more likely. In clusters of three plosives or two plosives plus a fricative, the middle plosive may disappear, so that the following pronunciations result: 'acts' æks; 'looked back' lʊk bæk; 'scripts' skrɪps.

iv) Loss of final v in 'of' before consonants.
     Examples: 'lots of them' lɒts ə ðəm; 'waste of money' weɪst ə mʌni.

v) It is difficult to know whether **contractions** of grammatical words should be regarded as examples of elision or not. The fact that they are regularly represented with special spelling forms makes them seem rather different from the above examples. The best-known cases are:

– 'Had', 'would': spelt 'd, pronounced d (after vowels), əd (after consonants).

– 'Is', 'has': spelt 's, pronounced s (after fortis consonants), z (after lenis consonants), except that after s, z, ʃ, ʒ, tʃ, dʒ 'is' is pronounced ɪz and 'has' is pronounced əz in contracted form.

– 'Will': spelt 'll, pronounced l (after vowels', l̩ (after consonants).

– 'Have': spelt 've, pronounced v (after vowels), əv (after consonants).

– 'Not': spelt n't, pronounced nt (after vowels), n̩t (after consonants).

(There are also vowel changes associated with n't, e.g. 'can' kæn – 'can't' kɑːnt, 'do' duː – 'don't' dəʊnt.)

– 'Are': spelt 're, pronounced ə after vowels, usually with some change in the preceding vowel, e.g. 'you' juː – 'you're' jʊə, 'we' wiː – 'we're' wɪə, 'they' ðeɪ – 'they're' ðeə; linking r is used when a vowel follows, as explained in the next section. Contracted 'are' is also pronounced as ə or ər when following a consonant.

14.4 Linking

In our hypothetical "mechanical speech" all words would be separate units placed next to each other in sequence; in real connected speech, however, we sometimes link words together. The most familiar case is the use of **linking r**; the phoneme r cannot occur in syllable-final position in RP, but when a word's spelling *suggests* a final r, and a word beginning with a vowel follows, the usual pronunciation for RP speakers is to pronounce with r. For example:

'here' hɪə	*but*	'here are' hɪər ə	
'four' fɔː	*but*	'four eggs' fɔːr egz	

Many RP speakers use r in a similar way to link words ending with a vowel even when there is no "justification" from the spelling, as in:

'Formula A' fɔːmjələr eɪ
'Australia all out' ɒstreɪlɪər ɔːl aʊt
'media event' miːdɪər ɪvent

This has been called **intrusive r**; some English speakers and teachers still regard this as incorrect or sub-standard pronunciation, but it is undoubtedly widespread.

"Linking " and "intrusive r" are special cases of **juncture**; this name refers to the relationship between one sound and the sounds that immediately precede and follow it, and has been given some importance in phonological theory. If we take the two words 'my turn' maɪ tɜːn, the relationship between m and aɪ, between t and ɜː and between ɜː and n is said to be one of **close juncture**. m is preceded by silence and n is followed by silence, and so m and n are said to be in a position of **external open juncture**. The problem lies in deciding what the relationship is between aɪ and t; since we do not usually pause between words, there is no silence (or external open juncture) to indicate word division and to justify the space left in the transcription. But if English speakers hear maɪ tɜːn they can usually recognise this as 'my turn' and not 'might earn'. This is where the problem of **internal open juncture** (usually just called "juncture" for short) becomes apparent. What *is* it that makes perceptible the difference between maɪ tɜːn and maɪt ɜːn? The answer is that in the one case the t is aspirated (initial in 'turn'), and in the other case it is not (being final in 'might'). In addition to this, the aɪ diphthong is shorter in 'might', but we will ignore this for the sake of a simpler argument. If a difference in meaning is caused by the difference between aspirated and unaspirated t, how can we avoid the conclusion that English has a phonemic contrast between aspirated and unaspirated t? The answer is, of course, that the position of a word boundary has some effect on the realisation of the t phoneme; this is one of the many cases in which the occurrence of different allophones can only be properly explained by making reference to units of grammar (something which was for a long time disapproved of by many phonologists).

Many ingenious minimal pairs have been invented to show the significance of juncture, a few of which are given below:

a) 'might rain' maɪt reɪn (r voiced when initial in 'rain', aɪ short)
b) 'my train' maɪ treɪn (r voiceless following t in 'train')

a) 'all that I'm after today' ɔːl ðət aɪm ɑːftə tədeɪ (t unaspirated when final in 'that')
b) 'all the time after today' ɔːl ðə taɪm ɑːftə tədeɪ (t aspirated when initial in 'time')

a) 'he lies' hiː laɪz ("clear l" initial in 'lies')
b) 'heal eyes 'hiːl aɪz ("dark l" final in 'heal')

a) 'keep sticking' kiːp stɪkɪŋ (t unaspirated after s; iː short)
b) 'keeps ticking' kiːps tɪkɪŋ (t aspirated in 'ticking')

Of course, the context in which the words occur almost always makes it clear where the boundary comes, and the juncture information is then redundant.

It should by now be clear that there is a great deal of difference between the way words are pronounced in isolation and in the context of connected speech. It would not be practical or useful to teach all learners of English to produce assimilations; practice in making elisions is more useful, and it is clearly valuable to do exercises related to rhythm and linking. Perhaps the most important consequence of what has been described in this chapter is that learners of English must be made very clearly aware of the problems that they will meet in listening to colloquial, connected speech.

Notes on problems and further reading

14.1   English rhythm is a controversial subject on which widely differing views have been expressed. On one side there are writers such as Abercrombie (1964) and Halliday (1967) who have set out an elaborate theory of the rhythmical structure of English speech (including foot theory). On the other side there are sceptics like Crystal (1969) who reject the idea of an inherent rhythmical pattern. The distinction between physically measurable time-intervals and subjective impressions of rhythmicality is discussed in Roach (1982) (in which figures are presented from a laboratory study of six different languages) and Lehiste (1977); see also Dauer (1983). Adams (1979) presents a review and experimental study of the subject, and concludes that despite the theoretical problems, there is practical value in teaching rhythm to learners of English. The treatment of rhythmicality as a matter of degree, or a characteristic which may or may not be present, is presented in Crystal (1969), pp. 161–5. For some writers concerned with English language teaching, the notion of rhythm is a more practical matter of making a sufficiently clear difference between strong and weak syllables, rather than concentrating on a rigid timing pattern, as I suggest at the end of 14.1. See, for example, Taylor (1981); Mortimer (1984) contains practice material on rhythm.

The treatment of rhythmical hierarchy is based on the comparatively recent theory of **metrical phonology**. Hogg and McCully (1987) give a full explanation of this, but it is difficult material. Goldsmith (1990), chapter 4, and Katamba (1989), chapter 11.1, are briefer and somewhat simpler. James (1988) explores the relevance of metrical phonology to language learning.

14.2   Assimilation of place with specific reference to alveolar consonants is described in Gimson (1960). I think it is important to realise that the traditional view of assimilation as a change from one phoneme to another is naive; modern instrumental studies in the broader field of *coarticulation* show that when assimilation happens one can often show how there is some sort of combination of articulatory gestures. In 'good girl', for example, it is not a simple matter of the first word ending *either* in d *or* in g, but rather a matter of the extent to which alveolar and/or velar closures are achieved. There may be an alveolar closure immediately preceding and overlapping with a velar closure; there may be simultaneous alveolar and velar closure, or a velar closure followed by slight contact but not closure in the alveolar region. There are many other possibilities. An experimental study of coarticulation in consonant clusters which shows some of the above articulatory events is described in Hardcastle and Roach (1979).

14.4 An essential part of acquiring fluency in English is learning to produce connected speech without gaps between words, and this is the practical importance of linking. For practical work, see Mortimer (1984). From the theoretical point of view, however, I personally do not find the question of 'intrusive' and 'linking' r in RP very interesting (one might perhaps class it as a matter similar to the grammatical and stylistic question of whether or not to use 'whom') but anyone who wishes to go into the subject could read Windsor Lewis (1975a), Pring (1976), Windsor Lewis (1977a) and Fox (1978).

An obvious question to be asked in relation to juncture is whether 'internal open juncture' can actually be heard. Jones (1931) implies that it can, but experimental work (e.g. O'Connor and Tooley (1964)) suggests that in many cases it is not perceptible unless a speaker is deliberately trying to avoid ambiguity. It is interesting to note that some phonologists of the 1950s and 1960s felt it necessary to invent a 'phoneme' of juncture in order to be able to transcribe minimal pairs like 'grey tape' / 'great ape' unambiguously without having to refer to grammatical boundaries; see for example Trager and Smith (1951).

Notes for teachers

There is a lot of disagreement about the importance of the various topics in this chapter from the language teacher's point of view. My feeling is that two separate matters sometimes get mixed up: the practice and study of connected speech is agreed by everyone to be of great importance, but this can sometimes result in some relatively unimportant aspects of speech (e.g. assimilation, juncture) being given more emphasis than they should.

In looking at the importance of studying aspects of speech above the segmental level some writers have claimed that learners can come to identify an overall "feel" of the pronunciation of the language being learned. Differences between languages have been described in terms of their **articulatory settings**, that is, overall articulatory posture, by

Honikman (1964). She describes such factors as lip mobility and tongue-setting for English, French and other languages. The notion seems a useful one, though it is difficult to confirm these settings scientifically.

Tape Unit 14 is liable to come as something of a surprise to students who have not had the experience of examining colloquial English speech before. The main message to get across is that concentration on selective, analytic listening will help them to recognise what is being said, and that practice usually brings confidence.

Written exercises

1. Divide the following sentences up into feet, using the | mark as a boundary symbol. If a sentence starts with an unstressed syllable, leave it out of consideration – it doesn't belong in a foot.

   a) A bird in the hand is worth two in the bush.
   b) Over a quarter of a century has elapsed since his death.
   c) Computers consume a considerable amount of money and time.
   d) Most of them have arrived on the bus.
   e) Newspaper editors are invariably underworked.

2. Try to draw tree diagrams of the rhythmical structure of the following phrases.

   a) Christmas present
   b) Rolls Royce
   c) Pet food dealer
   d) Rolls-Royce rally event

3. The following sentences are given in spelling and in a "slow, careful" phonemic transcription. Rewrite the phonemic transcription as a "broad phonetic" one so as to show likely assimilations, elisions and linking.

   a) One cause of asthma is supposed to be allergies
      wʌn kɔːz əv æsθmə ɪz səpəʊzd tə bi æːlədʒɪz
      [   ]
   b) What the urban population could use is better trains
      wɒt ði ɜːbən pɒpjʊleɪʃn̩ kʊd juːz ɪz betə treɪnz
      [   ]
   c) She acts particularly well in the first scene
      ʃi ækts pətɪkjələli wel ɪn ðə fɜːst siːn
      [   ]

15 Intonation 1

Many of the previous chapters have been concerned with the description of phonemes, and in 5.2 it was pointed out that the subject of phonology includes not just this aspect (which is usually called **segmental phonology**) but also several others. In Chapters 10 and 11, for example, we studied stress. Clearly, stress has linguistic importance and is therefore an aspect of the phonology of English that must be described, but it is not usually regarded as something that is related to individual segmental phonemes; normally, stress is said to be something that is applied to (or is a property of) syllables, and is therefore part of the **suprasegmental phonology** of English. Another part of suprasegmental phonology is **intonation**, and the next five chapters are devoted to this subject.

What is intonation? No definition is completely satisfactory, but any attempt at a definition must recognise that the **pitch** of the voice plays the most important part. Only in very unusual situations do we speak with fixed, unvarying pitch, and when we speak normally the pitch of our voice is constantly changing. One of the most important tasks in analysing intonation is to listen to the speaker's pitch and recognise what it is doing; this is not an easy thing to do, and it seems to be a quite different skill from that acquired in studying segmental phonetics. We describe pitch in terms of **high** and **low**, and some people find it difficult to relate what they hear in someone's voice to a scale ranging from low to high. We should remember that "high" and "low" are arbitrary choices for end-points of the pitch scale. It would be perfectly reasonable to think of pitch as ranging instead from "light" to "heavy", for example, or from "left" to "right", and people who have difficulty in "hearing" intonation patterns are generally only having difficulty in relating what they hear (which is the same as what everyone else hears) to this "pseudo-spatial" representation.

It is very important to make the point that we are not interested in *all* aspects of a speaker's pitch; the only things that should interest us are those which carry some linguistic information. If a speaker tries to talk while riding fast on a horse, the speaker's pitch will make a lot of sudden rises and falls as a result of the irregular movement; this is something which is outside the speaker's control and therefore cannot be linguistically significant. Similarly, if we take two speakers at random we will almost certainly find that one speaker typically speaks with lower pitch than the other; the difference between the two speakers is not linguistically significant because their habitual pitch level is determined by their physical structure. But individual speakers *do* have control over their own pitch, and may choose to speak with a higher than normal pitch; this is something which *is* potentially of linguistic significance.

We have established that for pitch differences to be linguistically significant, it is a necessary condition that they should be under the speaker's control. There is another necessary condition and that is that a pitch difference must be **perceptible**; it is possible to detect differences in the **frequency** of the vibration of a speaker's voice by means of laboratory instruments, but these differences may not be great enough to be heard by a listener as differences in pitch. Finally, it should be remembered that in looking for linguistically significant aspects of speech we must always be looking for *contrasts*; one of the most important things about any unit of phonology or grammar is the set of items it contrasts with. We know how to establish what phonemes are in contrast with b in the context – ɪn; we can substitute other phonemes (e.g. p, s) to change the identity of the word from 'bin' to 'pin' to 'sin'. Can we establish such units and contrasts in intonation?

15.1 Form and function in intonation

To summarise what was said above, we want to know the answers to two questions about English speech:

i)   What can we observe when we study pitch variations?
ii) What is the linguistic importance of the phenomena we observe?

These questions might be rephrased more briefly as:

i)   What is the **form** of intonation?
ii) What is the **function** of intonation?

We will begin by looking at intonation in the shortest piece of speech we can find – the single syllable. At this point a new term will be introduced: we need a name for a continuous piece of speech beginning and ending with a clear pause, and we will call this an **utterance**. In this chapter, then, we are going to look at the intonation of one-syllable utterances. These are quite common, and give us a comparatively easy introduction to the subject.

Two common one-syllable utterances are 'yes' and 'no'. The first thing to notice is that we have a choice of saying these with the pitch remaining at a constant level, or with the pitch changing from one level to another. The word we use for the overall behaviour of the pitch in these examples is **tone**; a one-syllable word can be said with either a **level tone** or a **moving tone**. If you try saying 'yes' or 'no' with a level tone (rather as though you were trying to sing them on a steady note) you may find the result does not sound natural, and indeed English speakers do not use level tones on one-syllable utterances very frequently. Moving tones are more common; if English speakers want to say 'yes' or 'no' in a definite, final manner they will probably use a **falling** tone – one which descends from a higher to a lower pitch. If they want to say 'yes?' or 'no?' in a questioning manner they may say it with a **rising** tone – a movement from a lower pitch to a higher one.

Notice that already, in talking about different tones, some idea of function has been introduced; speakers are said to select from a choice of tones according to how they want the utterance to be heard, and it is implied that the listener will hear one-syllable utterances said with different tones as sounding different in some way. During the development of modern phonetics in the present century it was for a long time hoped that scientific study of intonation would make it possible to state what the function of each different aspect of intonation was, and that foreign learners could then be taught rules to enable them to use intonation in the way that native speakers use it. Few people now believe this to be possible. It is certainly possible to produce a few general rules, and some will be given in this course, just as a few general rules for word stress were given in Chapters 10 and 11. However, these rules are certainly not adequate as a practical guide to how to use English intonation. My treatment of intonation is based on the belief that foreign learners of English at advanced levels who may use this course should be given training to make them better able to recognise and copy English intonation; the only really efficient way to learn to use the intonation of a language is the way a child acquires the intonation of its first language, and the training referred to above should help the adult learner of English to acquire English intonation in a similar (though much slower) way – through listening to and talking to English speakers. It is perhaps a discouraging thing to say, but learners of English who are not able to talk regularly with native speakers of English, or who are not able at least to listen regularly to colloquial English, are not likely to learn English intonation, though they may learn very good pronunciation of the segments and use stress correctly.

15.2 **Tone and tone languages**

TU 15,
Exs 1–3

In the preceding section we mentioned three simple possibilities for the intonation used in pronouncing the one-word utterances 'yes' and 'no'. These were: level, fall and rise. It will often be necessary to use symbols to represent tones, and for this we will use marks placed before the syllable in the following way (phonemic transcription will not be used in these examples – words are given in spelling):

Level	_yes	_no
Falling	ˏyes	ˏno
Rising	ˌyes	ˌno

Obviously, this simple system for tone transcription could be extended, if we wished, to cover a greater number of possibilities. For example, if it was important to distinguish between a high level and low level tone for English we could do it in this way:

High level	ˉyes	ˉno
Low level	_yes	_no

Although in English we do on occasions say ˉyes or ˉno and on other occasions _yes or _no, no speaker of English would say that the meaning of the words 'yes' and 'no' was different with the different tones. (As will be seen below, we will not use the symbols for high and low level tones in the description of English intonation.) But there are many languages in which the tone *can* determine the meaning of a word, and changing from one tone to another can completely change the meaning. For example, in Kono, a language of West Africa, we find the following (meanings given in brackets):

High level	ˉbɛŋ ('uncle')	ˉbuu ('horn')
Low level	_bɛŋ ('greedy')	_buu ('to be cross')

Similarly, while we can hear a difference between English _yes, ˌyes and ˏyes, and between _no, ˌno and ˏno, there is not a difference in meaning in such a clear-cut way as in Chinese (Peking dialect), where, for example, ˉma means 'mother', ˌma means 'hemp' and ˏma means 'scold'. Languages such as the above are called **tone languages**; although to most speakers of European languages they may seem strange and exotic, such languages are in fact spoken by a very large proportion of the world's population. In addition to the many dialects of Chinese, many other languages of South-East Asia (e.g. Thai, Vietnamese) are tone languages; so are very many African languages, particularly those to the South and West, and a considerable number of Amerindian languages. English is, of course, *not* a tone language, and the function of tone is much more difficult to define than in a tone language.

15.3 **Complex tones and pitch height**

We have introduced three simple tones that can be used on one-syllable English utterances: level, fall and rise. However, other more complex tones are also used. One that is quite frequently found is the **fall–rise** tone, where the pitch descends and then rises again; another complex tone, much less frequently used, is the **rise–fall** in which the pitch follows the opposite movement. We will not consider any more complex tones, since these are not often encountered and are of little importance.

One further complication should be mentioned here. Each speaker has his or her own normal pitch range: a top level which is the highest pitch normally used by the speaker, and a bottom level that the speaker's pitch normally does not go below. In ordinary speech, the intonation tends to take place within the lower part of the speaker's pitch range, but in situations where strong feelings are to be expressed it is usual to make use of extra pitch height. For example, if we represent the pitch range by drawing two parallel lines representing the highest and lowest limits of the range, then a normal unemphatic 'yes' could be diagrammed like this:

but a strong, emphatic 'yes' like this:

We will use a new symbol ↑ (a vertical arrow) to indicate **extra pitch height,** so that we can distinguish between:

ˏyes   and   ↑ ˏyes

Any of the tones presented in this chapter may be given extra pitch height, but since this course is based on normal, unemotional speech, it will not be necessary to use the symbol very frequently.

15.4 **Some functions of English tones**

In this chapter only a very small part of English intonation has been
introduced. We will now see if it is possible to state in what
circumstances the different tones are used within the very limited
context of the words 'yes' and 'no' said in isolation. We will look at
some typical occurrences; no examples of extra pitch height will be
considered here.

TU 15,
Ex 4

Fall ˎyes ˎno

This is the tone about which least needs to be said, and which is usually
regarded as more or less "neutral". If someone is asked a question and
replies ˎyes or ˎno it will be understood that the question is now
answered and that there is nothing more to be said. The fall could be
said to give an impression of "finality".

Rise ˏyes ˏno

In a variety of ways, this tone conveys an impression that something
more is to follow; a typical occurrence in a dialogue between two
speakers whom we shall call A and B might be the following:

A (wishing to attract B's attention): Excuse me.
B: ˏyes

(B's reply is, perhaps, equivalent to 'what do you want?')
Another quite common occurrence would be:

A: Do you know John Smith?

One possible reply from B would be ˏyes, inviting A to continue with
what she intends to say about John Smith after establishing that B
knows him. To reply instead ˎyes would give a feeling of "finality", of
"end of the conversation"; if A *did* have something to say about John
Smith, the response with a fall would make it difficult for A to continue.
We can see similar "invitations to continue" in someone's response
to a series of instructions or directions. For example:

A: You start off on the ring road . . .
B: ˏyes
A: turn left at the first roundabout . . .
B: ˏyes
A: and ours is the third house on the left.

Whatever B replies to this last utterance of A, it would be most unlikely to be ˌyes again, since A has clearly finished her instructions and it would be pointless to "prompt" her to continue.

With 'no', a similar function can be seen. For example:

A: Have you seen Ann?

If B replies ˎno, he implies quite clearly that he has no interest in continuing with that topic of conversation. But a reply of ˌno would be an invitation to A to explain why she is looking for Ann, or why she does not know where she is.

Similarly, someone may ask a question that implies readiness to present some new information. For example:

A: Do you know what the longest balloon flight was?

If B replies ˌno he is inviting A to tell him, while a response of ˎno could be taken to mean that he does not know and is not expecting to be told. This is, in fact, a common cause of misunderstanding in English conversation, when a question such as A's above might be a request for information *or* an offer to provide some.

Fall–rise ˎˌyes ˎˌno

The fall–rise is used a lot in English and has some rather special functions. In the present context we will only consider one fairly simple one, which could perhaps be described as "limited agreement" or "response with reservations". Examples may make this clearer:

A: I've heard that it's a good school.
B: ˇyes

B's reply would be taken to mean that he would not completely agree with what A said, and A would probably expect B to go on to explain *why* he was reluctant to agree. Similarly:

A: It's not really an expensive record, is it?
B: ˇno

The fall–rise in B's reply again indicates that he would not completely agree with A. Fall–rise in such contexts almost always indicates both something "given" or "conceded" and at the same time some "reservation" or "hesitation". This use of intonation will be returned to in Chapter 19.

Rise–fall ˆyes ˆno

This is used to convey rather strong feelings of approval, disapproval or surprise. It is not usually considered to be an important tone for foreign learners to acquire, though it is still useful practice to learn to distinguish it from other tones. Here are some examples:

A: *You* would't do an awful thing like that, would you?
B: ˎno

A: Isn't the view lovely!
B: ˎyes

A: I think you said it was the best so far.
B: ˎyes

Level ˍyes ˍno

This tone is certainly used in English, but in a rather restricted context: it almost always conveys (on single-syllable utterances) a feeling of saying something routine, uninteresting or boring. A teacher calling the names of pupils from a register will often do so using a level tone on each name, and the pupils would be likely to respond with ˍyes when their name was called. Similarly, if one is being asked a series of routine questions for some purpose such as applying for an insurance policy, one might reply to each question of a series like 'Have you ever been in prison?', 'Do you suffer from any serious illness?', 'Is your eyesight defective?', etc., with ˍno.

A few "meanings" have been suggested for the five tones that have been introduced, but each tone may have many more such meanings. Moreover, it would be quite wrong to conclude that in the above examples only the tones given would be appropriate; it is, in fact, almost impossible to find a context where one could not substitute a different tone. This is not the same thing as saying that *any* tone can be used in *any* context; the point is that no particular tone has a unique "privilege of occurrence" in a particular context. When we come to look at more complex intonation patterns, we will see that defining intonational "meanings" does not become any easier.

Notes on problems and further reading

To devote five chapters to intonation may seem excessive, but I feel that this is necessary since the subject is difficult and complex, and needs to be explained at considerable length if the explanation is to be intelligible. The study of intonation has gone through many changes during this century. The most intensive theoretical development began during the 1940s. In the United States the theory that evolved was based on 'pitch phonemes' (Wells, 1945; Pike, 1945): four contrastive pitch levels were established and intonation was described basically in terms of a series of movements from one of these levels to another. This approach was further developed in Trager and Smith (1951). Although this 'pitch phoneme' theory became an orthodoxy, it was consistently attacked by one American linguist, D. Bolinger (e.g. Bolinger, 1951). In Britain the 'tone-unit' or 'tonetic' approach begun by H. E. Palmer in the 1920s (Palmer, 1924) was developed by (among others) Kingdon (1958a), O'Connor and Arnold (1962) and Halliday (1967). These two different theoretical approaches became gradually more elaborate; in the American case perhaps the most elaborate exposition was in Trager (1964), while O'Connor and Arnold produced an extended version of their treatment in their second edition (1973). However, since the 1970s it has become clear that such frameworks are inadequate for dealing with natural spontaneous speech; in Britain the most influential work leading to this recognition was Crystal (1969); another good example of the same attitude is Brown *et al.* (1980). I have tried in this course to reflect some of the more recently developed ideas for dealing with intonation, though the treatment remains essentially within the conventions of the British tradition. The best explanation of theoretical issues in intonation is Cruttenden (1986).

A word of caution is needed in connection with the word *pitch*. Strictly speaking, this should be used to refer to an auditory sensation experienced by the hearer. The rate of vibration of the vocal cords – something which is physically measurable, and which is related to activity on the part of the speaker – is the *fundamental frequency** of voiced sounds, and should not be called 'pitch'. However, as long as this distinction is understood, it is generally agreed that the term 'pitch' is a convenient one to use informally to refer both to the subjective sensation and to the objectively measurable fundamental frequency.

15.1 The notion of *tone* is best understood by dealing with single syllables at first. Eventually the number of tones used in this course is five: fall, rise, fall–rise, rise–fall and level.

15.2 The amount of time to be spent on learning about tone languages should depend to some extent on your background. Those whose native language is a tone language should be aware of the considerable linguistic importance of tone in such languages; often it is extremely difficult for people who have spoken a tone language all their life to learn to observe their own use of tone objectively. The study of tone languages is less important for native speakers of non-tone languages, but most students seem to find it an interesting subject. A good introduction is Ladefoged (1982), pp. 226–32. The classic work on the

---

* 'fundamental frequency' is often abbreviated to FO.

subject is Pike (1948), while more modern treatments are Hyman (1975), pp. 212–29 and Katamba (1989), Chapter 10.

15.3   Many analyses within the British approach to intonation include among tones both 'high' and 'low' varieties. For example, O'Connor and Arnold (1973) distinguished between 'high fall' and 'low fall' (the former starting from a high pitch, the latter from mid), and also between 'low rise' and 'high rise' (the latter rising to a higher point than the former). Some writers have high and low versions of all tones. Compared with the proposed establishing of a separate feature of 'extra pitch height' (which is explained more fully in 18.1), this is unnecessary duplication. Of course, if one adds extra pitch height to a tone, one has not given all possible detail about it. If we take as an example a fall–rise without extra pitch height:

then something symbolised as ↑ ˬ could be any of the following:

It would be possible to extend our framework to distinguish between these possibilities, but I do not believe it would be profitable to do so.

Crystal (1969) includes in his set of tones fall–rise–fall and rise–fall–rise; I have seldom felt the need to recognise these as distinct from rise–fall and fall–rise respectively. Halliday (1967) has a rather odd-looking set of tones:

1.   \ falling
2.   { / rising
      { \/ falling–rising
3.   ⌐/ rising
4.   ∿/ (rising–)<u>falling</u>–rising
5.   ⋁\ (falling–)<u>rising</u>–falling

There is, of course, no particular reason to expect linguistic systems to be tidy and symmetrical, but I find it hard to see why Halliday chose these particular tones.

15.4   I will leave discussion of the functions (or supposed functions) of tones until later, except for the fall–rise. It seems to be generally agreed that this is in some way 'special', and peculiar to English. This may not be true, but certainly in listening to conversational English one does encounter a very large number of these and they do seem to the native speaker to have some perhaps indefinable 'feel' of something negative present in the background, as suggested above, on p. 139). The clearest attempt to explain this is, in my opinion, O'Connor (1957).

Note for teachers

As explained above, some students may be perfectly well able to discriminate between tones, but have difficulty in labelling them as 'fall', 'rise', etc. I find that about 5 per cent of the students I teach are never able to overcome this difficulty (even though they may have perfect hearing and in some cases a high level of linguistic and musical ability); of the remainder, a few are especially gifted and cannot understand how anyone could find the task difficult, and most others eventually learn after five or ten hours of practical classes. Many students find it very helpful to sit in the phonetics laboratory looking at a computer display showing a picture of their pitch movements.

Written exercise

In the following sentences and bits of dialogue, each underlined syllable must be given an appropriate tone mark. Write a tone mark just in front of each of the syllables.

1. This train is for <u>Leeds</u>, <u>York</u>, <u>Dar</u>lington and <u>Dur</u>ham
2. Can you give me a <u>lift</u>?
   <u>Poss</u>ibly Where <u>to</u>?
3. <u>No</u>! Certainly <u>not</u>! Go <u>away</u>!
4. Did you know he'd been convicted of drunken <u>dri</u>ving?
   <u>No</u>!
5. If I give him <u>mo</u>ney he goes and <u>spends</u> it
   If I lend him the <u>bike</u> he <u>lo</u>ses it
   He's completely unre<u>li</u>able

16 Intonation 2

16.1 The tone-unit

In the last chapter it was explained that some of the world's languages are "tone languages", in which substituting one distinctive tone for another on a particular word or morpheme can cause a change in the dictionary ("lexical") meaning of that word or morpheme, or in some aspect of its grammatical categorisation. English is one of the languages that do *not* use tone in this way though tones or pitch differences *are* used for other purposes; such languages are sometimes called **intonation languages**. In tone languages the main suprasegmental contrastive unit is the tone, which is usually linked to the phonological unit that we call the syllable. It could be said that someone analysing the function and distribution of tones in a tone language would be mainly occupied in examining utterances syllable by syllable, looking at each syllable as an independently variable item. In the last chapter, five tones found on English one-syllable utterances were introduced, and if English was spoken in isolated monosyllables, the job of tonal analysis would be a rather similar one to that described for tone languages. However, when we look at continuous speech in English utterances we find that these tones can only be identified on a small number of particularly prominent syllables. For the purposes of analysing intonation, a unit generally greater in size than the syllable is needed, and this unit is called the **tone-unit**; in its smallest form the tone-unit may consist of only one syllable, so it would in fact be wrong to say that it is always composed of more than one syllable. The tone-unit is difficult to define, and one or two examples may help to make it easier to understand the concept. (As explained in the last chapter, examples used to illustrate intonation transcription are usually given in spelling form, and you will notice that no punctuation is used; the reason for this is that intonation and stress are the vocal equivalents of written punctuation, so that when these are transcribed it would be unnecessary or even confusing to include punctuation as well.)

Let us begin with a one-syllable utterance:

,<u>you</u>

TU 16,
Exs 1 & 2

We will underline syllables that carry a tone. Now consider this three-syllable utterance:

is it ‿you

The third syllable is more prominent than the other two and carries a rising tone. The other two syllables will normally be much less prominent, and be said on a level pitch. Why do we not say that each of the syllables 'is' and 'it' carries a level tone? This is a difficult question that will be examined more fully later; for the present I will answer it (rather unsatisfactorily) by saying that it is unusual for a syllable said on a level pitch to be so prominent that it would be described as carrying a level *tone*. To summarise the analysis of 'is it ‿you' so far, it is an utterance of three syllables, composed of one tone-unit; the only syllable that carries a tone is the third one. From now on, a syllable which carries a tone will be called a **tonic syllable**. It has been mentioned several times that tonic syllables have a high degree of prominence; prominence is, of course, a property of stressed syllables, and a tonic syllable not only carries a tone (which is something related to intonation) but also a type of stress that will be called **tonic stress**. (Some writers use the terms **nucleus** and **nuclear stress** for **tonic syllable** and **tonic stress**.)

The example can now be extended:

‿John is it ‿you

(a fall–rise is used quite commonly in calling someone's name out). If there is a clear pause (silence) between '‿John' and 'is it ‿you', then according to the definition of an utterance given in the last chapter, there are two utterances; however, it is quite likely that a speaker would say '‿John is it ‿you' with no pause, so that the four syllables would make up a single utterance. In spite of the absence of any pause, the utterance would normally be regarded as divided into two tone-units: '‿John' and 'is it ‿you'. Since it is very difficult to lay down the conditions for deciding where the boundaries between tone-units exist, the discussion of this matter must wait until later.

It should be possible to see now that the tone-unit has a place in a range of phonological units that are in a **hierarchical relationship**: speech consists of a number of **utterances** (the largest unit that we shall consider); each utterance consists of one or more **tone-units**; each tone-unit consists of one or more **feet**; each foot consists of one or more **syllables**; each syllable consists of one or more **phonemes**.

16.2 The structure of the tone-unit

In Chapter 8 the structure of the English syllable was examined in some detail. Like the syllable, the tone-unit has a fairly clearly-defined internal structure, but the only component that has been mentioned so far is the tonic syllable. The first thing to be done is to make more precise the role of the tonic syllable in the tone-unit. Most tone-units are of a type that we call **simple**, and the sort that we call **compound** are not discussed in this chapter. Each simple tone-unit has one and only one tonic syllable; this means that the tonic syllable is an obligatory component of the tone-unit. (Compare the role of the vowel in the syllable.) We will now see what the other components may be.

The head

Consider the following one-syllable utterance:

ˌthose

We can find the same tonic syllable in a long utterance (still of one tone-unit):

'give me ˌthose

The rest of the tone-unit in this example is called the **head**. Notice that the first syllable has a stress mark; this is important. A head is all that part of a tone-unit that extends from the first stressed syllable up to (but not including) the tonic syllable. It follows that if there is no stressed syllable before the tonic syllable, there cannot be a head. In the above example, the first two syllables (words) are the head of the tone-unit. In the following example, the head is the first five syllables:

'Bill 'called to 'give me ˌthose

As was said a little earlier, if there is no stressed syllable preceding the tonic syllable, there is no head. This is the case in the following example:

in an ˌhour

Neither of the two syllables preceding the tonic syllable is stressed. The syllables 'in an' form a **pre-head**, which is the next component of the tone-unit to be introduced.

The pre-head

The **pre-head** is composed of all the unstressed syllables in a tone-unit preceding the first stressed syllable. Thus pre-heads are found in two main environments:

i) When there is no head (i.e. no stressed syllable preceding the tonic syllable), as in the example 'in an ˌhour'.

ii) When there is a head, as in the following example:

    in a 'little 'less than an ˎhour

In this example, the pre-head consists of 'in a', the head consists of ''little 'less than an', and the tonic syllable is 'ˎhour'.

The tail

It often happens that some syllables follow the tonic syllable. Any syllables between the tonic syllable and the end of the tone-unit are called the **tail**. In the following examples, each tone-unit consists of an initial tonic syllable and a tail:

    ˎlook at it   ˏwhat did you say
    ˎboth of them were here

When it is necessary to mark stress in a tail, we will use a special symbol, a raised dot · for reasons that will be explained later. The above examples should, then, be transcribed as follows:

    ˎlook at it   ˏwhat did you ·say
    ˎboth of them were ·here

This completes the list of tone-unit components. If we use brackets to indicate optional components (that is, components which may be present or may be absent), we can summarise tone-unit structure as follows:

    (pre-head)   (head)   tonic syllable   (tail)

or, more briefly, as:

    (PH)   (H)   TS   (T)

To illustrate this more fully, let us consider the following passage, which is transcribed from a tape-recording of spontaneous speech (the speaker is describing a picture). When we analyse longer stretches of speech, it is necessary to mark the places where tone-unit boundaries occur (that is, where one tone-unit ends and another begins, or where a tone-unit ends and is followed by a pause, or where a tone-unit begins following a pause). It was mentioned above that tone-units are sometimes separated by silent pauses and sometimes not; pause-type boundaries can be marked by double vertical lines like this ‖ and non-pause boundaries with a single line |. In practice it is not usually important to mark pauses at the beginning and end of a passage; in the rest of the book I put no lines on short examples and only single lines around longer ones; the boundaries *within* a passage are much more important.

‖ and then 'nearer to the ͺfront ‖ on the ˎleft | theres 'bit of ˎforest |
'coming 'down to the ˎwaterside ‖ and then a 'bit of a ˌbay ‖

We can mark their structure as follows:

‖ PH	H	TS ‖	PH	TS	PH
‖ and then	'nearer to the	ˎfront ‖	on the	ˎleft	theres a

H	TS	T	H	TS	T
'bit of	ˎfo	rest	'coming 'down to the	ˎwa	terside ‖

PH	H	TS‖
and then a	'bit of a	ˌbay ‖

The above passage contains five tone-units. Notice that in the third
tone-unit, since it is the tonic syllable rather than the word that carries
the tone, it is necessary to divide the word 'forest' into two parts, 'fo' fɒ
and 'rest' rɪst (it could be argued that the syllables should be divided
'for' and 'est', but this is not important here). This example shows
clearly how the units of phonological analysis can sometimes be seen to
differ from those of grammatical analysis.

16.3 Pitch possibilities in the simple tone-unit

It has been said several times in this chapter that tone is carried by the
tonic syllable, and it is now necessary to examine this statement more
carefully. Before doing this, another general statement will be made
(and will also need further explanation): intonation is carried by the
tone-unit.

In a one-syllable utterance, the single syllable must have one of the
five tones described in the last chapter. In a tone-unit of more than one
syllable, the tonic syllable must have one of those tones. If the tonic
syllable is the final syllable, the tone will not sound much different from
that of a corresponding one-syllable tone-unit. For example, the word
'here' will be said in much the same way in the following:

ˌhere   'shall we 'sit ˌhere

However, if there are other syllables following the tonic syllable (i.e.
there is a tail), we find that the pitch movement of the tone is not
completed on the tonic syllable. If, for example, a tail follows a tonic
syllable that has a rising tone, it will almost always be found that the
syllable or syllables of the tail will continue to move upwards from the
pitch of the tonic syllable. For example, if the word 'what' is said on a
rising tone, 'ˌwhat', it might have a pitch movement that could be
diagrammed like this:

The four syllables in '‚what did you say' might be said like this:

with the pitch of the syllables in the tail getting progressively higher. In such cases, the tonic syllable is the syllable on which the pitch movement of the tone begins, but that pitch movement is completed over the rest of the tone unit (i.e. the tail). If, in rising progressively higher, the pitch reaches the highest part of the speaker's normal pitch range, subsequent syllables will continue at that level.

We find a similar situation with the falling tone. On a single syllable '‚why', the pitch movement might be of this sort:

but if there are syllables following, the fall may not be completed on the tonic syllable: ‚why did you go

Again, if the speaker's lowest pitch is reached before the end of the tail, the pitch continues at the bottom level. In the case of a level tone, syllables following in the tail will, of course, continue at the same level; since level tone is to be treated as a rather unusual type of tone, we will not examine it in more detail at this stage. The situation is more complicated when we have a tail following a fall–rise or a rise–fall, and this will be described in the next chapter.

Notes on problems and further reading

Almost all British analyses use a unit similar or identical to what I call a *tone-unit*, and many writers see this unit as having a crucial role in linking intonation to higher-level grammatical units. It is possible to represent intonation as a simple sequence of tonic and non-tonic stressed syllables, and pauses, with no higher-level organisation; an example of this is Windsor Lewis (1977b). An early attempt at defining intonation units was that of Jones (1975, Chapter 30), where stretches of speech between pauses were called 'breath-groups' and marked with double vertical lines ||, and smaller stretches within these, called 'sense-groups', bounded by places where 'pauses *may* be made' and consisting of 'a few words in close grammatical connexion'. Trim (1959)* criticises this proposal, saying that Jones' 'sense-group' is defined in semantic terms and the 'breath-group' in physiological terms, whereas we should be concerned with phonetic and phonological units and definitions. Instead, he proposes that the unit used should be the 'tone-group', defined in terms of rhythm and pitch movements, and that we should distinguish between 'major' and 'minor' tone-groups. The minor tone-group corresponds to the tone-unit used in this course, and the idea of a larger unit (the major tone-unit) is a valuable one that will be discussed further in the notes on Chapter 19. Different writers use different names: Halliday and his followers use 'tone-group', O'Connor and Arnold use 'sense-group' and Crystal, Brazil *et al.* and I use 'tone-unit'. On tone-unit structure and pitch possibilities in the tone-unit, see chapter 5 in Crystal (1969), chapter 1 in Crystal (1975), Halliday (1967), and chapter 1 in O'Connor and Arnold (1973).

Note for teachers

The move from tones to tone-units is a difficult one, and I feel it is advisable at this stage to use only slow, careful speech for exercises (**Tape Units 15 and 16**). More difficult exercises follow later (**Tape Units 18 and 19**).

---

* Not surprisingly, the fact that Trim's article is written in phonemic transcription with many words not separated by spaces makes it hard to read.

Written exercises

1. Here is a list of single tonic syllables. Add a number of extra syllables (as specified by the number in brackets) to make a tail. Example: <u>go</u> (2) *answer:* <u>go</u> for it
   a) <u>buy</u> (3)
   b) <u>hear</u> (1)
   c) <u>talk</u> (2)
(The answers section gives some possible versions.)
2. Now expand the following tonic syllables by putting heads in front of them, containing the number of stressed syllables indicated in brackets. Example: (2) <u>dark</u> *answer:* 'John was a'fraid of the <u>dark</u>
   a) (1) <u>step</u>
   b) (3) <u>train</u>
   c) (2) <u>hot</u>
3. The following sentences are given with intonation transcribed. Draw underneath them a diagram of the pitch movements, leaving a gap between each syllable. Example:
      'would you 'like some 'more ͵<u>milk</u>

a) 'Only when the ͵<u>wind</u> blows

b) ͵<u>When</u> did you say

c) 'What was the ͵<u>name</u> of the place

F

17 Intonation 3

In the last chapter the structure of the tone-unit was introduced and it was explained that when a tonic syllable is followed by a tail, that tail continues and completes the tone begun on the tonic syllable. Examples were given to show how this happens in the case of rising and falling tones. We now go on to consider the rather more difficult cases of fall–rise and rise–fall tones.

17.1 Fall–rise and rise–fall tones followed by a tail

TU 17,
Exs 1 & 2

A rising or a falling tone is quite easy to identify, whether it falls on a single syllable or extends over more syllables in the case of a tonic syllable followed by a tail. Fall–rise and rise–fall tones, however, can be quite difficult to recognise when they are extended over tails, since their characteristic pitch movements are often broken up or distorted by the structure of the syllables they occur on. For example, the pitch movement on ‚some will be something like this:

If we add a syllable, the "fall" part of the fall–rise is usually carried by the first syllable and the "rise" part by the second. The result may be a continuous pitch movement very similar to the one-syllable case, if there are no voiceless medial consonants to cause a break in the voicing. For example:

‚some ·men

If the continuity of the voicing is broken, however, the pitch pattern might be more like this:

‚some ·chairs

In this case it would be possible to say that there is a falling tone on 'some' and a rise on 'chairs'. However, most English speakers seem to feel that the pitch movement in this case is the same as that in the previous two examples; it can be said that there is a parallel with rhyming. Just as 'balloon' rhymes with 'moon', so we might say that '‚some chairs' has what could be called a **tonal rhyme** with '‚some'.

If there is a tail of two or more syllables, the normal pitch movement is for the pitch to fall on the tonic syllable and to remain low until the last stressed syllable in the tail. The pitch then rises from that point up to the end of the tone-unit. If there is *no* stressed syllable in the tail, the rise happens on the final syllable. Here are some examples:

a) I ‚might ·buy it

I ‚might have ·thought of ·buying it

b) ‚most of them

‚most of it was for them

With the rise–fall tone we find a similar situation: if the tonic syllable is followed by a single syllable in the tail, the "rise" part of the tone takes place on the first (tonic) syllable and the "fall" part is on the second. Thus:

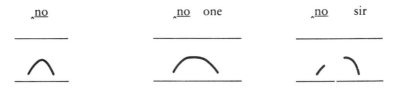

When there are two or more syllables in the tail, the syllable immediately following the tonic syllable is always higher and any following syllables are low. For example:

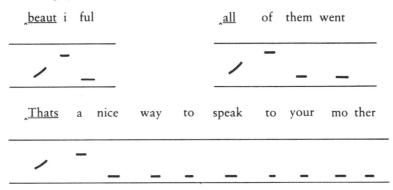

It should be clear by now that the speaker does not have a choice in the matter of the pitch of the syllables in the tail. This is completely determined by the choice of tone for the tonic syllable.

17.2 **High and low heads**

TU 17,
Ex 3

The **head** was defined in the last chapter as "all that part of a tone-unit that extends from the first stressed syllable up to, but not including, the tonic syllable". In our description of intonation up to this point, the only pitch contrasts found in the tone-unit are the different possible choices of tone for the tonic syllable. However, we can identify different pitch possibilities in the head, though these are limited to two which we will call **high head** and **low head**. In the case of the high head, the stressed syllable which begins the head is high in pitch; usually it is higher than the beginning pitch of the tone on the tonic syllable. For example:

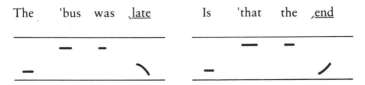

In the low head the stressed syllable which begins the head is low in pitch; usually it is lower than the beginning pitch of the tone on the tonic syllable. To mark this stressed syllable in the low head we will use a different symbol, ˌ as in ˌlow. As an example, the heads of the above sentences will be changed from high to low:

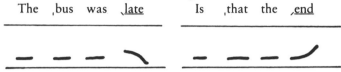

The two different versions (high and low head) will usually sound slightly different to English listeners, though it it not easy to say just what the difference *is*, as will be made clear in the next chapter.

It is usual for unstressed syllables to continue the pitch of the stressed syllable that precedes them. In the following example, the three unstressed syllables 'if it had' continue at the same pitch as the stressed syllable 'asked':

a) with high head
  We 'asked if it had ˌcome

b) with low head
  We ˌasked if it had ˌcome

When there is more than one stressed syllable in the head there is usually a slight change in pitch from the level of one stressed syllable to that of the next, the change being in the direction of the beginning pitch of the tone on the tonic syllable. We will use some long examples to illustrate this, though heads of this length are not very frequently found in natural speech. In the first example the stressed syllables in the high head step downwards progressively to approach the beginning of the tone:

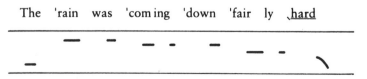

In the next example the head is low; since the tone also starts low, being a rise, there is no upward movement in the head:

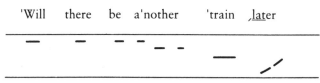

,Thats ,not the ,sto ry you ,told in ,court

When there is a low head followed by a falling tone, successive stressed syllables in the head will tend to move upwards towards the beginning pitch of the tone:

,I could have ,bought it for ,less than a ,pound

When a high head is followed by a rise the stressed syllables tend to move downwards, as one would expect, towards the beginning pitch of the tone:

'Will there be a'nother 'train ,later

Of course, when we examine the intonation of polysyllabic heads we find much greater variety than these simple examples suggest. However, the division into high and low heads as general types is probably the most basic that can be made, and it would be pointless to set up a more elaborate system to represent differences if these differences were not recognised by most English speakers. Some writers on intonation claim that the intonation pattern starting at a fairly high pitch, with a gradual dropping down of pitch during the utterance, is the most basic, normal, "unmarked" intonation pattern; this movement is often called **declination**. The claim that declination is universally unmarked in English, or even in all languages, is a strong one. As far as English is concerned, it would be good to see more evidence from the full range of regional and national varieties in support of the claim.

It should be noted that the two marks ' and , are being used for two different purposes in this course, as they are in many phonetics books. When stress is being discussed, the ' mark indicates primary stress and , indicates secondary stress. For the purposes of marking intonation, however, the mark ' indicates a stressed syllable in a high head and the mark , indicates a stressed syllable in a low head. In practice this is not usually found confusing as long as one is aware of whether one is marking stress levels or intonation. Of course, when the high and low marks ' and , are being used to indicate intonation it is no longer possible to mark two different levels of stress within the word. However, when looking at speech at the level of the tone-unit we are not usually interested in this; a much more important difference here is that between tonic stress (marked by underlining the tonic syllable and placing before it one of the five tone-marks) and non-tonic stressed syllables (marked ' or ˌ in the head or ˙in the tail).

It needs to be emphasised that in marking intonation, only stressed syllables are marked; this implies that intonation is carried entirely by the stressed syllables of a tone-unit and that the pitch of unstressed syllables is either predictable from that of stressed syllables or is of so little importance that it is not worth marking. Remember that the additional information given in the examples above by drawing pitch levels and movements between lines is only included here to make the examples clearer and is not normally given with our system of transcription, so all the important information about intonation *must* be given by the marks placed in the text.

17.3 Problems in analysing the form of intonation

The analysis of intonational form presented in this chapter and the two previous ones is similar in most respects to the approaches used in many British studies of English intonation. There are certain difficulties that all of these studies have had to confront, and it is useful to have a brief summary of what the major difficulties are.

Identifying the tonic syllable

It is often said that the tonic syllable can be identified because it is the only syllable in the tone-unit that carries a movement in pitch; this is in fact not always true. We have seen how when the tonic syllable is followed by a tail the tone is carried by the tonic plus tail together in such a way that in some cases practically no pitch movement is detectable on the tonic syllable itself. In addition it has been claimed that one of the tones is the *level* tone, which by definition may not have any pitch movement. It is therefore necessary to say in this particular case that the tonic syllable is identified simply as the most prominent syllable.

In addition, it sometimes seems as if some tone-units (though only a small number) contain not one but *two* tonic syllables, almost always with the first syllable having a fall on it and the other a rise. An example is:

Ive ˌseen ˌhim
_____

i)

— ＼ ／
_____

In this example there seems to be equal prominence on 'seen' and 'him'. Of course, it could be claimed that this was the same thing as:

Ive ˌseen him
_____

ii)

— ＼ ／
_____

but it has been pointed out that the two versions are different in several ways. Since 'him' has greater prominence in (i), it cannot occur in its weak form ɪm, but must be pronounced hɪm, whereas in (ii) the pronunciation is likely to be aɪv ˌsiːn ɪm. The two versions are said to convey different meanings, too. Version (i) might be said in conversation on hearing someone's name, as in this example:

A: John Cleese is a very funny actor.
B: 'Oh ˌyes |Ive ˌseen ˌhim

In version (ii), on the other hand, the word 'seen' is given the greatest prominence, and it is likely to sound as though the speaker has some reservation, or has something further to say:

A: Have you seen my father yet?
B: Ive ˌseen him |but I 'havent had ' time to ˌtalk to him

The same is found with 'her', as in

Ive ˌseen ˌher
aɪv ˌsiːn ˌhɜː

compared with

Ive ˌseen her
aɪv ˌsiːn ə

This is a difficult problem, since it weakens the general claim made earlier that each tone-unit contains only one tonic syllable.

Identifying tone-unit boundaries

It is a generally accepted principle in the study of grammar that utterances may contain one or more sentences, and that one can identify on grammatical grounds the places where one sentence ends and another begins. In a similar way in suprasegmental phonology it is claimed that utterances may be divided up into tone-units, and that one can identify on phonetic or phonological grounds the places where one tone-unit ends and another tone-unit begins. However, giving rules for determining where the boundaries are placed is not easy, except in cases where a clear pause separates tone-units. Two principles are usually mentioned: one is that it is possible in most cases to detect some sudden change from the pitch level at the end of one tone-unit to the pitch level that starts the following tone-unit, and recognition of the start of the following tone-unit is made easier by the fact that speakers tend to "return home" to a particular pitch level at the beginning of a tone-unit. The second principle used in tone-unit boundary identification is a rhythmical one: it is claimed that *within* the tone-unit, speech has a regular rhythm, but that rhythm is broken or interrupted at the tone-unit boundary. Both the above principles are useful guides, but one regularly finds, in analysing natural speech, cases where it remains difficult or impossible to make a clear decision; the principles may well also be factually correct, but it should be emphasised that at present there is no conclusive evidence from instrumental study in the laboratory that they are.

Anomalous tone-units

However comprehensive one's descriptive framework may be (and the one given in this course is very limited), there will inevitably be cases which do not fit within it. For example other tones such as fall –rise–fall or rise–fall–rise are occasionally found. In the head, we sometimes find cases where the stressed syllables are not all high or all low, as in the following example:

ˌAfter ˌone of the 'worst 'days of my ˌlife

It can also happen that a speaker is interrupted and leaves a tone-unit incomplete – for example, lacking a tonic syllable. To return to the analogy with grammar, one often finds in natural speech, sentences which are grammatically anomalous or incomplete, but this does not deter the grammarian from describing "normal" sentence structure. Similarly, though there are inevitably problems and exceptions, we continue to treat the tone-unit as something that can be described, defined and recognised.

Notes on problems and further reading

The main concern of this chapter is to complete the description of intonational form, including analysis of perhaps the most difficult aspect, that of recognising fall–rise and rise–fall tones when they are extended over a number of syllables. This is necessary since no complete analysis of intonation can be done without having studied these "extended tones".

The most detailed discussion of the difference between fall–rise and the "compound" fall–plus–rise is Sharp (1958), though this is not easy reading and many will find it hard to follow some of the examples. It is interesting that Brazil et al. (1980) exclude compound tone completely from their analysis.

On tone-unit boundaries, there is a clear explanation of the problems in Cruttenden (1986), pp. 35–42, and in more detail in Crystal (1969), pp. 204–7. Brazil et al. make it clear (pp. 45–6) that they attach little importance to the identification of such boundaries. The study of Scottish English by Brown et al. (1980) gives ample evidence that tone-units in real life are not by any means always like tone-units in text-books.

Declination was given importance by Pierrehumbert (1979, 1987); see Cruttenden (1986), pp. 67–72 for a summary.

Notes for teachers

I would like to emphasise how valuable an exercise it is for students and teachers to attempt to analyse some recorded speech for themselves. For beginners it is best to start on slow, careful speech, such as that of newsreaders, before attempting conversational speech. One can learn more about intonation in an hour of this work than in days of reading text-books on the subject, and one's interest in and understanding of theoretical problems becomes much more profound.

Written exercises

1. The following sentences are given with intonation marks. Sketch the pitch within the lines below, leaving a gap between each syllable.
   a) 'Which was the ˌcheap one did you say

   _____

   _____

   b) I 'only 'want to ˌtaste it

   _____

   _____

   c) ˌShe would have ˌthought it was ˌobvious

   _____

   _____

   d) There 'wasnt 'even a 'piece of ˌbread in the ·house

   _____

   _____

   e) ˌNow will you be ·lieve me

   _____

   _____

2. This exercise is similar, but here you are given polysyllabic words and a tone; you must draw an appropriate pitch movement between the lines.
   a) (rise)   opportunity

   _____

   b) (fall–rise)   actually

   _____

   c) (fall)   confidently

   _____

   _____

   d) (rise–fall)   magnificent

   _____

   _____

e)   (rise)   relationship

_____

_____

f)   (fall–rise)   afternoon

_____

_____

18 Functions of intonation 1

The form of intonation has now been described in some detail, and we will move on to look more closely at its functions. Perhaps the best way to start on this is to ask ourselves what would be lost if we were to speak *without* intonation: you should try to imagine speech in which every syllable was said on the same level pitch, with no pauses and no changes in speed or loudness. This is the sort of speech that would be produced by a "mechanical speech" device (as described at the beginning of Chapter 14) that made sentences by putting together recordings of isolated words. To put it in the broadest possible terms, we can see that intonation makes it easier for a listener to understand what a speaker is trying to convey. The ways in which intonation does this are very complex, and many suggestions have been made for ways of isolating different functions. Among the most often proposed are the following:

i) Intonation enables us to express emotions and attitudes as we speak, and this adds a special kind of "meaning" to spoken language. This is often called the **attitudinal function** of intonation.

ii) Intonation helps to produce the effect of prominence on syllables that need to be perceived as stressed, and in particular the placing of tonic stress on a particular syllable marks out the word to which it belongs as the most important in the tone-unit. This has been called the **accentual function** of intonation.

iii) The listener is better able to recognise the grammar and syntactic structure of what is being said by using the information contained in the intonation: for example, such things as the placement of boundaries between phrases, clauses or sentences, the difference between questions and statements and the use of grammatical subordination may be indicated. This has been called the **grammatical function** of intonation.

iv) Looking at the act of speaking in a broader way, we can see that intonation can signal to the listener what is to be taken as "new" information and what is already "given", can suggest when the speaker is indicating some sort of contrast or link with material in another tone-unit and, in conversation, can convey to the listener what kind of response is expected. Such functions are examples of intonation's **discourse function**.

The attitudinal function has been given so much importance in past work on intonation that it will be discussed separately in this chapter, though it should eventually become clear that it overlaps considerably with the discourse function. In the case of the other three functions, it will be argued that it is difficult to see how they could be treated as separate: for example, the placement of tonic stress is closely linked to the presentation of "new" information, while the question/statement distinction and the indication of contrast seem to be equally important in grammar and discourse. What seems to be common to accentual, grammatical and discourse functions is the indication, by means of intonation, of the relationship between some linguistic element and the context in which it occurs. The word used in linguistics for this type of relationship is **syntagmatic**, and I will refer to the accentual, grammatical and discourse functions as **syntagmatic functions** of intonation. The fact that they overlap with each other to a large degree is not so important if one does not insist on discovering several distinct functions.

The rest of this chapter is concerned with a critical examination of the attitudinal function.

18.1 The attitudinal function of intonation

Many writers have expressed the view that intonation is used to convey our feelings and attitudes; for example, the same sentence can be said in different ways, which might be labelled "angry", 'happy", "grateful", "bored", and so on. It has also been widely observed that the form of intonation is different in different languages; for example, the intonation of languages such as Swedish, Italian or Hindi is instantly recognisable as being different from that of English. Not surprisingly, it has often been said that foreign learners of English need to learn English intonation; some have gone further than this and claimed that, unless the foreign learner learns the appropriate way to use intonation in a given situation, there is a risk that he or she may unintentionally give offence; for example, the learner might use an intonation suitable for expressing boredom or discontent when what was needed was an expression of gratitude or affection. This misleading view of intonation must have caused unnecessary anxiety to many learners of the language.

Let us begin by considering how one might analyse the attitudinal function of intonation. One possibility would be for the analyst to invent a large number of sentences and try saying them with different intonation patterns (i.e. different combinations of head and tone), noting what attitude was supposed to correspond to the intonation in each case; of course, the results are then very subjective, and based on an artificial performance that has little resemblance to conversational speech. Alternatively, the analyst could say these different sentences to a group of listeners and ask them all to write down what attitudes they thought were being expressed; however, we have a vast range of adjectives available for labelling attitudes and the members of the group would probably produce a very large number of such adjectives, leaving the analyst with the problem of deciding whether pairs such as 'pompous' and 'stuck-up', or 'obsequious' and 'sycophantic' were synonyms or represented different attitudes. To overcome this difficulty, one could ask the members of the group to choose among a small number of adjectives (or "labels") given by the analyst; the results would then inevitably be easier to quantify (that is, the job of counting the different responses would be simpler) but the results would no longer represent the listeners' free choice of label. An alternative procedure would be to ask a lot of speakers to say a list of sentences in different ways according to labels provided by the analyst, and see what intonational features are found in common (for example, one might count how many speakers used a low head in saying something in a "hostile" way). The results of such experiments are usually very variable and difficult to interpret, not least because the range of acting talent in a randomly selected group is considerable.

A much more useful and realistic approach is to study recordings of different speakers' natural, spontaneous speech and try to make generalisations about attitudes and intonation on this basis. Many problems remain, however. In the method described previously, the analyst tries to select sentences (or passages of some other size) whose meaning is fairly "neutral" from the emotional point of view, and will tend to avoid material such as 'Why don't you leave me alone?' or 'How can I ever thank you enough?' because the lexical meaning of the words used already makes the speaker's attitude pretty clear, whereas sentences such as 'She's going to buy it tomorrow' or 'The paper has fallen under the table' are less likely to prejudice the listener. The choice of material is much less free for someone studying natural speech. Nevertheless, if we are ever to make new discoveries about intonation, it will be as a result of studying what people actually say rather than inventing examples of what they *might* say.

The notion of "expressing an emotion or attitude" is itself a more complex one than is generally realised. Firstly, an emotion may be expressed involuntarily or voluntarily; if I say something in a "happy" way, this may be because I *feel* happy, or because I want to convey to *you* the *impression* that I am happy. Secondly, an attitude that is expressed could be an attitude towards the listener (e.g. if I say something in a "friendly" way), towards what is being said (e.g. if I say something in a "sceptical" or "dubious" way) or towards some external event or situation (e.g. "regretful" or "disapproving").

However, one point is much more important and fundamental than all the problems discussed above. To understand this point you should imagine (or even actually *perform*) your pronunciation of a sentence in a number of different ways: for example, if the sentence was 'I want to buy a new car' and you were to say it in the following ways: "pleading", "angry", "sad", "happy", "proud", it is certain that at least *some* of your performances will be different from some others, but it is also certain that the technique for analysing and transcribing intonation introduced earlier in the course will be found inadequate to represent the different things you do. You will have used variations in *loudness* and *speed*, for example; almost certainly you will have used different *voice qualities* for different attitudes. You may have used your pitch range (which was introduced in 15.3) in different ways: your pitch movements may have taken place within quite a narrow range (**narrow pitch range**) or using the full range between high and low (**wide pitch range**); if you did not use wide pitch range, you may have used different **keys**: **high key** (using the upper part of your pitch range), **mid key** (using the middle part of the range) or **low key** (the lower part). It is very likely that you will have used different **facial expressions** and even **gestures** and **body movements**. These factors are all of great importance in conveying attitudes and emotions, yet the traditional handbooks on English pronunciation have almost completely ignored them.

If we accept the importance of these factors it becomes necessary to consider how they are related to intonation, and what intonation itself consists of. We can isolate three distinct types of suprasegmental variable:

SEQUENTIAL

These components of intonation are found as elements in sequences of other such elements occurring one after another (never simultaneously). These are:

i) pre-heads, heads, tonic syllables and tails (with their pitch possibilities)
ii) pauses
iii) tone-unit boundaries.

These have all been introduced in previous chapters.

PROSODIC

These components are characteristics of speech which are constantly present and observable while speech is going on. The most important are:

i)   width of pitch range
ii) key
iii) loudness
iv) speed
v)   voice quality.

It is not possible to speak without one's speech having some degree or type of pitch range, loudness, speed and voice quality (with the possible exception that pitch factors are largely lost in whispered speech). Different speakers do, of course, have their own typical pitch range, loudness, voice quality, etc., and contrasts among prosodic components should be seen as relative to these "background" speaker characteristics.

Each of these prosodic components needs a proper framework for categorisation, and this is an interesting area of current research. One example of the prosodic component "width of pitch range" has already been mentioned in 15.3, when "extra pitch height" was introduced, and the "rhythmicality" discussed in 14.1 could be regarded as another prosodic component. Prosodic components should be regarded as part of intonation along with sequential components.

PARALINGUISTIC

Mention was made above of facial expressions, gestures and body movements. People who study human behaviour use the term **body language** for such activity. One could also mention certain **vocal effects** such as laughs and sobs. These are obviously relevant to the act of speaking but could not themselves properly be regarded as components of speech. Again, they need a proper descriptive and classificatory system, but this is not something that comes within the scope of this course, nor in my opinion should they be regarded as components of intonation.

What advice, then, can be given to the foreign learner of English who wants to learn "correct intonation"? It is certainly true that a few generalisations can be made about the attitudinal functions of some components of intonation. Within tone, for example, most books agree on some basic meanings; here are some examples:

1. *Fall*
   Finality, definiteness: That is the end of the ˎnews
                           I'm absolutely ˎcertain
                           Stop ˎtalking
2. *Rise*
   Most of the functions attributed to rises are nearer to grammatical

than attitudinal, as in the first three examples given below; they are
included here mainly to give a fuller picture of intonational function.

General questions: Can you ˌhelp̲ me

Is it ˌo̲ver

Listing: ˌR̲ed, ˌb̲rown, ˌy̲ellow or ˌb̲lue

(fall is normal on the last item)

"More to follow": I phoned them right aˌw̲ay

(and they agreed to come)

You must write it aˌg̲ain

(and this time, get it right)

Encouraging: It wont ˌh̲urt

3. *Fall–rise*

Uncertainty, doubt: You ˬm̲ay be right

Its ˬp̲ossible

Requesting: Can I ˬb̲uy it

Will you ˬl̲end it to me

4. *Rise–fall*

Surprise, being impressed: You were ˄f̲irst

˄A̲ll of them

Generalisations such as these are, however, too broad, and foreign
learners do not find it easy to learn to use intonation through studying
them. Similarly, within the area of prosodic components most
generalisations tend to be very broad and obvious: wider pitch range
tends to be used in excited or enthusiastic speaking, slower speed is
typical of the speech of someone who is tired or bored, and so on. Most
of the generalisations one could make are probably true for a lot of
other languages as well. In short, of the rules and generalisations that
could be made about conveying attitudes through intonation, those
which are not actually wrong are likely to be too trivial to be worth
learning. I have witnessed many occasions when foreigners have
unintentionally caused misunderstanding or even offence in speaking to
an English person, but can remember very few occasions when this
could be attributed to "using the wrong intonation" except when a
mistake caused a difference in apparent grammatical meaning (something that is dealt with in the next chapter).

It should not be concluded that intonation is not important for
conveying attitudes. What is being claimed here is that, though it *is* of
great importance, the complexity of the total set of sequential and
prosodic components of intonation and of paralinguistic features
makes it a very difficult thing to teach. One might compare the difficulty
with that of trying to write rules for how one might indicate to someone
of the opposite sex that one finds them attractive; while psychologists
and biologists might make detailed observations and generalisations
about how human beings of a particular culture behave in such a

situation, most people would rightly feel that studying these generalisations would be no substitute for practical experience, and that relying
on a text-book could lead to hilarious consequences. The attitudinal
use of intonation is something that is best acquired through talking
with and listening to English speakers, and this course aims simply to
train learners to be more aware of and sensitive to the way English
speakers use intonation.

Notes on problems and further reading

Perhaps the most controversial question concerning English intonation
is what its function is; pedagogically speaking, this is a very important
question, since one would not wish to devote time to teaching
something without knowing what its value was likely to be. At the
beginning of the chapter I list four commonly cited functions; it is
possible to construct a longer list: Lee (1958), for example, proposes
ten.

For general introductory reading on the attitudinal function of
intonation, see O'Connor and Arnold (1973), Chapter 2; Gimson
(1989). Critical views are expressed in Brazil et al. (1980), pp. 98–103
and Crystal (1969), pp. 282–308 and there is a good survey in
Cruttenden (1986), pp. 95–126.

Few people have actually done experiments on listeners' perception
of attitudes through intonation. The experiments reported in Crystal
(1969), chapter 7, are only small-scale pilot experiments. Uldall (1960,
1964) used a speech synthesiser to vary pitch and elicit listeners'
judgments. Lieberman and Michaels (1962) found that they could get
reasonably accurate recognition of attitudes using short recording of
sentences spoken in different ways, but that when the recordings were
distorted in such a way that most acoustic information was removed
(e.g. the speech sounds, voice quality, loudness variations etc.) leaving
only the pitch information – that part traditionally equated with
intonation – listeners' ability to recognise the attitudes was seriously
reduced.

Once one has recognised the importance of features other than pitch,
it is necessary to devise a framework for categorising these features. In
writing this course I have found it necessary to do this in a way which is
somewhat different from other writers' proposals. The framework set
out in Crystal and Quirk (1964) is unsatisfactory in two ways: firstly, no
explicit distinction is made between sequential and prosodic variables
and the choice between, say, rising as opposed to falling tone is
presented as a choice of the same type as the choice between fast and
slow speed (tempo), which I feel is confusing. Secondly, paralinguistic

features of the 'vocal effect' type are treated as part of intonation, and it is not made sufficiently clear how these are to be distinguished from prosodic features. Crystal (1969) defines paralinguistic features as: '...vocal effects which are primarily the result of physiological mechanisms other than the vocal cords, such as the direct results of the workings of the pharyngeal, oral or nasal cavities' but this does not seem to me to fit the facts. In my view, 'paralinguistic' implies 'outside the system of contrasts used in spoken language' – which does not, of course, necessarily mean 'non-vocal'. I would therefore treat prosodic variables as linguistic, and consequently part of intonation, while vocal effects like laughs or sobs are non-linguistic vocal effects to be classed with gestures and facial expressions. Brown (1990), on the other hand, uses 'paralinguistic' to include what I call 'prosodic', and appears to have no separate term for non-linguistic vocal effects.

The term 'voice quality' needs comment, as it tends to be used to refer to three different things:

i)   The personal, 'background' characteristics that make one person's voice recognisably different from another. Crystal (1969), pp. 100–4, uses it in this sense; see also Nolan (1973).
ii) The result of different types of vocal fold vibration.
iii) The auditory quality resulting from the complex interaction of laryngeal and supralaryngeal features.

The last use is the basis of the major work in this field, the treatment by Laver (1968, 1980); if one adopts this as the meaning of 'voice quality' it is preferable to use the term 'phonation type' (see Catford, 1964) for (ii), and in any case I would prefer to use 'personal speaker characteristics' for (i).

Note for teachers

Tape Unit 18 consists of extracts from a recording of spontaneous dialogue. Students usually feel that listening to these unfamiliar voices chopped up into small pieces is hard work, but generally the transcription exercise is not found nearly as difficult as expected.

Written exercises

In the following bits of conversation, you are supplied with an "opening line" and a response that you must imagine saying. You are given an indication in brackets of the feeling or attitude expressed, and you must mark on the text the intonation you think is appropriate (mark only the response). As usual in intonation work in this book, punctuation is left out, since it can cause confusion.

1. It looks nice for a ˏswim   Its rather cold *(doubtful)*
2. Why not get a ˏcar   Because I cant afford it *(impatient)*
3. Ive lost my ˏticket   Youre silly then *(stating the obvious)*
4. You cant have an ice ˏcream   Oh please *(pleading)*
5. What times are the ˏbuses   Seven o'clock seven thirty and eight *(listing)*
6. She got eight ˏ'A' levels   Eight *(impressed)*
7. How much ˏwork have you got to do   Ive got to do the shopping *(and more things after that)*
8. Will the ˏchildren go   Some of them might *(uncertain)*

19 Functions of intonation 2

In the previous chapter a distinction was made between the attitudinal function of intonation and several other functions that were given the collective names of **syntagmatic functions**. They include accentual, grammatical and discourse functions, and these are discussed below.

19.1 The accentual function of intonation

The term **accentual** is derived from "accent", a word used by some writers to refer to what in this course is called "stress". When writers say that intonation has accentual function they imply that the placement of stress is something that is determined by intonation. It is possible to argue against this view: in Chapters 10 and 11, word stress was presented as something quite independent of intonation, and subsequently (p. 157) it was said that "intonation is carried entirely by the stressed syllables of a tone-unit". This means that in the presentation so far it has been implied that the placing of stress is independent of and prior to the choice of intonation. However, one particular aspect of stress *could* be regarded as part of intonation: this is the placement of the tonic stress within the tone-unit. It would be reasonable to suggest that while word stress was independent of intonation, the placement of tonic stress was a function (the accentual function) of intonation. Some older pronunciation handbooks refer to this area as "sentence stress", which is not an appropriate name: the sentence is a unit of grammar, while the location of tonic stress is a matter which concerns the tone-unit, a unit of phonology.

The location of the tonic syllable is of considerable linguistic importance. The most common position for this is on the last lexical word (e.g. noun, adjective, verb, adverb as distinct from the function words introduced in Chapter 12, p. 102) of the tone-unit. For contrastive purposes, however, any word may become the tonic syllable. In the following pairs of examples, (a) represents normal placement and (b) contrastive:

a) | I ˌwant to ˌknow ˌwhere hes ˎtraˉvelling to |
(The word 'to', being a preposition and not a lexical word, is not stressed.)
b) (I 'dont want to 'know where hes 'travelling ˎfrom)
| I ˌwant to ˌknow ˌwhere hes ˌtravelling ˎto |

a) | She was 'wearing a 'red ˎdress |
b) (She 'wasnt 'wearing a ˎgreen ·dress) | She was 'wearing a ˎred ·dress |

Similarly, for the purpose of emphasis we may place the tonic stress in other positions; in these examples, (a) is non-emphatic and (b) is emphatic:

a) | It was 'very ˎboring |
b) | It was ˎvery ·boring |

a) | You 'mustnt 'talk so ˎloudly |
b) | You ˎmustnt ·talk so ·loudly |

However, it would be wrong to say that the only cases of departure from putting tonic stress on the last lexical word were cases of contrast or emphasis. There are quite a few situations where it is normal for the tonic syllable to come earlier in the tone-unit. A well-known example is the sentence 'I have plans to leave'; this is ambiguous:

a) | I have 'plans to ˎleave | (i.e. I am planning to leave.)
b) | I have ˎplans to ·leave | (i.e. I have some plans/diagrams/drawings that I have to leave.)

Version (b) could not be described as contrastive or emphatic. There are many examples similar to (b); perhaps the best rule to give is that the tonic syllable will *tend* to occur on the last lexical word in the tone-unit, but may be placed earlier in the tone-unit if there is a word there with greater importance to what is being said. This can quite often happen as a result of the last part of the tone-unit being already "given" (i.e. something which has already been mentioned or is completely predictable), for example:

a) | 'Heres that ˎbook you ·asked me to bring | (The fact that you asked me to bring it is not new.)
b) | Ive ˌgot to ˌtake the ˎdog for a ·walk | ('For a walk' is by far the most probable thing to follow 'I've got to take the dog'; if the sentence ended with 'to the vet' the tonic syllable would probably be 'vet'.)

Placement of tonic stress is, therefore, important and is closely linked to intonation. A question that remains, however, is whether one can and should treat this matter as separate from the other functions described below.

19.2 **The grammatical function of intonation**

The word "grammatical" tends to be used in a very loose sense in this context. It is usual to illustrate the grammatical function by inventing sentences which when written are ambiguous, and whose ambiguity can only be removed by using differences of intonation. A typical example is the sentence "Those who sold quickly made a profit". This can be said in at least two different ways:

a) | 'Those who 'sold ˌquickly | ˌmade a ˌprofit |
b) | 'Those who ˌsold | ˌquickly ˌmade a ˌprofit |

The difference caused by the placement of the tone-unit boundary is seen to be equivalent to giving two different paraphrases of the sentences, as in:

a)   A profit was made by those who sold quickly.
b)   A profit was quickly made by those who sold.

Let us look further at the role of tone-unit boundaries, and the link between the tone-unit and units of grammar. There is a strong tendency for tone-unit boundaries to occur at boundaries between grammatical units of higher order than words; it is extremely common to find a tone-unit boundary at a sentence boundary, as in:

|I 'wont have any ˌtea |I 'dont ˌlike it |

In sentences with a more complex structure, tone-unit boundaries are often found at phrase and clause boundaries as well, as in:

|In ˌFrance |where ˌfarms ˌtend to be ˌsmaller |the 'subsidies are 'more imˌportant |

It is very unusual to find a tone-unit boundary at a place where the only grammatical boundary is between words. It would, for example, sound distinctly odd to have a tone-unit boundary between an article and a following noun, or between auxiliary and main verbs if they are adjacent (though we may on occasions hesitate or pause in such places within a tone-unit; some people who do a lot of arguing, notably politicians and philosophers, develop the skill of pausing for breath in such intonationally unlikely places because they are less likely to be interrupted than if they pause at the end of a sentence). Tone-unit boundary placement can, then, indicate grammatical structure to the listener and we can find minimal pairs such as the following:

a) | The Con'servatives who ˌlike the pro·posal | are ˌpleased |
b) | The Conˌservatives | who ˌlike the pro·posal | are ˌpleased |

The intonation makes clear the difference between (a) "restrictive" and (b) "non-restrictive" relative clauses; (a) implies that only *some* Conservatives like the proposal, while (b) implies that *all* the Conservatives like it.

Another component of intonation that can be said to have grammatical significance is the choice of tone on the tonic syllable. One example that is very familiar is the use of a rising tone with questions. Many languages have the possibility of changing a statement into a question simply by changing the tone from falling to rising. This is, in fact, not used very much by itself in the variety of English being described here, where questions are usually grammatically marked. Thus the sentence "The price is going up" can be said as a statement like this:

|The ˏprice is going up|

(the tonic stress could equally well be on 'up'). It would be quite acceptable in some dialects of English (e.g. many varieties of American English) to ask a question like this:

(Why do you want to buy it now?) |The ˏprice is going up|

But speakers in England would be more likely to ask the question like this:

(Why do you want to buy it now?) |Is the ˏprice going up|

It is by no means true that a rising tone is always used for questions in English; it is quite usual, for example, to use a falling tone with questions beginning with one of the "wh-question-words" like 'what', 'which', 'when', etc. Here are two examples with typical intonations, where (a) does not start with a "wh- word" and has a rising tone and (b) begins with 'where' and has a falling tone.

a) | 'Did you 'park the ˏcar |
b) | 'Where did you 'park the ˎcar |

However, the fall in (b) is certainly not obligatory, and a rise is quite often heard in such a question. A fall is also possible in (a).

The intonation of **question-tags** (e.g. 'isn't it', 'can't he', 'should she', 'won't they', etc.) is often quoted as a case of a difference in meaning being due to the difference between falling and rising tone. In the following example, the question-tag is 'aren't they'; when it has a falling tone, as in (a), the implication is said to be that the speaker is comparatively certain that the information is correct, and simply expects the listener to provide confirmation, while the rising tone in (b) is said to indicate a lesser degree of certainty, so that the question-tag functions more like a request for information.

a) | They 'are 'coming on ˎTuesday | ˎarent they |

b) | They'are 'coming on ˏTuesday | ˏarent they |

The difference illustrated here could reasonably be said to be as much attitudinal as grammatical. Certainly there is overlap between these two function.

19.3   **The discourse function of intonation**

A comparatively new area of study is becoming increasingly important in the description of natural speech. If we think of linguistic analysis as usually being linked to the sentence as the maximum unit of grammar, then the study of discourse attempts to look at the larger contexts in which sentences occur. For example, consider the four sentences in the following:

A: Have you got any free time this morning?
B: I might have later on if that meeting's off.
A: They were talking about putting it later.
B: You can't be sure.

Each sentence could be studied in isolation and be analysed in terms of grammatical construction, lexical content and so on. But it is obvious that the sentences form part of some larger act of conversational interaction between two speakers; the sentences contain several references that presuppose shared knowledge (e.g. 'that meeting' implies that both speakers know which meeting is being spoken about), and in some cases the meaning of a sentence can only be correctly interpreted in the light of knowledge of what has preceded it in the conversation (e.g. 'You can't be sure').

If we consider how intonation may be studied in relation to discourse, we can identify two main areas: one of them is the use of intonation to focus the listener's attention on aspects of the message that are most important, and the other is concerned with the regulation of conversational behaviour. We will look at these in turn.

In the case of "attention focussing", the most obvious use has already been described: this is the placing of tonic stress on the appropriate syllable of one particular word in the tone-unit. In many cases it is easy to demonstrate that the tonic stress is placed on the word that is in some sense the "most important", as in:

|She 'went to ˏScotland|

Sometimes it seems more appropriate to describe tonic stress placement in terms of "information content": the more predictable a word's occurrence is in a given context, the lower its information content is, and tonic stress will tend to be placed on words with high information content. This is the explanation that would be used in the case of the sentences suggested in 19.1:

a) |Ive ,got to ,take the ˎdog for a ·walk|
b) |Ive ,got to ,take the ,dog to the ˎvet|

The word 'vet' is less predictable (has a higher information content) than 'walk'. However, we still find many cases where it is difficult to explain tonic placement in terms of "importance" or "information". For example, in messages like:

> Your coat's on fire　　　　The wing's breaking up
> The radio's gone wrong　　Your uncle's died

probably the majority of English speakers would place the tonic stress on the subject noun, though it is difficult to see how this is more important than the last lexical word in each of the sentences. The placement of tonic stress is still to some extent an unsolved mystery; it is clear, though, that it is at least partly determined by the larger context (linguistic and non-linguistic) in which the tone-unit occurs.

We can see at least two other ways in which intonation can assist in focussing attention. The tone chosen can indicate whether the tone-unit in which it occurs is being used to present new information or to refer to information which is felt to be already possessed by speaker and hearer. For example, in the following sentence:

> | 'Since the ˎlast time we met | when we had that 'huge ˎdinner | Ive 'been on a ˎdiet |

the first two tone-units present information which is relevant to what the speaker is saying, but which is not something new and unknown to the listener. The final tone-unit, however, does present new information. Writers on discourse intonation have proposed that the falling tone indicates new information while rising (including falling–rising) tones indicate "shared" or "given" information.

Another use of intonation connected with the focussing of attention is **intonational subordination**; we can signal that a particular tone-unit is of comparatively low importance and as a result give correspondingly greater importance to adjacent tone-units. For example:

a) | As I ex,pect youve ˎheard | theyre 'only ad'mitting eˏmergency ·cases |
b) | The ,Japaˎnese | for ,some ,reason or ˏother | 'drive on the ˎleft | like ˏus |

In a typical conversational pronunciation of these sentences, the first tone-unit of (a) and the second and fourth tone-units of (b) might be treated as intonationally subordinate; the prosodic characteristics marking this are usually (i) a drop to a lower part of the pitch range ("low key"), (ii) increased speed, (iii) narrower range of pitch and (iv) lower loudness, relative to the non-subordinate tone-unit(s). The use of these components has the result that the subordinate tone-units are less easy to hear. Native speakers can usually still understand what is said, if necessary by guessing at inaudible or unrecognisable words on the basis of their knowledge of what the speaker is talking about; foreign learners of English, on the other hand, having in general less "common ground" or shared knowledge with the speaker, often find that these subordinate tone-units, with their "throw-away", parenthetic style, cause serious difficulties in understanding.

We now turn to the second main area of intonational discourse function, the regulation of conversational behaviour. We have already seen how the study of sequences of tone-units in the speech of one speaker can reveal information carried by intonation which would not have been recognised if intonation was analysed only at the level of individual tone-units. Intonation is also important in the conversational interaction of two or more speakers. Most of the research on this has been on conversational interaction of a rather restricted kind, such as between doctor and patient, teacher and pupil or between the various speakers in court cases. In such material it is comparatively easy to identify what each speaker is actually *doing* in speaking – for example, questioning, challenging, advising, encouraging, disapproving, etc. It is likely that other forms of conversation can be analysed in the same way, though this is considerably more difficult. In a more general way, it can be seen that speakers use various prosodic components to indicate to others that they have finished speaking, that another person is expected to speak, that a particular type of response is required, and so on. A very familiar example is that quoted above (p. 175), where the difference between falling and rising intonation on question-tags is supposed to indicate to the listener what sort of response is expected. It seems that key (the part of the pitch range used) is important in signalling information about conversational interaction. We can observe many examples in non-linguistic behaviour of the use of signals to regulate **turn-taking**: in many sports, for example, it is necessary to do this – footballers can indicate that they are looking for someone to pass the ball to, or that they are ready to receive the ball, and doubles partners in tennis can indicate to each other who is to play a shot. Intonation, in conjunction with "body language" such as eye-contact, facial expression, gestures and head-turning, is used for similar purposes in speech, as well as for establishing or confirming the status of the participants in a conversation.

19.4 **Conclusions**

It seems clear that studying intonation in relation to discourse makes it possible to explain much more comprehensively the uses that speakers make of intonation. Practically all the separate functions traditionally attributed to intonation (attitudinal, accentual and grammatical) could be seen as different aspects of discourse function. The risk, with such a broad approach, is that one might end up making generalisations that were *too* broad and had little power to predict with any accuracy the intonation that a speaker would use in a particular context. It is too early yet to say how useful the discourse approach will be, but even if it achieves nothing else, it can at least be claimed to have shown the inadequacy of attempting to analyse the function of intonation on the basis of isolated sentences or tone-units, removed from their linguistic and situational context.

Notes on problems and further reading

19.1 In Britain, the most important work on the placement of tonic stress is Halliday (1967); his term for this is 'tonicity', and he adopts the widely-used linguistic term 'marked' for tonicity that deviates from what I have called (for the sake of simplicity) 'normal'. Within generative phonology there has been much debate about whether one can put tonic ('primary') stress in the right place without referring to the non-linguistic context in which the speaker says something. This debate is well summarised and criticised in Schmerling (1976), but see Bolinger (1972).

19.2 Opinions differ about whether intonation has a grammatical function. Cruttenden (1970) argues that intonation is affected by and reflects the grammar of what is said, but does not alter it or contribute to it. Consequently, it is wrong to say that it has a grammatical function. I think Cruttenden's arguments are in many ways convincing, but one must recognise that if intonation is influenced by and reflects the grammar, it follows that it must be a help to listeners in interpreting the grammar of what they hear, and perhaps more importantly, if a speaker's intonation is inappropriate in relation to the grammar, listeners will find it more difficult to interpret the grammar, and may be confused.

19.3 One of the most interesting developments of recent years has been the emergence of a theory of *discourse intonation*. Readers unfamiliar with the study of discourse may find some initial difficulty in understanding some of the principles involved; the best way to begin is to read Coulthard (1977), paying particular attention to the chapter on intonation, then go on to study Brazil *et al.* (1980). I have not been able to do more than suggest the rough outline of this approach.

The treatment of intonational subordination is based not on the work of Brazil but on Crystal and Quirk (1964), pp. 52–6 and Crystal (1969), pp. 235–52. The basic philosophy is the same, however, in that both views illustrate the fact that there is in intonation some organisation at a level higher than the isolated tone-unit; this was pointed out in the discussion of Trim (1959) (notes on Chapter 16 above); see also Fox (1973). A parallel might be drawn with the relationship between the sentence and the paragraph in writing. It seems likely that a considerable amount of valuable new research on pronunciation will grow out of the study of discourse.

Note for teachers

The comment about Tape Unit 18 made above applies also to **Tape Unit 19**: at first hearing it seems very difficult, but when worked on step by step it is far from impossible. In fact, although this passage sounds rapid and colloquial it is still easier to analyse than a full-speed conversational interchange.

Written exercises

1. In the following exercise, read the "opening line" and then decide the most suitable place for tonic stress placement (underline the syllable) in the response.
   a) I'd like you to ˎhelp me ... (right) can I do the shopping for you
   b) I hear you're offering to do the ˎshopping for someone ... (right) can I do the shopping for you
   c) What was the first thing that ˎhappened ... first the professor explained her theory
   d) Was the theory explained by ˏstudents ... no first the professor explained her theory
   e) Tell me how the ˎtheory was presented ... first she explained her theory
   f) I think it starts at ten to ˎthree ... no ten past three
   g) I think it starts at quarter past ˏthree ... no ten past three
   h) I think it starts at ten past ˎfour ... no ten past three

2. The following sentences are given without punctuation. Underline the appropriate tonic syllable places and mark tone-unit boundaries where you think they are appropriate.
   a) *(he wrote the letter in a sad way)* he wrote the letter sadly
   b) *(it's regrettable that he wrote the letter)* he wrote the letter sadly
   c) four plus six divided by two equals five
   d) four plus six divided by two equals seven
   e) we broke one thing after another fell down
   f) we broke one thing after another that night

20 Further areas of study in phonetics and phonology

This chapter completes the course by looking at three further areas of study; each is important in its own way, and each is an area on which students working at an advanced level in phonetics and phonology spend a considerable amount of time.

20.1 Distinctive features

Many references have been made to phonology in this course, with the purpose of making use of the concepts and analytical techniques of that subject to help explain various facts about English pronunciation as efficiently as possible. One might call this "applied phonology"; however, the phonological analysis of different languages raises a great number of difficult and interesting theoretical problems, and for a long time the study of phonology "for its own sake" has been regarded as an important area of theoretical linguistics. Within this area of what could be called "pure phonology", problems are examined with little or no reference to their relevance to the language learner. Many different theoretical approaches have been developed, and no area of phonology has been free from critical examination. The very fundamental notion of the phoneme, for example, has been treated in many different ways.

One approach that has been given a lot of importance is **distinctive feature analysis**, which is based on the principle that phonemes should be regarded not as independent and indivisible units, but instead as combinations of different features. For example, if we consider the English d phoneme, it is easy to show that it differs from the plosives b and g in its place of articulation (alveolar), from t in being lenis, from s and z in not being fricative, from n in not being nasal, and so on. If we look at each of the consonants just mentioned and see which of the features each one has, we get a table like this, where + means that a phoneme does possess that feature and − means that it does not:

	d	b	g	t	s	z	n
alveolar	+	−	−	+	+	+	+
bilabial	−	+	−	−	−	−	−
velar	−	−	+	−	−	−	−
lenis	+	+	+	−	−	+	(+)*
plosive	+	+	+	+	−	−	−
fricative	−	−	−	−	+	+	−
nasal	−	−	−	−	−	−	+

*Since there is no fortis/lenis contrast among nasals this could be left blank

If you look carefully at this table, you will see that the combination of + and − values for each phoneme is different; if two sounds were represented by exactly the same +'s and −'s, then by definition they could not be different phonemes. In the case of the limited set of phonemes used for this example, not all the features are needed: if one wished, it would be possible to get rid of, for example, the feature "velar" and the feature "nasal". The g phoneme would still be distinguished from b and d by being *neither* alveolar *nor* bilabial, and n would be distinct from plosives and fricatives simply by being *neither* plosive *nor* fricative. Of course, to produce a complete analysis of all the phonemes of English, other features would be needed for representing other types of consonant and for vowels and diphthongs. In distinctive feature analysis the features themselves thus become important components of the phonology.

Let us look at how the full set of English vowels might be analysed in terms of a small number of distinctive features. We could begin with a feature called **short** to make the fundamental distinction between ɪ, e, æ, ʌ, ɒ, ʊ, ə (+short), and iː, ɑː, ɔː, ɜː, uː, eɪ, aɪ, ɔɪ, əʊ, aʊ, ɪə, eə, ʊə (−short). Then to distinguish pure vowels from diphthongs we could have the feature **pure**; ɪ, e, æ, ʌ, ɒ, ʊ, ə, iː, ɑː, ɔː, ɜː, uː would be (+pure) and all the diphthongs would be (−pure). The feature **close** would have the value + for ɪ, ʊ, iː, uː, and we could also use this for ɪə and ʊə if we adopt the convention that most of the features will be used to classify the *first part* of the diphthongs. All the other vowels and diphthongs would then be (−close). We could also have the feature **open**; æ, ʌ, ɒ, ɑː, aɪ, aʊ would be (+open), all the others being (−open). All vowels and diphthongs that are neither close nor open, i.e. e, ə, ɔː, ɜː, eɪ, ɔɪ, əʊ, eə, must be distinguished from each other by other features. Some of the vowels that are (−close, −open) are central and some are not; the feature **central** would identify ʌ, ə, ɜː, əʊ, all others being (−central). With the features introduced so far, we still do not have complete distinctiveness for all vowels: æ and ɒ, for example, are identical in feature specification so far, as are ɪ and ʊ, iː and uː, eɪ and ɔɪ. We can use the feature **round** to separate these pairs, so that in each case the former is (−round) and the latter (+round). The only remaining problem is that we have three different sorts of diphthong:

183

G

those which glide to ɪ (eɪ, aɪ, ɔɪ), those which glide to ʊ (əʊ, aʊ) and those which glide to ə (ɪə, eə, ʊə). The obvious approach would be to have two additional features: **gliding to ɪ** and **gliding to ʊ**; ɪə, eə and ʊə would be (−gliding to ɪ, −gliding to ʊ). In fact, however, it turns out that if we have only the former of these two features, that is, gliding to ɪ, all the diphthongs which are (−gliding to ɪ) can be distinguished from each other in terms of their beginnings, using the features we have already introduced. This can all be seen in Table 5, which you should look at carefully. This is only one possible analysis, and many others, using quite different features, are equally efficient.

It has been claimed by some writers that distinctive feature analysis is not irrelevant to the study of language learning, and that pronunciation difficulties experienced by learners are better seen as due to the need to learn a particular feature or combination of features than as the absence of particular phonemes. For example, English speakers learning French or German have to learn to produce front rounded vowels. In English it is not necessary to be able to class a vowel as (+front, +round), whereas this *is* necessary for French and German; it could be said that the major task for the learner in this case is to learn the combination of these features, not to learn the individual vowels y, ø and (in French) œ.* English, on the other hand, has to be able to distinguish dental from labiodental and alveolar places of articulation for θ to be distinct from f and s and for ð to be distinct from v and z; this requires an additional feature that most languages do not need, and this could be seen as specific task for the learner of English. Distinctive feature phonologists have also claimed that when children are learning their first language, they acquire features rather than individual phonemes.

20.2 **Experimental phonetics**

Experimental phonetics has been an important part of phonetics for almost a century, and experimental work in phonetics laboratories has produced many important discoveries about how speech is produced and perceived. Too often, however, this area of the subject is regarded as a mysterious world where incomprehensible things are done with expensive equipment. There is reason to hope that in coming years the

---

* The phonetic symbols represent the following sounds: y is a close front rounded vowel (e.g. the vowel in French *tu*, German *bühne*); ø is a half-close front rounded vowel (e.g. French *peu*, German *schön*); œ is a half-open front rounded vowel (e.g. French *œuf*).

fields of pronunciation teaching and of experimental phonetics will become much more closely linked.

In explaining the subject-matter of experimental phonetics it is usual to start by mentioning the **speech chain**, which may be diagrammed in simplified form like this:

speaker's brain	→ speaker's vocal tract	→ transmission of sound through air	→ listener's ear	→ listener's brain
1	2	3	4	5
	articulatory phonetic	acoustic phonetic	auditory phonetic	

With currently available equipment we are not able to discover what goes on in detail in the brain when someone is speaking, though we can make guesses based on evidence such as speech errors ("slips of the tongue") and the effects on speech production of different sorts of brain damage. Much more is known about stage 2, the articulatory aspect of speech production. Many special instruments have been developed to help us to find out about such things as the pressure of air in the lungs and the vocal tract, the flow of air out of the mouth and nose, the opening and closing of the vocal folds and of the soft palate, and the movement of articulators like the lips and the lower jaw. Recently-developed, safer X-ray techniques can help us to observe articulatory movements taking place within the vocal tract, and contact between the tongue and the palate can be measured electrically. Additionally, it is possible to detect the electrical activity that is produced when muscles contract, and we can thus observe the complex co-ordination of activity in the muscles controlling speech production. Although most of these techniques are expensive and difficult to use, it is possible that at least some of them may become more easily available; they can be very useful both for discovering in detail how English speakers produce their speech sounds, and for demonstrating to learners of English their pronunciation errors in a way that helps them to correct them. To give a brief example, recording the airflow from speakers' mouths can show how successfully they are producing the aspiration appropriate for p, t and k.

The third stage, the transmission of sound waves through the air, is studied by acoustic analysis; much has been discovered about the sounds of speech in this way. We can discover the physical events that produce the perceptual effect of vowel quality, we can measure the intensity of different sounds (which is closely related to the loudness that we perceive), and the fundamental frequency of voiced sounds (which is closely related to pitch) can be extracted from the speech signal. Until recently, the acoustic analysis of speech has been such a

Table 5. *A distinctive feature analysis of the English vowel system*

	ɪ	e	æ	ʌ	ɒ	ʊ	ə	iː	ɑː	ɔː	ɜː	uː	eɪ	aɪ	ɔɪ	əʊ	aʊ	ɪə	eə	ʊə
short	+	+	+	+	+	+	+	−	−	−	−	−	−	−	−	−	−	−	−	−
pure	+	+	+	+	+	+	+	+	+	+	+	+	−	−	−	−	−	−	−	−
close	+	−	−	−	−	+	−	+	−	−	−	+	−	−	−	−	−	+	−	+
open	−	−	+	+	+	−	−	−	+	−	−	−	−	+	−	−	+	−	−	−
central	−	−	−	+	−	−	+	−	−	−	+	−	−	−	−	+	−	−	−	−
gliding to ɪ	−	−	−	−	−	−	−	−	−	−	−	−	+	+	+	−	−	−	−	−
round	−	−	−	−	+	+	−	−	−	+	−	+	−	−	+	−	−	−	−	+

slow and laborious business that only small samples of speech could be analysed, but recent developments in the use of computers are making it possible to carry out analysis on a much larger scale. Not only is it possible to get an accurate computer analysis of the fundamental frequency of speech (which can be displayed on a screen for someone doing practice on intonation, or can be used in the study of the intonation of large samples of natural speech), but it is now possible to get a computer to produce a simple phonetic transcription of what is said to it. If such techniques are further developed, it should be possible to use computers to provide additional pronunciation training at times when a human teacher is not available.

Finally, it is of great importance to discover more about how the listener's brain identifies what it receives from the ear (stages 4 and 5); many experiments have shown how sensitive we are to very slight acoustic differences and how flexible we are in being able to adjust to very different speakers. We are also very strongly influenced by our expectations; if we have heard and understood half a sentence, it seems that our brain is already guessing at what the rest of it will be before it is heard, and is certainly not acting in a passive way like a simple machine. To help in discovering the organisation and the capabilities of our faculty for perceiving speech, we need to be able to produce very small and finely-controlled differences in speech sounds, and experimental phonetics has made much use of speech produced by machines called **speech synthesisers**. Here again, developments in computers are bringing about rapid changes. The best speech synthesisers are capable of producing speech of such high quality that only an expert can distinguish it from a recording of a human being's speech; less sophisticated synthesisers are becoming so cheap that they can now be bought for attaching to ordinary micro-computers. It is possible that synthetic speech may have a useful role to play in testing language learners' ability to perceive important segmental and suprasegmental distinctions in the language they are learning.

20.3 The study of variety

Differences among accents of English have been mentioned several times in the course, and this is a subject that many students of English find interesting and wish to know more about. For a long time, the study of accents was part of the subject of **dialectology**, which aimed to identify all the ways in which a language differed from place to place. Dialectology in its traditional form is therefore principally interested in geographical differences; its best-known data-gathering technique has been to send researchers (usually called "field-workers") mainly into rural areas (where the speakers were believed to be less likely to have been influenced by other accents), to find elderly speakers (whose speech was believed to have been less influenced by other accents and to preserve older forms of the dialect) and to use lists of questions to find information about vocabulary and pronunciation, the questions being chosen to concentrate on items known to vary a lot from region to region. Surveys of this kind can provide the basis for many generalisations about geographical variation, but they have serious weaknesses, which will be discussed later.

Differences between accents are of two main sorts, **phonetic** and **phonological**. When two accents differ from each other only phonetically, we find the same number of phonemes in both accents, but some or all of the phonemes are realised differently. There may also be differences in stress or intonation, but not such as would cause a change in meaning. As an example of phonetic differences at the segmental level, it is said that Australian English has the same set of phonemes and phonemic contrasts as RP, yet Australian pronunciation is so different from RP that it is easily recognised as such. A word of caution should be given here: it is all too easy to talk about such things as "Australian English", and ignore the great variety that inevitably exists within such a large community of speakers. Every individual's speech is different from any other's; it follows from this that no one speaker can be taken to represent a particular accent or dialect, and it also follows that the idea of a "standard Received Pronunciation" is a convenient fiction, not a scientific fact.

Many accents of English also differ noticeably in intonation without the difference being such as would cause a difference in meaning; some Welsh accents, for example, have a tendency for unstressed syllables to be higher in pitch than stressed syllables. Such a difference is, again, a phonetic one. An example of a phonetic (non-phonological) difference in stress would be the stressing of verbs ending in '-ise' in some Scots and Northern Irish accents (e.g. 'realise' rɪəˈlaɪz).

Phonological differences are of various types: again, we can divide these into segmental and suprasegmental. Within the area of segmental phonology the most obvious type of difference is where one accent has a different number of phonemes (and hence of phonemic contrasts) from another. Many speakers with Northern English accents, for example, do not have a contrast between ʌ and ʊ, so that 'luck' and 'look' are pronounced identically (both as lʊk); in the case of consonants, many accents do not have the phoneme h. The phonemic system of such accents is different from that of RP. On the other hand, some accents differ from others in having *more* phonemes and phonemic contrasts. For example, many Northern English accents have a long e: sound as the realisation of the phoneme symbolised eɪ in RP (which is a simple phonetic difference); but in some Northern accents there is an eɪ diphthong phoneme *and* a contrasting long vowel phoneme that could be symbolised eː. Words like 'eight' and 'reign' are pronounced eɪt, reɪn, while 'late', 'rain' (with no 'g' in the spelling) are pronounced leːt, reːn.

A more complicated kind of difference is where, without affecting the overall set of phonemes and contrasts, a phoneme has a distribution in one accent that is different from the "same" phoneme's distribution in another accent. The obvious example is r, which is restricted to occurring in pre-vocalic position in RP but in many other accents is not restricted in this way. Another example is the occurrence of j between a consonant and uː, ʊ or ʊə; in RP we can find the following: 'pew' pjuː, 'tune' tjuːn, 'queue' kjuː. However, in many American accents and in some English accents of the South and East we find that, while 'pew' is pronounced pjuː and 'queue' as kjuː, 'tune' is pronounced tuːn; this absence of j is found after the other alveolar consonants, hence: 'due' duː; 'new' nuː.

We also find another kind of variation: in the example just given above, the occurrence of the phonemes being discussed was determined by their phonological context, but sometimes the determining factor is lexical rather than phonological. For example, in many accents of the Midlands and North-Western England a particular set of words contains a vowel (represented by 'o' in the spelling) which is pronounced as ʌ in RP but as ɒ in these other accents; the list of words includes 'one', 'none', 'nothing', 'tongue', 'mongrel' and 'constable'. One of the results of this difference is that such accents have different pronunciations for the two members of pairs of words that are pronounced identically (i.e. are **homophones**) in RP, e.g. 'won' and 'one', 'nun' and 'none'.

It would be satisfying to be able to list examples of phonological differences between accents in the area of stress and intonation, but unfortunately, straightforward examples are not available; we do not yet know enough about the phonological functions of stress and intonation, and too little work has been done on comparing accents in terms of these factors. It would be necessary to show how one accent was able to make some difference in meaning with stress or intonation that another accent was unable to make. It is very probable that such differences do exist, and will be identified by suitable research work.

It was mentioned earlier that there were weaknesses in the description of accents in terms of geographical variation alone; the study of **sociolinguistics** has shown the importance of considering other sources of variation. We can find differences in pronunciation (as well as in other fields of linguistic analysis) resulting from various factors that we could call **static** influences including (in addition to geographical origin) one's age and sex, social class, educational background, occupation and personality. In addition, various **situational** factors influence pronunciation, such as the social relationship between speaker and hearer, whether one is speaking publicly or privately and the purposes for which one is using language. Some people (who usually turn out to do well in phonetic training) find that in speaking to someone with a different accent their pronunciation gets progressively more like that of the person they are speaking to, like a chameleon adapting its colour to its environment.

Among the situational factors influencing variation, it is possible to pick out some which could be described as **stylistic**, and many linguists have attempted to produce frameworks for the analysis of style in language. We will not consider this in detail, but should note that for foreign learners a typical situation – regrettably, an almost inevitable one – is that they learn a style of pronunciation which could be described as careful and formal. Probably their teachers will speak to them in this style, though what the learners are likely to encounter when they join in conversations with native speakers is what we have referred to previously as a "rapid, casual" style. Young children have an enviable ability to acquire the rapid, casual pronunciation of a language apparently without effort if they are provided with the necessary social contact with native speakers and meaningful communication situations. It has been claimed that adults can also "pick up" spoken language in this way (**second language acquisition**) better than by the traditional classroom approach (**second language learning**) if the conditions are similar to those experienced by young children. This is an attractive idea, but for most adults the goal of learning through communicating naturally in the language throughout the day will, sadly, never be a practical one; we have to continue to make use of something like formal classroom teaching because of the limited time and resources available.

It should now be clear that the pronunciation described in this course is only one of a vast number of possible varieties. The choice of a slow, careful style is made for the sake of convenience and simplicity; learners of English need to be aware of the fact that this style is far from being the only one they will meet, and teachers of English to foreigners should do their best to expose their pupils to other varieties.

Notes on problems and further reading

20.1 Students learning about distinctive features face two main difficulties: one is understanding the basic principles and the other is learning the meanings of the rather confusing feature labels used by most writers. I have chosen to reduce the latter problem by using labels already familiar from earlier chapters, but some information about the other labels is given here. The idea of distinctive features was put forward in the early 1930s by Bloomfield (1933) and Trubetzkoy (various publications leading up to 1939); however, in early work and in present-day functional phonology, the features are worked out individually for the language being studied. Later, under Jakobson, the idea emerged of a set of features that could be used for every language, and a set of about twelve such features was proposed in Jakobson *et al.* (1952), later reworked in more readable form in Jakobson and Halle (1956).

A universal set of features is an attractive idea, but the price one pays is that each feature has to do many jobs, and the meaning associated with it gets spread thinner and thinner, like a small amount of butter on a large amount of bread. The definition of the Jakobsonian features is thus very difficult to understand. The principle of whether features should or should not be binary (i.e. ' + ' or ' − ', 'yes' or 'no') has been much argued about, but this is too big a question to go into here (Hyman (1975), pp. 32–3, 55–8). In the 1960s it became apparent that a revision of the features was needed, and the new set was introduced in Chomsky and Halle (1968), pp. 293–329, rather pretentiously called 'The Universal Set of Phonetic Features'. Unfortunately the definitions of many of these features are also very difficult to understand and there are twice as many of them. If one does not like these features, one can use features that are designed to have a more clearly-defined phonetic meaning (Ladefoged (1982), chapter 11), or alternatively, abandon phonetically meaningful feature labels altogether (Fudge, 1967).

There is a good review of approaches to distinctive features in Clark and Yallop (1990), chapter 9 and pp. 364–8.

20.2   As far as I know there is no introductory book that explains the principles of experimental phonetics, in the sense of how to design and carry out experiments and to interpret the results in terms that are meaningful to other phoneticians. There are, however, good books that explain the speech chain and the aspects of the speech that are measurable. Denes and Pinson (1973) is entitled *The Speech Chain*, and is clear and interesting. Outlines of acoustic phonetics are given in O'Connor (1973), chapter 3, and Ladefoged (1982), chapter 8. There is fuller treatment of speech production, speech acoustics and speech perception in Borden and Harris (1984) and Lieberman and Blumstein (1988).

20.3   On the study of variety, the list of references could become enormous. Those given in the section "Suggestion for further reading" should be enough for most readers; the same is true for sociolinguistics, but I feel that any reading beyond basic introductory material ought to include some work by Labov, whose influence on the subject has been profound. See, for example, Labov (1972).

The distinction between second language learning and second language acquisition is one that has been proposed by Krashen; see for example Krashen (1981).

Note for teachers

Tape Unit 20 is short and intensive. It is meant primarily to give a final reminder that English spoken at something like full conversational speed is very different from the slow, careful pronunciation of the early Tape Units. If there is time, students should now be encouraged to go back to some of the more difficult Tape Units dealing with connected speech (say from Tape Unit 12 onwards, missing out Tape Unit 15); they will probably discover a lot of things they did not notice before.

Written exercises

1. Distinctive feature analysis looks at different properties of segments and classes of segments. In the following exercise you must find what feature or features certain groups of segments have in common; you will probably find it useful to look at the IPA chart on pp. 40–1. You are not restricted to using feature labels given in Chapter 20.
   a) k g ʔ h
   b) English iː ɪ uː ʊ Cardinal vowels i e u o
   c) t d n l s tʃ dʒ ʃ ʒ r
   d) p b f v k g h
   e) p t k f θ s ʃ tʃ
   f) uː ɔː əʊ aʊ
   g) l r w j

2. Phonological differences between accents are of various types. For each of the following sets of data, based on non-RP accents, say what you can conclude about the phonology of that accent.

   a) 'sing'   sɪŋ   'finger'   fɪŋgə
      'sung'   sʌŋ   'running' rʌnɪn
      'singing' sɪŋɪn   'ring'   rɪŋ
   b) 'day'   deː   'you'   juː
      'buy'   baɪ   'me'   miː
      'go'   goː   'more'   mɔː
      'now'   naʊ   'fur'   fɜː

c) 'mother'   mʌvə   'father'   fɑːvə
    'think'   fɪŋk   'breath'   bref
    'lip'   lɪp   'pill'   pɪw
    'help'   ewp   'hill'   ɪw
d) 'mother'   mʌðər   'father'   fɑːðər
    'car'   kɑːr   'cart'   kɑːrt
    'area'   ɛːɾəl   'aerial'   ɛːɾəl
    'idea'   aɪdɪəl   'ideal'   aɪdɪəl
    'India'   ɪndɪəl   'Norma'   nɔːrməl
e) 'cat'   kat   'plaster'   plaːstər
    'cart'   kɑːrt   'grass'   graːs
    'calm'   kɑːm   'gas'   gas

Recorded exercises

These exercises are mainly intended for students whose native language is not English; however, those exercises which involve work with transcription (exercises 2.2, 3.3, 3.5, 3.7, 4.5, 5.3, 5.4, 6.2, 7.6, 9.5, 10.1, 10.2, 10.3, 11.5, 12.3, 13.1, 13.2, 13.3, all of Tape Unit 14 and exercise 20.2) and those which give practice in intonation (Tape Units 15, 16, 17, 18 and 19, and exercise 20.3) will be useful to native speakers as well.

Each Tape Unit corresponds to a chapter of this book, with the exception that there is no Tape Unit 1 to correspond to Chapter 1. As far as possible, I have tried to relate the contents of each Tape Unit to the subject-matter of the chapter, but where the chapter is devoted to theoretical matters I have taken advantage of this to produce revision exercises going back over some of the subjects previously worked on.

The best way of listening to the tapes is in a language laboratory, where you can record your voice and later listen to it, if possible with the assistance of a tutor. However, if this is not possible, you can use the tapes on an ordinary domestic cassette recorder. If it is possible for you to use headphones you will find the sound quality, even on a cheap machine, very much better than that of the loudspeaker.

In some of the exercises you are asked to put stress or intonation marks on the text. It would obviously be sensible to do this in a way that will make it possible for you, or someone else, to erase these marks and use the exercise again.

As with the chapters of the book, the tapes are intended to be worked through from first to last. Those at the beginning are concerned with individual vowels and consonants, and the words containing them are usually pronounced in isolation in a slow, careful style. Pronouncing isolated words in this way is, of course, a very artificial practice, but the recorded exercises are designed to lead the student towards the study of comparatively natural and fluent speech by the end of the course. In some of the later exercises you will find it necessary to stop the tape in order to allow yourself enough time to write a transcription.

After Tape Unit 20, there is an answers section. Two symbols are used throughout the Tape Units: ■ means "Stop your tape" and ▶ means "Start your tape".

The exercises in this Tape Unit practise the six short vowels introduced in Chapter 2. When pronouncing them, you should take care to give the vowels the correct length *and* the correct quality.

Exercise 1   Repetition

Listen and repeat:

ɪ

bit **bɪt**	bid **bɪd**	him **hɪm**	miss **mɪs**

e

bet **bet**	bed **bed**	hen **hen**	mess **mes**

æ

bat **bæt**	bad **bæd**	ham **hæm**	mass **mæs**

ʌ

cut **kʌt**	bud **bʌd**	bun **bʌn**	bus **bʌs**

ɒ

pot **pɒt**	cod **kɒd**	Tom **tɒm**	loss **lɒs**

ʊ

put **pʊt**	wood **wʊd**	pull **pʊl**	push **pʊʃ**

Exercise 2   Identification

Write the symbol for the vowel you hear in each word. (1 ... 10)
Check your answers.

Exercise 3   Production

When you hear the number, pronounce the word (which is given in spelling and in phonetic symbols). Repeat the correct pronunciation when you hear it. *Example*: 1. 'Mad'

1. mad **mæd**	7. put **pʊt**
2. mud **mʌd**	8. pot **pɒt**
3. bit **bɪt**	9. men **men**
4. bet **bet**	10. man **mæn**
5. cut **kʌt**	11. fun **fʌn**
6. cot **kɒt**	12. fan **fæn**

Exercise 4 Short vowels contrasted

Listen and repeat (words given in spelling):

ɪ and	e	e and	æ	æ and	ʌ
bit	bet	hem	ham	lack	luck
tin	ten	set	sat	bad	bud
fill	fell	peck	pack	fan	fun
built	belt	send	sand	stamp	stump
lift	left	wreck	rack	flash	flush

ʌ and	ɒ	ɒ and	ʊ
dug	dog	lock	look
cup	cop	cod	could
rub	rob	pot	put
stuck	stock	shock	shook
luck	lock	crock	crook

Tape Unit 3 Long vowels diphthongs and triphthongs

Long vowels

Exercise 1 Repetition

Listen and repeat:

iː
| beat biːt | bead biːd | been biːn | beef biːf |

ɑː
| heart hɑːt | hard hɑːd | harm hɑːm | hearth hɑːθ |

ɔː
| caught kɔːt | cord kɔːd | corn kɔːn | course kɔːs |

uː
| root ruːt | rude ruːd | room ruːm | roof ruːf |

ɜː
| hurt hɜːt | heard hɜːd | earn ɜːn | earth ɜːθ |

Exercise 2   Production

When you hear the number, pronounce the word. Repeat the correct pronunciation when you hear it.

1. heard hɜːd
2. been biːn
3. root ruːt
4. hearth hɑːθ
5. caught kɔːt
6. heart hɑːt
7. cord kɔːd
8. beef biːf
9. rude ruːd
10. earn ɜːn

Exercise 3   Transcription

Write the symbol for the vowel you hear in each word.
(1 ... 10)

■   Check your answers.

▶ ## Exercise 4   Long-short vowel contrasts

Listen and repeat (words in spelling):

iː and ɪ		ɑː and ʌ		ɑː and æ	
feel	fill	calm	come	part	pat
bead	bid	cart	cut	lard	lad
steel	still	half	huff	calm	Cam
reed	rid	lark	luck	heart	hat
been	bin	mast	must	harms	hams

ɔː and ɒ		uː and ʊ		ɜː and ʌ		ɑː and ɒ	
caught	cot	pool	pull	hurt	hut	dark	dock
stork	stock	suit	soot	turn	ton	part	pot
short	shot	Luke	look	curt	cut	lark	lock
cord	cod	wooed	wood	girl	gull	balm	bomb
port	pot	fool	full	bird	bud	large	lodge

Exercise 5   Transcription

Write the symbol for the vowel (long or short) you hear in each word.
(1 ... 10)

■   Check your answers.

▶ **Diphthongs**

Exercise 6   Repetition

Listen and repeat, making sure that the second part of the diphthong is weak.

eɪ

mate meɪt	made meɪd	main meɪn	mace meɪs

aɪ

right raɪt	ride raɪd	rhyme raɪm	rice raɪs

ɔɪ

quoit kɔɪt	buoyed bɔɪd	Boyne bɔɪn	Royce rɔɪs

əʊ

coat kəʊt	code kəʊd	cone kəʊn	close kləʊs

aʊ

gout gaʊt	loud laʊd	gown gaʊn	louse laʊs

ɪə

	feared fɪəd	Ian ɪən	fierce fɪəs

eə

	cared keəd	cairn keən	scarce skeəs

ʊə

	moored mʊəd	fuel fjʊəl	

Exercise 7   Transcription

Write the symbol for the diphthong you hear in each word.
(1 . . . 12)

■ Check your answers.

Triphthongs

▶ *Exercise 8   Repetition*

Listen and repeat:

eɪə	layer leɪə	əʊə	lower ləʊə
aɪə	liar laɪə	aʊə	tower taʊə
ɔɪə	loyal lɔɪəl		

Tape Unit 4 Plosives

Exercise 1 Repetition of initial plosives

INITIAL FORTIS p, t, k

Each word begins with a fortis plosive; notice that the plosive is aspirated. Listen and repeat:

paw	pɔ:	care	keə
tea	ti:	two	tu:
car	kɑ:	key	ki:
pie	paɪ	tar	tɑ:
toe	təʊ	pay	peɪ

INITIAL LENIS b, d, g

Each word begins with a lenis plosive; notice that there is practically no voicing of the plosive. Listen and repeat:

bee	bi:	gear	gɪə
door	dɔ:	boy	bɔɪ
go	gəʊ	dear	dɪə
bear	beə	bough	baʊ
do	du:	day	deɪ

INITIAL sp, st, sk

The plosive must be unaspirated. Listen and repeat:

spy	spaɪ	score	skɔ:
store	stɔ:	spear	spɪə
ski	ski:	stay	steɪ
spare	speə	sky	skaɪ
steer	stɪə	spar	spɑ:

Exercise 2 Repetition of final plosives

In the pairs of words in this exercise one word ends with a fortis plosive and the other ends with a lenis plosive. Notice the length difference in the vowel. Listen to each pair and repeat:

Fortis followed by lenis		*Lenis followed by fortis*	
mate made	meɪt meɪd	code coat	kəʊd kəʊt
rope robe	rəʊp rəʊb	bid bit	bɪd bɪt
leak league	liːk liːg	lobe lope	ləʊb ləʊp
cart card	kɑːt kɑːd	heard hurt	hɜːd hɜːt
back bag	bæk bæg	brogue broke	brəʊg brəʊk

Exercise 3   Identification of final plosives

You will hear the twenty words of Exercise 2. Each will be one of a pair. You must choose whether the word is one ending with a fortis plosive or the one ending with a lenis plosive; when you hear the word, say "fortis" if you heard the word on the left, or "lenis" if you heard the word on the right. You will then hear the correct answer and the word will be said again for you to repeat.

Example: 'coat'

FORTIS	LENIS	FORTIS	LENIS
coat kəʊt	code kəʊd	mate meɪt	made meɪd
leak liːk	league liːg	coat kəʊt	code kəʊd
hurt hɜːt	heard hɜːd	leak liːk	league liːg
bit bɪt	bid bɪd	rope rəʊp	robe rəʊb
mate meɪt	made meɪd	hurt hɜːt	heard hɜːd
lope ləʊp	lobe ləʊb	broke brəʊk	brogue brəʊg
back bæk	bag bæg	lope ləʊp	lobe ləʊb
cart kɑːt	card kɑːd	bit bɪt	bid bɪd
broke brəʊk	brogue brəʊg	back bæk	bag bæg
rope rəʊp	robe rəʊb	cart kɑːt	card kɑːd

Each of the words which follow ends with a plosive. Write the symbol for each plosive when you hear the word. Each will be said twice. (1 ... 10)

■   Check your answers.

▶ Exercise 4   Repetition of words containing plosives

The following words contain several plosives. They are given in spelling and in transcription. Listen and repeat:

potato pəteɪtəʊ	carpeted kɑːpɪtɪd
topic tɒpɪk	bodyguard bɒdɪgɑːd
petticoat petɪkəʊt	tobacco təbækəʊ
partake pɑːteɪk	doubted daʊtɪd
cupboard kʌbəd	decode diːkəʊd
decapitated dɪkæpɪteɪtɪd	bigoted bɪgətɪd
pocket pɒkɪt	about əbaʊt

Exercise 5 Reading of words in transcription

When you hear the number, pronounce the word given in transcription taking care to pronounce the plosives correctly and putting the strongest stress on the syllable preceded by the stress mark '. You will then hear the correct pronunciation, which you should repeat.

1. dɪ'beɪt
2. 'kɒpɪd
3. 'bʌtəkʌp
4. 'kʊkuː
5. dɪ'keɪd

6. 'gɑːdɪd
7. 'dedɪkeɪtɪd
8. 'pædək
9. buː'tiːk
10. 'æpɪtaɪt

(You will find these words in spelling form in the answers section.)

Tape Unit 5 Revision

Exercise 1 Vowels and diphthongs

Listen and repeat (words given in spelling):

ɑː and ɜː		eɪ and e		aɪ and ɑː	
barn	burn	fade	fed	life	laugh
are	err	sale	sell	tight	tart
fast	first	laid	led	pike	park
cart	curt	paste	pest	hide	hard
lark	lurk	late	let	spike	spark

ɔɪ and ɔː		əʊ and ɔː		ɪə and iː	
toy	tore	phone	fawn	fear	fee
coin	corn	boat	bought	beard	bead
boil	ball	code	cord	mere	me
boy	bore	stoke	stork	steered	steed
foil	fall	bowl	ball	peer	pea

eə and eɪ		eə and ɪə		ʊə and ɔː	
dare	day	fare	fear	poor	paw
stared	stayed	pair	pier	sure	shore
pairs	pays	stare	steer	moor	more
hair	hay	air	ear	dour	door
mare	may	snare	sneer	tour	tore

Exercise 2 Triphthongs

Listen and repeat:
eɪə player pleɪə
aɪə tyre taɪə
ɔɪə loyal lɔɪəl
əʊə mower məʊə
aʊə shower ʃaʊə

Exercise 3 Transcription of words

You should now be able to recognise all the vowels, diphthongs and triphthongs of English, and all the plosives. In the next exercise you will hear one-syllable English words composed of these sounds. Each word will be said twice. You must transcribe these words using the phonemic symbols that you have learned in the first three chapters. When you hear the word, write it with phonemic symbols.
(1 . . . 20)
Now check your answers.

Exercise 4 Production

The following are all English words; they are given only in phonemic transcription. When you hear the number you should say the word; you will then hear the correct pronunciation, which you should repeat. If you want to see how these words are spelt when you have finished the exercise, you will find them in the answers section.

1. kiːp	11. dʌk
2. bəʊt	12. kəʊp
3. kʌp	13. dɒg
4. dɜːt	14. kaʊəd
5. baɪk	15. beɪk
6. kæb	16. taɪd
7. geɪt	17. brəd
8. keəd	18. pʊt
9. taɪəd	19. bʌg
10. bɜːd	20. daʊt

Exercise 5 Fortis/lenis discrimination

When you hear the word, say "fortis" if you hear it as ending with a fortis consonant, and "lenis" if you hear it as ending with a lenis consonant. You will then hear the correct answer and the word will be said again for you to repeat.

	FORTIS	LENIS
1.	right raɪt	ride raɪd
2.	bat bæt	bad bæd
3.	bet bet	bed bed
4.	leak liːk	league liːg
5.	feet fiːt	feed fiːd
6.	right raɪt	ride raɪd
7.	tack tæk	tag tæg
8.	rope rəʊp	robe rəʊb
9.	mate meɪt	made meɪd
10.	beat biːt	bead biːd

Tape Unit 6   Fricatives and affricates

Exercise 1   Repetition of words containing fricatives

Listen and repeat (words given in spelling and transcription):

f	fin fɪn	offer ɒfə	laugh lɑːf
v	vat væt	over əʊvə	leave liːv
θ	thing θɪŋ	method meθəd	breath breθ
ð	these ðiːz	other ʌðə	breathe briːð
s	sad sæd	lesser lesə	moss mɒs
z	zoo zuː	lazy leɪzi	lose luːz
ʃ	show ʃəʊ	washing wɒʃɪŋ	rush rʌʃ
ʒ		measure meʒə	rouge ruːʒ
h	hot hɒt	beehive biːhaɪv	

Exercise 2   Identification

Write the symbol for the fricative you hear in each word.
a) initial position: (1 ... 5)
b) medial position (6 ... 10)
c) final position (11 ... 15)

■ Now check your answers.

▶ *Exercise 3 Production*

When you hear the number, pronounce the word, giving particular attention to the fricatives. You will then hear the correct pronunciation, which you should repeat.

1. ðiːz these
2. feɪθ faith
3. heðə heather
4. siːʃɔː seashore
5. feðəz feathers
6. fɪfθ fifth
7. ʃɪvəz shivers
8. bɪheɪv behave
9. siːʒə seizure
10. læʃɪz lashes

Exercise 4 Repetition of fricative and affricate pairs

Listen and repeat:

a) Initial ʃ and tʃ
   ʃɒp tʃɒp (shop, chop)
   ʃiːt tʃiːt (sheet, cheat)
   ʃuːz tʃuːz (shoes, choose)

b) Medial ʃ and tʃ
   liːʃɪz liːtʃɪz (leashes, leaches)
   wɒʃɪŋ wɒtʃɪŋ (washing, watching)
   bæʃɪz bætʃɪz (bashes, batches)

c) Final ʃ and tʃ
   mæʃ mætʃ (mash, match)
   kæʃ kætʃ (cash, catch)
   wɪʃ wɪtʃ (wish, witch)

d) Medial ʒ and dʒ
   leʒə ledʒə (leisure, ledger)
   pleʒə pledʒə (pleasure, pledger)
   liːʒən liːdʒən (lesion, legion)

Exercise 5 Discrimination between fricatives and affricates

You will hear some of the words from Exercise 4. When you hear the word, say "A" if you hear the word on the left or "B" if you hear the word on the right. You will then hear the correct answer and the word will be said again for you to repeat.

A	B
ʃɒp	tʃɒp
kæʃ	kætʃ
wɒʃɪŋ	wɒtʃɪŋ
ʃuːz	tʃuːz
liːʒən	liːdʒən
bæʃɪz	bætʃɪz
ʃiːt	tʃiːt
leʒə	ledʒə
liːʃɪz	liːtʃɪz
wɪʃ	wɪtʃ
pleʒə	pledʒə
mæʃ	mætʃ

Tape Unit 7   Further consonants

Exercise 1 Repetition of words containing a velar nasal

Listen and repeat; take care not to pronounce a plosive after the velar nasal.

hæŋ	hæŋə
sɪŋɪŋ	rɒŋ
rʌŋ	bæŋɪŋ
θɪŋ	rɪŋ

Exercise 2 ŋ with and without g

Words of one morpheme		*Words of two morphemes*	
Listen and repeat:		Listen and repeat:	
fɪŋgə	finger	sɪŋə	singer
æŋgə	anger	hæŋə	hanger
bæŋgə	Bangor	lɒŋɪŋ	longing
hʌŋgə	hunger	rɪŋɪŋ	ringing
æŋgl	angle	bæŋə	banger

205

Exercise 3 "Clear" and "dark" l

"Clear l" before vowels

Listen and repeat:

laɪ lie	ləʊ low
luːs loose	laʊd loud
liːk leak	lɔː law

"Dark l" before pause

Listen and repeat:

fɪl fill	peɪl pale
bel bell	maɪl mile
niːl kneel	kɪl kill

"Dark l" before consonants

Listen and repeat:

help help	feɪld failed
fɪlθ filth	mɪlk milk
belt belt	welʃ Welsh

Exercise 4 r

Listen and repeat, concentrating on not allowing the tongue to make contact with the roof of the mouth in pronouncing this consonant:

eərɪŋ airing	reərə rarer
riːraɪt rewrite	herɪŋ herring
terərɪst terrorist	mɪrə mirror
ærəʊ arrow	rɔːrɪŋ roaring

Exercise 5 j and w

Listen and repeat:

juː you	weɪ way
jɔːn yawn	wɔː war
jɪə year	wɪn win
jʊə your	weə wear

Exercise 6   Dictation of words

When you hear the word, write it down using phonemic symbols. Each word will be said three times; you should stop your tape if you need more time for writing.
(1 . . . 12)

■   Check your answers.

Tape Unit 8   Consonant clusters

Exercise 1   Devoicing of l, r, w, j

When l, r, w, j follow p, t or k in syllable-initial position they are produced as voiceless, slightly fricative sounds.
Listen and repeat:

pleɪ play	treɪ tray	klɪə clear
preɪ pray	twɪn twin	kraɪ cry
pju: pew	tju:n tune	kju: queue

Exercise 2   Repetition of initial clusters

TWO CONSONANTS

Listen and repeat:

spɒt spot	plaʊ plough
stəʊn stone	twɪst twist
skeɪt skate	kri:m cream
sfɪə sphere	pjʊə pure
smaɪl smile	fleɪm flame
snəʊ snow	ʃrɪŋk shrink
slæm slam	vju: view
swɪtʃ switch	θwɔ:t thwart

THREE CONSONANTS

Listen and repeat:

spleɪ splay	streɪ stray	skru: screw
spreɪ spray	stju: stew	skwɒʃ squash
spju: spew		skju: skew

Exercise 3 Final plosive-plus-plosive clusters

a) When one plosive is followed by another at the end of a syllable, the second plosive is usually the only one that can be clearly heard. In this exercise, take care not to make an audible release of the first plosive.

Listen and repeat:

pækt packed	rɪgd rigged
bægd bagged	dʌkt duct
drɒpt dropped	lept leapt
rɒbd robbed	græbd grabbed

b) It is difficult to hear the difference between, for example, 'dropped back' and 'drop back', since in the normal pronunciation only the last plosive of the cluster (the b of bæk) is audibly released. The main difference is that the three-consonant cluster is longer.

Listen and repeat:

A	B
græbd bəʊθ grabbed both	græb bəʊθ grab both
laɪkt ðəm liked them	laɪk ðəm like them
hɒpt bæk hopped back	hɒp bæk hop back
lʊkt fɔːwəd looked forward	lʊk fɔːwəd look forward
pegd daʊn pegged down	peg daʊn peg down
wɪpt kriːm whipped cream	wɪp kriːm whip cream

Exercise 4 Recognition

Look at the items of Exercise 3(b) above. When you hear one of them, say "A" if you hear an item from the left-hand column, or "B" if you hear one from the right-hand column. You will then hear the correct answer and the item will be said again for you to repeat.
(1 . . . 6)

Exercise 5 Final clusters of three and four consonants

Listen and repeat:

helps helps	nekst next
sɪksθ sixth	reɪndʒd ranged
θæŋkt thanked	rɪsks risks
edʒd edged	riːtʃt reached
twelfθs twelfths	teksts texts

Exercise 6   Pronouncing consonant clusters

When you hear the number, say the word. You will then hear the correct pronunciation which you should repeat.

1. skreɪpt   5. krʌnʃt
2. grʌdʒd   6. θraʊnz
3. kləʊðz   7. plʌndʒd
4. skrɪpts   8. kwenʃ

(The spelling of these words is given in the answers section.)

Tape Unit 9   Weak syllables

Exercise 1   "Schwa" ə

TWO-SYLLABLE WORDS WITH WEAK FIRST SYLLABLE AND STRESS ON THE SECOND SYLLABLE

Listen and repeat:
Weak syllable spelt 'a'

about ə'baʊt	ahead ə'hed	again ə'gen

Spelt 'o'

obtuse əb'tjuːs	oppose ə'pəʊz	offend ə'fend

Spelt 'u'

suppose sə'pəʊz	support sə'pɔːt	suggest sə'dʒest

Spelt 'or'

forget fə'get	forsake fə'seɪk	forbid fə'bɪd

Spelt 'er'

perhaps pə'hæps	percent pə'sent	perceive pə'siv

Spelt 'ur'

survive sə'vaɪv	surprise sə'praɪz	survey (verb) sə'veɪ

TWO-SYLLABLE WORDS WITH WEAK SECOND SYLLABLE AND STRESS ON THE FIRST SYLLABLE

Listen and repeat:
Weak syllable spelt 'a'

ballad 'bæləd	Alan 'ælən	necklace 'nekləs

Spelt 'o'

melon 'melən	paddock 'pædək	purpose 'pɜːpəs

Spelt 'e'

hundred 'hʌndrəd	sullen 'sʌlən	open 'əʊpən

Spelt 'u'
    circus 'sɜːkəs   Autumn 'ɔːtəm   album 'ælbəm
Spelt 'ar'
    tankard 'tæŋkəd   custard 'kʌstəd   standard 'stændəd
Spelt 'or'
    juror 'dʒʊərə   major 'meɪdʒə   manor 'mænə
Spelt 'er'
    longer 'lɒŋgə   eastern 'iːstən   mother 'mʌðə
Spelt 'ure'
    nature 'neɪtʃə   posture 'pɒstʃə   creature 'kriːtʃə
Spelt 'ous'
    ferrous 'ferəs   vicious 'vɪʃəs   gracious 'greɪʃəs
Spelt 'ough'
    thorough 'θʌrə   borough 'bʌrə
Spelt 'our'
    saviour 'seɪvjə   succour 'sʌkə   colour 'kʌlə

THREE-SYLLABLE WORDS WITH WEAK SECOND SYLLABLE
AND STRESS ON THE FIRST SYLLABLE

Listen and repeat:
Weak syllable spelt 'a'
    workaday 'wɜːkədeɪ   roundabout 'raʊndəbaʊt
Spelt 'o'
    customer 'kʌstəmə   pantomime 'pæntəmaɪm
Spelt 'u'
    perjury 'pɜːdʒəri   venturer 'ventʃərə
Spelt 'ar'
    standardise 'stændədaɪz   jeopardy 'dʒepədi
Spelt 'er'
    wonderland 'wʌndəlænd   yesterday 'jestədeɪ

Exercise 2   Close front vowels

WEAK INITIAL SYLLABLES		WEAK FINAL SYLLABLES	
Listen and repeat:		Listen and repeat:	
excite ɪk'saɪt	resume rɪ'zjuːm	city 'sɪti	many 'meni
exist ɪg'zɪst	relate rɪ'leɪt	funny 'fʌni	lazy 'leɪzi
inane ɪ'neɪn	effect ɪ'fekt	easy 'iːzi	only 'əʊnli
device dɪ'vaɪs	ellipse ɪ'lɪps	busy 'bɪzi	lady 'leɪdi

Exercise 3   Syllabic ļ

Listen and repeat:
bottle 'bɒtļ	bottled 'bɒtļd	bottling 'bɒtļɪŋ
muddle 'mʌdļ	muddled 'mʌdļd	muddling 'mʌdļɪŋ
tunnel 'tʌnļ	tunnelled 'tʌnļd	tunnelling 'tʌnļɪŋ
wrestle 'resļ	wrestled 'resļd	wrestling 'resļɪŋ

Exercise 4   Syllabic ņ

Listen and repeat:
burden 'bɜːdņ	burdened 'bɜːdņd	burdening 'bɜːdņɪŋ
frighten 'fraɪtņ	frightened 'fraɪtņd	frightening 'fraɪtņɪŋ
listen 'lɪsņ	listened 'lɪsņd	listening 'lɪsņɪŋ

Exercise 5   Transcription

Transcribe the following words when you hear them, giving particular attention to the weak syllables. Each word will be said twice. If you need more time for writing, stop your tape and restart it when you are ready for the next word.
(1 ... 10)

■ Now check your answers.

Tape Unit 10   Word stress

Exercise 1   Stress marking

When you hear the word, repeat it, then place a stress mark ' before the stressed syllable.
enɪmi enemy	səbtrækt subtract
kəlekt collect	elɪfənt elephant
kæpɪtļ capital	əbzɜːvə observer
kɑːneɪʃņ carnation	prɒfɪt profit
pærədaɪs paradise	entəteɪn entertain

■ Now check your marking with the correct version.

▶ *Exercise 2   Pronouncing from transcription*

The following are British place-names. When you hear the number, pronounce them with the stress as marked. You will then hear the correct pronunciation, which you should repeat.

1. 'ʃrəʊzbr̩i
2. pɒl'perəʊ
3. æbə'diːn
4. wʊlvə'hæmptən
5. æbə'rɪstwəθ
6. 'bɜːmɪŋəm
7. nɔː'θæmptən
8. dʌn'diː
9. 'kæntəbr̩i
10. 'beɪzɪŋstəʊk

(The spelling for these names is given in the answers section.)

Exercise 3   Placing stress on verbs, adjectives and nouns

When you hear the number, pronounce the word with the appropriate stress. You will then hear the correct pronunciation, which you should repeat.

TWO-SYLLABLE WORDS

VERBS

1. dɪsiːv deceive
2. ʃɑːpən sharpen
3. kəlekt collect
4. prənaʊns pronounce
5. kɒpi copy
6. əbdʒekt object
7. kɒŋkə conquer
8. rɪkɔːd record
9. pɒlɪʃ polish
10. dɪpend depend

ADJECTIVES

1. iːzi easy
2. kəmpliːt complete
3. meɪdʒə major
4. ələʊn alone
5. bɪləʊ below
6. jeləʊ yellow
7. ɜːli early
8. səblaɪm sublime
9. hevi heavy
10. əlaɪv alive

NOUNS

1. bɪʃəp bishop
2. æspekt aspect
3. əfeə affair
4. kɑːpɪt carpet
5. dɪfiːt defeat
6. ɒfɪs office
7. əreɪ array
8. pətrəʊl patrol
9. dentɪst dentist
10. ɔːtəm Autumn

THREE-SYLLABLE WORDS

VERBS

1. entəteɪn entertain
2. rezərekt resurrect
3. əbændən abandon
4. dɪlɪvə deliver
5. ɪntərʌpt interrupt

6. ɪlɪsɪt elicit
7. kɒməndɪə commandeer
8. ɪmædʒɪn imagine
9. dɪtɜːmɪn determine
10. sepəreɪt separate

ADJECTIVES

1. ɪmpɔːtn̩t important
2. ɪnɔːməs enormous
3. derɪlɪkt derelict
4. desɪml̩ decimal
5. æbnɔːml̩ abnormal

6. ɪnsl̩ənt insolent
7. fæntæstɪk fantastic
8. negətɪv negative
9. ækjərət accurate
10. ʌnlaɪkli unlikely

NOUNS

1. fɜːnɪtʃə furniture
2. dɪzɑːstə disaster
3. dɪsaɪpl̩ disciple
4. æmbjələns ambulance
5. kwɒntɪti quantity

6. kəθiːdrəl cathedral
7. hɒləkɔːst holocaust
8. trænzɪstə transistor
9. æksɪdn̩t accident
10. təmɑːtəʊ tomato

Tape Unit 11 Complex word stress

Exercise 1   Stress-carrying suffixes

When you hear the number, pronounce the word with stress on the suffix. You will then hear the correct pronunciation which you should repeat.

1. -ain: entertain ˌentəˈteɪn
2. -ee: refugee ˌrefjʊˈdʒiː
3. -eer: mountaineer
   ˌmaʊntɪˈnɪə

4. -ese: Portuguese ˌpɔːtʃəˈgiːz
5. -ette: cigarette ˌsɪgəˈret
6. -esque: picturesque
   ˌpɪktʃəˈresk

213

When you hear the stem word, say the word with the given suffix, putting the stress on that suffix. In these examples, a secondary stress comes on the penultimate syllable of the stem.

employ + -ee	absent + -ee
engin + -eer	profit + -eer
Sudan + -ese	Pekin + -ese
usher + -ette	statue + -ette (statuette)

Exercise 2   Neutral suffixes

When you hear the stem word, add the suffix without changing the stress.

comfort + -able	power + -less
anchor + -age	hurried + -ly
refuse + -al (refusal)	punish + -ment
wide + -en (widen)	yellow + -ness
wonder + -ful	poison + -ous
amaze + -ing (amazing)	glory + -fy (glorify)
devil + -ish	other + -wise
bird + -like	fun + -y (funny)

Exercise 3   Stress-moving suffixes

When you hear the stem word, say it with the suffix added and put the stress on the last syllable of the stem.

advantage + -eous (advantageous)	injure + -ious (injurious)
photo + -graphy	tranquil + -ity (tranquillity)
proverb + -ial	reflex + -ive
climate + -ic (climatic)	embryo + -logy

Exercise 4   Compound words

When you hear the number, say the item.

a) First element adjectival, stress on second element.

1. loudspeaker	4. second-class
2. bad-tempered	5. three-wheeler
3. headquarters	

b) First element nominal, stress on first element.

1. typewriter	4. suitcase
2. car-ferry	5. tea-cup
3. sunrise	

c) Mixture of type (a) and (b).
1. long-suffering   4. red-blooded
2. gunman   5. gear-box
3. shoelace   6. overweight

Exercise 5   Word-class pairs

You will hear the number of the item and its word-class. Stress the second syllable if it is a verb; stress the first syllable if it is a noun or adjective.

1. abstract (Adjective)
2. conduct (Verb)
3. contract (Noun)
4. contrast (Verb)
5. desert (Noun)
6. escort (Noun)
7. export (Verb)
8. import (Noun)
9. insult (Verb)
10. object (Noun)
11. perfect (Adjective)
12. permit (Verb)
13. present (Adjective)
14. produce (Verb)
15. protest (Noun)
16. rebel (Verb)
17. record (Noun)
18. subject (Noun)

Tape Unit 12   Weak forms

Words occurring in their weak forms are printed in smaller type than stressed words and strong forms, e.g. 'We can wait' 'wiː kən 'weɪt

Exercise 1   Sentences for repetition

Listen and repeat:
We can 'wait for the 'bus   wi kən 'weɪt fə ðə 'bʌs
'How do the 'lights 'work?   'haʊ də ðə 'laɪts'wɜːk
There are some 'new 'books I must 'read   ðər ə səm 'nhuː 'bʊks aɪ məs 'riːd
She 'took her 'aunt for a 'drive   ʃi 'tʊk ər 'ɑːnt fər ə 'draɪv
The 'basket was 'full of 'things to 'eat   ðə 'bɑːskɪt wəz 'fʊl əv 'θɪŋz tu 'iːt
'Why should a 'man 'earn 'more than a 'woman?   'waɪ ʃəd ə 'mæn 'ɜːn 'mɔː ðən ə 'wʊmən
You 'ought to 'have your 'own 'car   ju 'ɔːt tə 'hæv jər 'əʊn 'kɑː

H

He 'wants to 'come and 'see us at 'home   hi 'wɒnts tə 'kʌm ən 'siː əs ət 'həʊm

'Have you 'taken them from 'that 'box?   'hæv ju 'teɪkən ðəm frəm 'ðæt 'bɒks

It's 'true that he was 'late, but his 'car could have 'broken 'down   ɪts 'truː ðət i wəz 'leɪt bət ɪz 'kɑː kəd əv 'brəʊkən 'daʊn

I shall 'take as 'much as I 'want   aɪ ʃl̩ 'teɪk əz 'mʌtʃ əz aɪ 'wɒnt

'Why am I 'too 'late to 'see him to'day?   'waɪ əm aɪ 'tuː 'leɪt tə 'siː ɪm tə'deɪ

Exercise 2 Weak forms with pre-vocalic and pre-consonantal forms

DIFFERENT VOWELS

When you hear the number, say the phrase, using the appropriate weak form:

the	1. the apple ði æpl̩	2. the pear ðə peə	
to	3. to Edinburgh tu edn̩brə	4. to Leeds tə liːdz	
do	5. so do I səʊ du aɪ	6. so do they səʊ də ðeɪ	

LINKING CONSONANT

a/an 7. an ear ən ɪə 8. a foot ə fʊt

(The other words in this section have "linking r".)

her	9. Her eyes hər aɪz	10. her nose hə nəʊz
your	11. your uncle jər ʌŋkl̩	12. your friend jə frend
for	13. for Alan fər ælən	14. for Mike fə maɪk
there	15. there aren't ðər ɑːnt	16. there couldn't ðə kʊdn̩t
are	17. these are ours ðiːz ər aʊəz	18. these are mine ðiːz ə maɪn
were	19. you were out juː wər aʊt	20. you were there juː wə ðeə

Exercise 3 Transcription

(*Note*: this exercise is a long one, and it is possible to go directly to Exercise 4 if wished)

Write the following sentences in transcription, taking care to give the correct weak forms for the words printed in smaller type.

1. 'Leave the 'rest of the 'food for 'lunch
2. 'Aren't there some 'letters for her to 'open?
3. 'Where do the 'eggs come from?
4. 'Read his 'book and 'write some 'notes
5. At 'least we can 'try and 'help

■ Now correct your transcription, using the version in the answers section.

▶ *Exercise 4   Pronunciation of weak forms*

This exercise uses the sentences of Exercise 3. When you hear the number, say the sentence, giving particular attention to the weak forms.
(1 ... 5)

Tape Unit 13 Revision

▶ *Exercise 1   Reading unfamiliar words from transcription*

The following are British place-names written in transcription.* When you hear the number, say the word, making sure that the stress is correctly placed. You will then hear the correct pronunciation which you should repeat.

1. 'kəʊltʃɪstə
2. kɑː'laɪl
3. 'herɪfəd
4. 'skʌnθɔːp
5. glə'mɔːgən
6. ˌhɒli'hed
7. 'fræmlɪŋəm
8. saʊθ'end
9. 'tʃeltn̩əm
10. ˌɪnvə'nes

Exercise 2   Transcription of unfamiliar words

The following are also place-names. Each will be said twice; write what you hear in transcription, including stress marks.
(1 ... 10)

■ Now check your transcriptions with the correct versions.

* Spelling is given in the answers section.

Exercise 3   Stress placement in sentences

Put a stress mark ' before each syllable you would expect to be stressed in the following sentences. For example, given the sentence 'I think I'll be late for work' you should mark the words 'think', 'late' and 'work' like this:

I 'think Ill be 'late for 'work

1. James decided to type the letter himself
2. The plane was approaching the runway at high speed
3. Try to see the other persons point of view
4. You put your brakes on when the light turns to red
5. In a short time the house was full of children

Now correct your stress marking by looking at the versions given in the answers section.

▶ Exercise 4   Pronunciation of stressed syllables

When you hear the number, say the sentence from the list in Exercise 3 taking care to stress the correct syllables. You will then hear the correct version, which you should repeat.

(1 . . . 5)

Exercise 5   Weak forms

In the following sentences, those words which are not stressed must be pronounced in their weak forms. When you hear the number, say the sentence:

1. 'Heres a 'present for your 'brother
2. 'These are 'all the 'pictures that are 'left
3. There 'could be a 'bit of 'rain at the 'end of the 'morning
4. A 'few 'people 'asked him a 'question
5. Col'lect your 'luggage be'fore 'leaving the 'train

Tape Unit 14 Elisions

READ THIS BEFORE STARTING YOUR TAPE

This Tape Unit gives you practice in recognising places where elision occurs in natural speech (i.e. where one or more phonemes which would be pronounced in careful speech are not pronounced). The examples are extracted from dialogues between speakers who are discussing differences between two similar pictures. Each extract is given three times. You must transcribe each item, using phonemic symbols so that the elision can be seen in the transcription. For example, if you heard 'sixth time' pronounced without the θ fricative at the end of the first word you would write **sɪks taɪm**, and the elision would be clearly indicated in this way. You can use the ʰ symbol to indicate a devoiced weak vowel, as in 'potato' **pʰteɪtəʊ**.

You will probably need to stop your tape to give yourself more time to write the transcription. This is a difficult exercise, but explanatory notes are given in the answers section.

▶ *Transcription*

ONE ELISION

1. a beautiful girl
2. we seem to have a definite one there
3. could it be a stool rather than a table
4. a fifth in
5. any peculiarities about that
6. and how many stripes on yours
7. well it appears to button up its got three
8. or the what do you call it the sill

TWO ELISIONS

9. by column into columns all right
10. diamond shaped patch
11. and I should think from experience of kitchen knives
12. what shall we do next go down

THREE ELISIONS

13. the top of the bottle is projecting outwards into the room

■ Now check your transcriptions.

Tape Unit 15   Tones

Exercise 1   Repetition of tones

Listen and repeat:

Fall:	ˎyes	ˎno	ˎwell	ˎfour
Rise:	ˏyes	ˏno	ˏwell	ˏfour
Fall–rise:	ˇyes	ˇno	ˇwell	ˇfour
Rise–fall:	ˆyes	ˆno	ˆwell	ˆfour
Level:	ˍyes	ˍno	ˍwell	ˍfour

Exercise 2   Production of tones

When you hear the number, say the syllable with the tone indicated:

1. ˏthem
2. ˇwhy
3. ˇwell
4. ˇJohn
5. ˏwhat
6. ˆno
7. ˇhere
8. ˇyou
9. ˏnow
10. ˎend

Exercise 3   Identification

You will hear each syllable twice. Write an appropriate tone symbol.
(1 ... 10)

■ Now check your answers.

▶ *Exercise 4   Production in context*

When you hear the sentence, say the response with the tone indicated.

Hello, is that 661071?	⸴yes
Do you know any scientists?	⸜some
Keep away from that road!	⸜why
How many dogs have you got?	⸜two
Have you ever heard such a terrible thing?	⸜no
What colour is your car?	⸜red
Do you want my plate?	⸴please
Don't you like it?	⸴yes
You haven't seen my watch, have you?	⸴no
What was the weather like?	⸜wet

Tape Unit 16   The tone-unit

Exercise 1   Identifying the tonic syllable

Listen and repeat, then underline the tonic syllable.
1. We could go by bus
2. Of course its broken
3. The car was where Id left it
4. How much is the biggest one
5. I knew it would go wrong
6. It was too cold
7. Here it is
8. That was a loud noise
9. We could go from Manchester
10. Have you finished

 Now check your answers.

▶ *Exercise 2   Pronouncing the tonic syllable*

When you hear the number, say the item with the tonic syllable in the
place indicated, using a falling tone:

1. Dont do <u>that</u>   8. Heres <u>my</u> pen
2. Dont <u>do</u> that   9. <u>Heres</u> my pen
3. <u>Dont</u> do that   10. Why dont you <u>try</u>
4. Write your <u>name</u>   11. Why dont <u>you</u> try
5. Write <u>your</u> name   12. Why <u>dont</u> you try
6. <u>Write</u> your name   13. <u>Why</u> dont you try
7. Heres my <u>pen</u>

Exercise 3   Repetition of tone-units

Listen and repeat, trying to copy the intonation exactly; no transcrip-
tion is given.
What time will they come
A day return to London
The North Pole would be warmer
Have you decided to buy it
I recorded them on cassette

Exercise 4   Partial analysis of tone-units

The items of Exercise 3 will now be said again twice, and you must do
the following things:
a)   Identify the tonic syllable and underline it.
b)   Identify the tone (in these items the only tones used are fall and rise)
       and place the appropriate tone-mark before the tonic syllable.
c)   Identify any stressed syllables preceding the tonic syllable and
       place a stress mark ' before each.
You may need to stop your tape to allow enough time to complete the
analysis of each item.
1. What time will they come
2. A day return to London
3. The North Pole would be warmer
4. Have you decided to buy it
5. I recorded them on cassette

■   Now check your transcription.

Tape Unit 17 Intonation

Exercise 1 Repetition of tonic syllable plus tail

Listen and repeat, taking care to continue the pitch movement of the tone over the tail:

˅Bill ·bought it   ˌ˅Four of them ·came   ˅Why do you ·do it

ˌBill ·bought it   ˌFour of them ·came   ˌWhy do you ·do it

˅Bill ·bought it   ˌFour of them ·came   ˌWhy do you ·do it

ˌBill ·bought it   ˌFour of them ·came   ˌWhy do you ·do it

Exercise 2 Production of tonic syllable plus tail

The items from Exercise 1 will be used again. When you hear the number, say the item with the tone that is marked:
(1 ... 12)

Exercise 3 High and low head

The following tone-units will be repeated with high and low heads. Listen and repeat:

'Taxes have 'risen by 'five per ˅cent

ˌTaxes have ˌrisen by ˌfive per ˅cent

'Havent you 'asked the 'boss for ˌmore

ˌHavent you ˌasked the ˌboss for ˌmore

We 'dont have 'time to 'read the ˅paper

We ˌdont have ˌtime to ˌread the ˅paper

'Wouldnt you 'like to 'read it on the ˌtrain

ˌWouldnt you ˌlike to ˌread it on the ˌtrain

Exercise 4 Transcription of tone-units

Each item will be pronounced as one tone-unit, and will be heard three times. You must do the following things:

a) Identify the tonic syllable and underline it.

b) Decide which tone it carries (only ˅, ˌ and ˌ are used in this exercise) and put the appropriate tone-mark before the tonic syllable.

c) Listen for stressed syllables preceding the tonic syllable and mark them high (') or low (ˌ).

d)   Listen for stressed syllables in the tail and mark them (if there are any) with a raised dot (·).

You will probably need to stop your tape to complete the transcription of each item.

1. Now heres the weather forecast
2. You didnt say anything about rates
3. A few years ago they were top
4. No-one could say the cinema was dead
5. Is there anything you wouldnt eat
6. Have you ever considered writing
7. That was what he claimed to be
8. We try to do our shopping in the market
9. But I never go there now
10. It wouldnt be difficult to find out

Now check your transcriptions. If there is time, you will find it useful to go back to the start of Exercise 4 and practise repeating the items while looking at the transcriptions.

Tape Unit 18   Intonation – extracts from conversation

The following extracts are from the same recorded conversations as were used in Tape Unit 14. Each extract will be heard three times, with four or five seconds between repetitions. Mark the intonation; the instructions for how to do this are given in the text for Tape Unit 17, Exercise 4. In addition, for numbers 10–16 you will need to use the vertical line | to separate tone-units. You should expect this tape to be more difficult than previous intonation tapes!

Transcription

ONE TONE-UNIT

1. it looks like a French magazine
2. the television is plugged in
3. does your colander have a handle
4. ('s) a flap on it
5. you tell me about yours
6. well dark hair
7. more than half way

8. but er not in the other corners
9. a sort of Daily Sketch format newspaper

TWO TONE-UNITS

10. on the top of the lid
11. well theyre on alternate steps theyre not on every step
12. what about the vent at the back
13. and a ladys handbag hanging on a nail on the wall
14. you do the left hand bit of the picture and Ill do the right hand bit
15. were being very particular but we just havent hit upon one of the differences yet

THREE TONE-UNITS

16. and what about your television two knobs in the front

■ Now check your intonation marking.

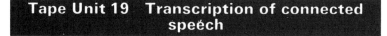

Tape Unit 19 Transcription of connected speech

Listen to the recording on which this exercise is based:
it was rather frightening because there there are scores of these bicycles and er you really have to have your wits about you all the time because the you know they stop suddenly and its awkward because the traffic regulations are more honoured in the breach than the observance I'm not in not really sure what regulations there are er for instance the er traffic lights red red lights do not apply if you're turning right erm which means that if you're coming up to a traffic light and there's erm someone stopped who wants to go straight on or turn left and you want to turn right then you pull out overtake them and then cut across in front

■ The above passage will now be heard divided up into 27 tone-units, each of which will be heard twice. Incomplete tone-units (those without a nucleus) are omitted. The main object of the exercise is to transcribe the intonation; however, for a harder exercise taking more time, you can also write a transcription using phonemic symbols plus any non-phonemic symbols you may need. The transcription given in the answers section is in this form.

▶ it was rather frightening
because there are scores
of these bicycles
you really have to
have your wits about you
all the time
because the you know they stop suddenly
its awkward
because the traffic regulations
are more honoured in the breach
than the observance
Im not in not really sure what
regulations there are
for instance
the er traffic lights
red red lights
do not apply
if youre turning right
which means that
if youre coming up to a traffic light
someone stopped
who wants to go straight on
or turn left
and you want to turn right
then you pull out
overtake them
and then cut across
in front

■ Now check your transcription.

Tape Unit 20 Further practice on connected speech

Exercise 1   Dictation

You will hear five sentences spoken rapidly. Each will be given three times. Write each sentence down *in normal spelling*.
(1 . . . 5)

■ Compare what you have written with the correct version.

▶ Exercise 2   Transcription

Now wind your tape back and listen to the above sentences again; this time *transcribe* what you hear, using mainly phonemic symbols but also using raised h (ʰ) to indicate a weak voiceless vowel, as in pʰteɪtəʊ. Do not mark intonation.
(1 . . . 5)

Exercise 3   Reading intonation

When you hear the number, say the sentence with the intonation indicated. You will then hear the correct pronunciation, which you should repeat.
1. I ˌthought you were on ˎholiday this ·week
2. ˎSome ·day | Im ˌgoing to get ˌround to ˌmending the ˎfuse
3. There were a ˎlot | 'not just 'one or ˎtwo
4. 'Didnt 'anyone 'try to ˎstop them
5. 'Leave it till 'after youve 'had some ˎtea | ˌotherwise youll be ˌtoo ˌfull to ˎeat

Chapter 2

1. *a)* Soft palate or velum
   b) Alveolar ridge
   c) Front of tongue
   d) Hard palate
   e) Lower lip
2. *a)* Close back rounded
   b) Close-mid front unrounded
   c) Open front unrounded
   d) Close front unrounded
   e) Close-mid back rounded

3.

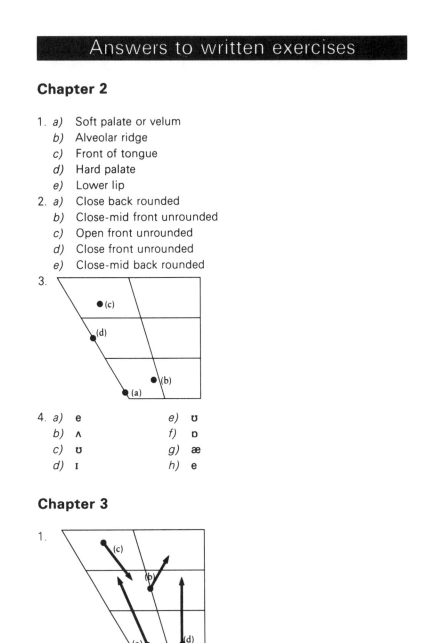

4. *a)* e   *e)* ʊ
   b) ʌ   *f)* ɒ
   c) ʊ   *g)* æ
   d) ɪ   *h)* e

Chapter 3

1.

2. *a)* ɔː   *d)* ɜː   *g)* ɜː
   b) ɔː   *e)* uː   *h)* iː
   c) ɑː   *f)* iː   *i)* ɜː
3. *a)* əʊ   *d)* eɪ   *g)* eə
   b) aɪ   *e)* ɪə   *h)* aɪ
   c) aʊ   *f)* ɔɪ   *i)* eɪ

Chapter 4

1. You will obviously not have written descriptions identical to the ones given below. The important thing is to check that the sequence of articulatory events is more or less the same.

   a) goat
   Starting from the position for normal breathing, the back of the tongue is raised to form a closure against the velum (soft palate). The lungs are compressed to produce higher air pressure in the vocal tract and the vocal folds are brought together in the voicing position. The vocal folds begin to vibrate, and the back of the tongue is lowered to allow the compressed air to escape. The tongue is moved to a mid central vowel and then moves in the direction of a closer, backer vowel; the lips are moderately rounded for the second part. The tongue blade is raised to make a closure against the alveolar ridge, the vocal folds are separated and voicing ceases. Then the compressed air is released quietly and the lips return to an unrounded shape.

   b) ape
   The tongue is moved slightly upward and forward and the vocal folds are brought together to begin voicing. The tongue glides to a slightly closer and more central vowel. Then the lips are pressed together making a closure and at the same time the vocal folds are separated so that voicing ceases. The lips are then opened and the compressed air is released quietly, while the tongue is lowered to the position for normal breathing.

2. *a)* tiː   *d)* dɑ̆ːk   *g)* eg
   b) mi̽ːt   *e)* kɑːd   *h)* ə̆ʊk
   c) təʊd   *f)* li̽p   *i)* ka̽ɪt

3. *a)* beɪk   *d)* bɔːt   *g)* bɔːd
   b) gəʊt   *e)* tɪk   *h)* gɑːd
   c) daʊt   *f)* baʊ   *i)* piːk

Chapter 5

a) 'speed'   spiːd   [spiːḍ]
b) 'partake'   pɑːteɪk   [pʰaˑtʰə̆ɪk]
c) 'book'   bʊk   [b̥ʊ̆k]
d) 'goat'   gəʊt   [g̥ə̆ʊt]
e) 'car'   kɑː   [kʰɑː]
f) 'bad'   bæd   [b̥æḍ]
g) 'appeared'   əpɪəd   [əpʰɪəḍ]
h) 'toast'   təʊst   [tʰə̆ʊst]
i) 'stalk'   stɔːk   [stɔˑk]

Chapter 6

1. *a)* fɪʃɪz   *e)* ətʃiːvz

   b) ʃeɪvə   *f)* ʌðəz

   c) sɪksθ   *g)* meʒə

   d) ðiːz   *h)* əhed

2. Starting from the position for normal breathing, the lower lip is brought into contact with the upper teeth. The lungs are compressed, causing air to flow through the constriction producing fricative noise. The tongue moves to the position for ɪ. The vocal folds are brought together, causing voicing to begin, and at the same time the lower lip is lowered. Then the tongue blade is raised to make a fairly wide constriction in the palato-alveolar region and the vocal folds are separated to stop voicing; the flow of air causes fricative noise. Next, the vocal folds are brought together to begin voicing again and at the same time the tongue is lowered from the constriction position into the ɪ vowel posture. The tongue blade is then raised against the alveolar ridge forming a constriction which results in fricative noise. This is initially accompanied by voicing, which then dies away. Finally, the tongue is lowered from the alveolar constriction, the vocal folds are separated and normal breathing is resumed.

Chapter 7

1. Plosives: **p t k b d g**

   Fricatives: **f θ s ʃ h v ð z ʒ**

   Affricates: **tʃ dʒ**

   Nasals: **m n ŋ**

   Lateral: **l**

   Approximants: **r w j**

   (This course has also mentioned the possibility of **ç** and **ʍ**)

2. *a)* səʊfə   *e)* skweə

   b) vɜːs   *f)* æŋgə

   c) stɪərɪŋ   *g)* bɔːt

   d) bredkrʌm   *h)* naɪntiːn

3. *a)* The soft palate is raised for the **b** plosive and remains raised for **æ**. It is lowered for **n**, then raised again for the final **ə**.

   b) The soft palate remains lowered during the articulation of **m**, and is then raised for the rest of the syllable.

   c) The soft palate is raised for the **æ** vowel, then lowered for **ŋ**. It is then raised for the **g** plosive and remains raised for the **l**.

Chapter 8

a)

PRE-INITIAL	INITIAL	POST-INITIAL	PEAK	FINAL	POST-FINAL
s	k	w	iː	l	d

ONSET   PEAK   CODA

(It would be possible to treat l as pre-final and d as final, but the above analysis is slightly preferable in that d here is a suffix and we know that l occurs finally in 'squeal' skwiːl.)

b)

	FINAL	POST-FINAL 1	POST-FINAL 2
eɪ	t	θ	s

PEAK   CODA

c)

PRE-INITIAL	INITIAL	POST-INITIAL		FINAL
s	p	l	æ	ʃ

ONSET   PEAK   CODA

d)

INITIAL		FINAL	POST-FINAL 1	POST-FINAL 2	POST-FINAL 3
t	e	k	s	t	s

ONSET   PEAK   CODA

Chapter 9

1. ə pətɪkjələ prɒbləm əv ðə bəʊt wəz ə liːk
2. əʊpn̩ɪŋ ðə bɒtl̩ prɪzentɪd nəʊ dɪfɪkl̩ti
3. ðər ɪz nəʊ ɒltɜːnətɪv tə ðə gʌvn̩mənts prəpəʊzl̩
4. wi ɔːt tə meɪk ə kəlekʃn̩ tə kʌvə ði ɪkspensɪz
   (also possible: kl̩ekʃn̩)
5. faɪnli ðeɪ əraɪvd ət ə haːbər ət ði edʒ əv ðə maʊntɪnz
   (haːbr̩ possible).

J

Chapter 10

1. a) pro'tect   prə'tekt
   b) 'clamber   'klæmbə
   c) fes'toon   fes'tu:n
   d) de'test   dɪ'test
   e) 'bellow   'beləʊ
   f) 'menace   'menɪs
   g) disco'nnect   dɪskə'nekt
   h) 'entering   'entərɪŋ   ('entr̩ɪŋ)
2. a) 'language   'læŋgwɪdʒ
   b) 'captain   'kæptɪn
   c) ca'reer   kə'rɪə
   d) 'paper   'peɪpə
   e) e'vent   ɪ'vent
   f) 'jonquil   'dʒɒŋkwɪl
   g) 'injury   'ɪndʒəri   ('ɪndʒr̩i)
   h) co'nnection   kə'nekʃən   (kə'nekʃn̩)

Chapter 11

1. and 2.
   a) 'shop ˌfitter   'ʃɒp ˌfɪtə
   b) ˌopen 'ended   ˌəʊpn̩ 'endɪd
   c) 'Java'nese   ˌdʒɑːvə'niːz
   d) 'birth ˌmark   'bɜːθ ˌmɑːk
   e) ˌanti 'clockwise   ˌænti 'klɒkwaɪz
   f) ˌconfir'mation   ˌkɒnfə'meɪʃn̩
   g) ˌeight 'sided   ˌeɪt 'saɪdɪd
   h) 'fruit ˌcake   'fruːt ˌkeɪk
   i) de'fective   dɪ'fektɪv
   j) 'roof ˌtimber   'ruːf ˌtɪmbə

Chapter 12

1. aɪ wɒnt ə tə pɑːk ðæt kɑːr əʊvə ðeə
2. əv ɔːl ðə prəpəʊzl̩z ðə wʌn ðət ju: meɪd ɪz ðə sɪliəst
3. dʒeɪn ən bɪl kəd əv drɪvn̩ ðəm tu: ən frɒm ðə pɑːti
   (kʊd is also suitable)
4. tə kʌm tə ðə pɔɪnt wɒt ʃl̩ wi du: fə ðə rest əv ðə wiːk
5. həz eniwʌn gɒt ən aɪdɪə weər ɪt keɪm frɒm
6. pədestrɪənz məst ɔːlwɪz ju:z ðə krɒsɪŋz prəvaɪdɪd
7. iːtʃ wʌn wəz ə pɜːfɪkt ɪgzɑːmpl̩ əv ðɪ ɑːt ðət əd biːn dɪveləpt ðeə

Chapter 13

1. In this data there is no evidence of ŋ contrasting with n, since ŋ never occurs except before k and g. So all phonetic ŋ consonants are phonemic n.
   - *a)* θɪŋg
   - *b)* θɪŋk
   - *c)* θɪŋkɪŋ
   - *d)* fɪŋgə
   - *e)* sɪŋə
   - *f)* sɪŋɪŋ
2. *a)* saʊnd
   - *b)* æŋgə
   - *c)* kɑːnt
   - *d)* kæmpə
   - *e)* bɒnd
3. /t/ is realised as [ɾ] when it occurs between vowels if the preceding vowel is stressed and the following vowel is unstressed.

Chapter 14

1. *a)* A | bird in the | hand is worth | two in the | bush
   - *b)* | Over a | quarter of a | century has e | lapsed since his | death
   - *c)* Com | puters con | sume a con | siderable a | mount of | money and | time
   - *d)* | Most of them have ar | rived on the | bus
   - *e)* | Newspaper | editors are in | variably | under | worked
2. *a)*   *b)*

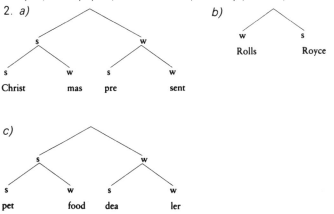

c)

d)

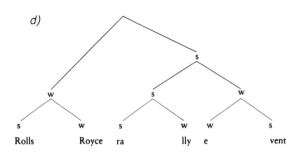

Rolls   Royce   ra   lly   e   vent

(The stress levels of 'Rolls' and 'Royce' are exchanged to avoid "stress clash" between 'Royce' and 'ra-'.)

3. *a)* wʌŋ kɔːz əv æsmənsspəʊstəbi æledʒɪz
   b) wɒt ði ɜːbm̩ pɒpjəleɪʃn̩ kədʒuːz ɪz betə treɪnz
   c) ʃi æks pətɪkjəli wel ɪn̩nə fɜːssiːn
   (The above represent just one possible pronunciation; many others are possible.)

Chapter 15

1. This train is for ˌLeeds ˌYork ˌDarlington and ˌDurham
2. Can you give me a ˌlift
   ˌPossibly   Wheɪə ˌto
3. ˌNo   Certainly ˌnot   Go a ˌway↑
4. Did you know hed been convicted of drunken ˌdriving ˌNo
5. If I give him ˌmoney he goes and ˌspends it
   If I lend him the ˌbike he ˌloses it
   Hes completely unreˌliable

Chapter 16

1. (This is an exercise where there is not one correct answer.)
   a) <u>buy</u> it for me
   b) <u>hear</u> it
   c) <u>talk</u> to him
2. *a)* 'mind the <u>step</u>
   b) 'this is the 'ten to 'seven <u>train</u>
   c) 'keep the 'food <u>hot</u>
3. *a)* 'Only when the ˌwind blows

b) ‚When did you say

c) 'What was the ‚name of the place

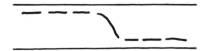

Chapter 17

1. a) 'Which was the ‚cheap one did you say

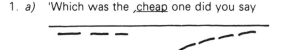

b) I 'only 'want to ‚taste it

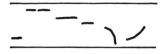

c) ‚She would have ‚thought it was ‚obvious

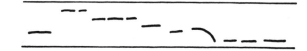

d) There 'wasnt 'even a 'piece of ‚bread in the ·house

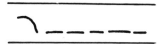

e) ‚Now will you be·lieve me

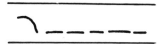

2. *a)* opport͵unity

b) ͵actually

c) ͵confidently

d) mag͵nificent

e) re͵lationship

f) after͵noon

Chapter 18

(The following are possible intonation patterns, but others could be correct.)

1. Its 'rather ͵cold
2. Be'cause I 'cant a͵fford it
3. Youre ͵silly then
4. Oh ͵please
5. ͵Seven o͵clock ͵seven ͵thirty and ͵eight
6. ͵Eight
7. Ive ͵got to ͵do the ͵shopping
8. ͵Some of them ·might

Chapter 19

1. *a)* <u>right</u> can I do the <u>shop</u>ping for you
   b) <u>right</u> can I do the shopping for <u>you</u>
   c) first the professor explained her <u>theory</u>
   d) <u>no</u> first the prof<u>ess</u>or explained her theory
   e) first she exp<u>lained</u> her theory
   f) <u>no</u> ten <u>past</u> three
   g) <u>no</u> <u>ten</u> past three
   h) <u>no</u> ten past <u>three</u>
2. *a)* he wrote the letter <u>sad</u>ly
   b) he wrote the <u>letter</u> | <u>sad</u>ly
   c) four plus <u>six</u> | divided by <u>two</u> | equals <u>five</u>
   d) <u>four</u> | plus six divided by <u>two</u> | equals <u>seven</u>
   e) we broke <u>one</u> thing | after another fell <u>down</u>
   f) we broke one thing after an<u>other</u> | that <u>night</u>

Chapter 20

1. *a)* All are made further back then the palatal region – they could be called "back" consonants.
   b) All the vowels are close or close mid (or between these heights).
   c) All require the tongue blade to be raised for their articulation, and all are in the alveolar or post-alveolar region.
   d) None of these requires the raising of the tongue blade – all are front or back articulations.
   e) All are voiceless.
   f) All are rounded or end with lip-rounding.
   g) All are approximants (they create very little obstruction to the airflow).
2. *a)* This accent has a distribution for ŋ similar to RP (i.e. a case can be made for a ŋ phoneme), except that in the case of the participial '-ing' ending n is found instead of ŋ.
   b) This accent has two additional long vowels (e: and o:) and, correspondingly, two fewer diphthongs (eɪ and əʊ). This situation is found in many Northern accents.
   c) The fricatives θ, ð and h are missing from the phoneme inventory, and f and v are used in their place. /l/ is realised as [w] where RP has "dark l". This is typical of a Cockney accent.
   d) This data is based on the traditional working-class accent of Bristol, where words of more than one syllable cannot end in ə. The accent is rhotic, so where there is an 'r' in the spelling (as in 'mother') a r is pronounced; where the spelling does not have 'r', a

/l/ sound is added, resulting in some loss of distinctiveness in words (cf. 'idea', 'ideal'; 'area', 'aerial').

e)   Here we appear to have three vowels where RP has two: the word 'cat' has the equivalent of æ, 'calm' has a vowel similar to ɑː while in the set of words that have æ in many Northern accents ('plaster', 'grass', etc.) an additional long vowel aː is used. This is found in Shropshire.

Tape Unit 2

Exercise 2

1. æ in bæn 'ban'
2. ʌ in hʌb 'hub'
3. ɪ in fɪl 'fill'
4. ɒ in mɒs 'moss'
5. e in led 'led'
6. ʊ in pʊt 'put'
7. ʌ in kʌm 'come'
8. ɪ in mɪd 'mid'
9. ɒ in bɒm 'bomb'
10. e in sel 'sell'

Tape Unit 3

Exercise 3

1. iː in siːt 'seat'
2. ɑː in dɑːk 'dark'
3. ɜː in bɜːd 'bird'
4. ɔː in fɔːt 'fought'
5. ɑː in pɑːt 'part'
6. uː in fuːd 'food'
7. ɜː in kɜːt 'curt'
8. ɑː in pɑːk 'park'
9. iː in niːd 'need'
10. ɔː in hɔːs 'horse'

Exercise 5

1. ɜː in hɜːd 'heard'
2. ɒ in sɒŋ 'song'
3. ɔː in sɔː 'saw'
4. ʌ in kʌm 'come'
5. ɑː in mɑːtʃ 'march'
6. ʊ in fʊl 'full'
7. ɑː in pɑːt 'part'
8. ɒ in dɒl 'doll'
9. ʌ in lʌv 'love'
10. ɜː in bɜːn 'burn'

Exercise 7

1. ɪə in fɪəs 'fierce'
2. eə in keəd 'cared'
3. ʊə in mʊəz 'moors'
4. eɪ in reɪd 'raid'
5. aɪ in taɪm 'time'
6. əʊ in kəʊt 'coat'
7. aɪ in kaɪt 'kite'
8. ɪə in bɪəd 'beard'
9. ʊə in tʊəz 'tours'
10. əʊ in bəʊn 'bone'
11. ɔɪ in bɔɪl 'boil'
12. aʊ in taʊn 'town'

Tape Unit 4

Exercise 3

1. p in 'harp' hɑːp
2. g in 'rogue' rəʊg
3. t in 'eight' eɪt
4. d in 'ride' raɪd
5. b in 'mob' mɒb

6. k in 'ache' eɪk
7. d in 'ode' əʊd
8. p in 'rip' rɪp
9. g in 'sag' sæg
10. t in 'feet' fiːt

Exercise 5

1. 'debate'
2. 'copied'
3. 'buttercup'
4. 'cuckoo'
5. 'decayed'

6. 'guarded'
7. 'dedicated'
8. 'paddock'
9. 'boutique'
10. 'appetite'

Tape Unit 5

Exercise 3

1. geɪt 'gate'
2. kəʊt 'coat'
3. bɪt 'bit'
4. taɪəd 'tired'
5. biːt 'beat'
6. pəʊk 'poke'
7. kɑːt 'cart'
8. kɔːt 'caught'
9. paʊə 'power'
10. kɔːd 'cord'

11. gæp 'gap'
12. bɪəd 'beard'
13. kɑː 'car'
14. peɪd 'paid'
15. gʌt 'gut'
16. daʊt 'doubt'
17. təʊd 'toad'
18. duː 'do'
19. peə 'pair'
20. dek 'deck'

Exercise 4

1. keep
2. boat
3. cup
4. dirt
5. bike
6. cab
7. gate
8. cared
9. tired
10. bird

11. duck
12. cope
13. dog
14. coward
15. bake
16. tied
17. beard
18. put
19. bug
20. doubt

Tape Unit 6

Exercise 2

a) initial position
1. ʃ in ʃəʊ 'show'
2. θ in θaɪ 'thigh'
3. z in zuː 'zoo'
4. f in fɑː 'far'
5. ð in ðəʊ 'though'

b) medial position
6. v in əʊvə 'over'
7. ʒ in meʒə 'measure'
8. s in aɪsɪŋ 'icing'
9. ʃ in eɪʃə 'Asia'
10. h in əhed 'ahead'

c) final position
11. ð in ləʊð 'loathe'
12. v in iːv 'Eve'
13. ʃ in æʃ 'ash'
14. f in rʌf 'rough'
15. θ in əʊθ 'oath'

Tape Unit 7

Exercise 6

1. juːʒʊəl 'usual'
2. rɪmeɪn 'remain'
3. eksəsaɪz 'exercise'
4. weərɪŋ 'wearing'
5. ɜːdʒənt 'urgent'
6. mɪnɪməm 'minimum'
7. vaɪələns 'violence'
8. emfəsɪs 'emphasis'
9. dʒentlɪ 'gently'
10. θɪŋkɪŋ 'thinking'
11. taɪpraɪtə 'typewriter'
12. jɪəlɪ 'yearly'

Tape Unit 8

Exercise 6 (Spellings)

1. 'scraped'
2. 'grudged'
3. 'clothes'
4. 'scripts'
5. 'crunched'
6. 'thrones'
7. 'plunged'
8. 'quench'

Tape Unit 9

Exercise 5

Note: The spelling is also given, but only the transcription was wanted for the correct answer.

1. 'gɑːdn̩ə 'gardener'
2. 'kɒləm 'column'
3. 'hændl̩z 'handles'
4. ə'laɪv 'alive'
5. prɪ'tend 'pretend'
6. 'sʌdn̩ 'sudden'
7. 'kæləs 'callous'
8. 'θretn̩ɪŋ threatening'
9. pə'laɪt 'polite'
10. 'pʌzl̩ 'puzzle'

Tape Unit 10

Exercise 1

1. 'enɪmi
2. kə'lekt
3. 'kæpɪtl̩
4. kɑː'neɪʃn̩
5. 'pærədaɪs
6. səb'trækt
7. 'elɪfənt
8. əb'zɜːvə
9. 'prɒfɪt
10. entə'teɪn

Exercise 2 (Spellings)

1. Shrewsbury
2. Polperro
3. Aberdeen
4. Wolverhampton
5. Aberystwyth
6. Birmingham
7. Northampton
8. Dundee
9. Canterbury
10. Basingstoke

Tape Unit 12

Exercise 3

1. 'liːv ðə 'rest əv ðə 'fuːd fə 'lʌnʃ
2. 'ɑːnt ðə səm 'letəz fər ə tu 'əʊpən
3. 'weə də ði 'egz kʌm frɒm
4. 'riːd ɪz 'bʊk ən 'raɪt səm 'nəʊts
5. ət 'liːst wi kən 'traɪ ən 'help

Tape Unit 13

Exercise 1 (Spellings)

1. Colchester
2. Carlisle
3. Hereford
4. Scunthorpe
5. Glamorgan
6. Holyhead
7. Framlingham
8. Southend
9. Cheltenham
10. Inverness

Exercise 2

1. ˈlestəʃə (Leicestershire)
2. dʌnˈfɜːmlɪn (Dunfermline)
3. ˈstiːvn̩dʒ (Stevenage)
4. penˈzæns (Penzance)
5. ˈgɪlfəd (Guildford)
6. kəʊlˈreɪn (Coleraine)
7. ˈhʌdəsfiːld (Huddersfield)
8. heɪlzˈəʊɪn (Halesowen)
9. ˈwɪlmzləʊ (Wilmslow)
10. ˈbɑːnstəpl̩ (Barnstaple)

Exercise 3

1. ˈJames deˈcided to ˈtype the ˈletter himˈself
2. The ˈplane was appˈroaching the ˈrunway at ˈhigh ˈspeed
3. ˈTry to ˈsee the ˈother ˈpersons ˈpoint of ˈview
4. You ˈput your ˈbrakes on when the ˈlight ˈturns to ˈred
5. In a ˈshort ˈtime the ˈhouse was ˈfull of ˈchildren

Tape Unit 14

Note: When recordings of conversational speech are used it is no longer possible to give definite decisions about "right" and "wrong" answers. Some problems, points of interest and alternative possibilities are mentioned.

1. ə bjuːtʰfl̩ gɜːl (Careful speech would have had bjuːtɪfl̩ or bjuːtɪfʊl.)
2. wi siːm tə hæv ə defnət wʌn ðeə (Careful speech would have defɪnɪt, defɪnət or defn̩ət; notice that this speaker uses a glottal stop at the end of 'definite' so the transcription – phonetic rather than phonemic – defnəʔ would be acceptable. There is a good example of assimilation in the pronunciation of 'one there'; as often happens when n and ð are combined, the n becomes dental n̪. In addition, the ð loses its friction – which is always weak – and becomes a dental nasal, so that this could be transcribed phonetically as wʌn̪n̪eə.)
3. kʊd ɪt bi ə stuːl rɑːððn̩ə teɪbl̩ (Careful speech would have rɑːðə ðən ə; the ð is long, so the symbol is written twice to indicate this.)

4. ə fɪθ ɪn (Careful speech would have fɪfθ; the transcription cannot, of course, show very fine details of articulation, but it is likely that though the sound one hears is most like θ there is some slight constriction between upper teeth and lower lip as well.)

5. eni pʰkjuːljærətɪz əbaʊt ðæt (The main elision is of the ɪ vowel in the first syllable of 'peculiarities'; a less noticeable case is that instead of having i before the æ in this word the speaker has a non-syllabic j; note the glottal stop at the end of 'about'.)

6. æn haʊ mni straɪps ɒn jɔːz (Careful speech would have meni; it is perhaps surprising that the speaker has æ rather than ə in 'and'; jɔːz is a frequently found alternative pronunciation to jʊəz.)

7. wel ɪt əpɪəz tə bʌtn̩ ʌp ɪs gɒt θriː (The elision is in 'its'; careful speech would have ɪts or, since this speaker uses glottal stops quite frequently – notice one between 'it' and 'appears' and another at the end of 'got' – ɪʔs.)

8. ɔːðə wɒtʃəkɔːl ɪt ðə sɪl ('What do you call it' or 'what d'you call it' is used frequently when speakers cannot remember a word.)

9. baɪ kɒləm ɪntʰ kɒləmz ɔːraɪt (Careful speech would have ɪntə and ɔːl raɪt.)

10. daɪəmən ʃeɪp pætʃ (Careful speech would have daɪəmənd ʃeɪpt pætʃ.)

11. ænd aɪ ʃd θɪŋk frəm ɪkspɪrɪəns f kɪtʃɪn naɪvz Careful speech would have ʃʊd or ʃəd and əv.)

12. wɒt ʃ wi duː: neks gəʊ daʊn (Careful speech would have ʃəl and nekst.)

13. ðiː tɒp f ðə bɒtl̩ ɪz pr̩dʒektɪŋ aʊtwədz ɪntʰ ðə ruːm (Careful speech would have əv, prədʒektɪŋ and ɪntə; the r in 'projecting' is devoiced as well as being syllabic; notice the glottal stops, one before the k in 'projecting' and another before the t in 'outwards'; the strong form of 'the' at the beginning is probably a sort of slight hesitation.)

Tape Unit 15

Exercise 3

1. ˶one	6. ˏsix
2. ˎtwo	7. ˎnow
3. ˏthree	8. ˶you
4. ˆfour	9. ˆmore
5. ˎfive	10. ˏus

Tape Unit 16

Exercise 1

1. We could go by <u>bus</u>
2. Of <u>course</u> its broken
3. The car was where Id <u>left</u> it
4. How much is the <u>biggest</u> one
5. I <u>knew</u> it would go wrong
6. It was too <u>cold</u>
7. <u>Here</u> it is
8. That <u>was</u> a loud noise
9. We could go from <u>Man</u>chester
10. Have you <u>finished</u>

Exercise 4

1. 'What 'time will they ‚<u>come</u>
2. A 'day re'turn to ‚<u>London</u>
3. The 'North ‚<u>Pole</u> would be warmer
4. 'Have you de'cided to ‚<u>buy</u> it
5. I re'corded them on cas‚<u>sette</u>

Tape Unit 17

Exercise 4

1. 'Now 'heres the ‚<u>weather</u> ·forecast
2. You ‚didnt say ‚anything about ‚<u>rates</u>
3. A ‚few ‚years ago they were ‚<u>top</u>
4. 'No-one could 'say the 'cinema was ‚<u>dead</u>
5. Is there ‚<u>anything</u> you ·wouldnt ·eat
6. 'Have you 'ever con'sidered ‚<u>writing</u>
7. ‚That was ‚what he ‚<u>claimed</u> to be
8. We 'try to do 'our 'shopping in the ‚<u>market</u>
9. But I ‚<u>never</u> ·go there ·now
10. It ‚wouldnt be ‚difficult to find ‚<u>out</u>

Tape Unit 18

Note: Since these extracts were not spoken deliberately for illustrating intonation, it is not possible to claim that the transcription given here is the only correct version. There are several places where other transcriptions would be acceptable, and suggestions about alternative possibilities are given with some items, in addition to a few other comments.

1. it 'looks like a 'French maga˛zine   (slight hesitation between 'looks' and 'like')
2. the 'television 'is plugged ˌin
3. 'does your 'colander have a ˛handle   ('does' possibly not stressed)
4. a ˌflap on it
5. 'you tell me about ˌyours   (narrow pitch movement on 'yours'; 'tell' may also be stressed)
6. 'well ˛dark hair
7. ˌmore than ˌhalf ˌway
8. but er 'not in the ˛other ·corners
9. a ˌsort of ˌDaily ˛Sketch ·format ·newspaper   ('sort' possibly not stressed)
10. 'on the ˛top | 'on the ˛lid   (both pronunciations of 'on' might be unstressed)
11. well theyre 'on alˌternate ·steps | theyre 'not on ˛every ·step
12. 'what about the ˛vent | at the ˛back
13. and a 'ladys ˛handbag | ˌhanging on a ˌnail on the ˛wall
14. 'you do the ˛left hand ·bit of the ·picture | and ˌIll do the ˛right hand ·bit
15. were being 'very parˌticular | but we 'just havent 'hit upon 'one of the ˛differences ·yet   (stress on 'just' is weak or absent)
16. and 'what about your teleˌvision | 'two ˌknobs | in the ˌfront |

Tape Unit 19

Note: transcription of natural speech involves making decisions that have the effect of simplifying complex phonetic events. The broad transcription given below is not claimed to be completely accurate, nor to be the only "correct" version.

ɪwəz 'rɑːðə ˛fraɪʔnɪŋ
bɪkəz ðə ðərə ˛skɔːz
ə ðiːz ˛baɪs k|z
ju 'riːli ˛hæv tʊ
'hæv jə wɪts əˌbaʊtʃu
'ɔːl ðə ˛taɪm
bɪkəz ðə jə nəʊ ðə ðeɪ ˛stɒp ·sʌdn̩li
ɪts -ɔːkwəd
bkəz ðə ˛træfɪk regjə·leɪʃn̩z
ˌɑːmɔː ˌɒnəd ɪn ðə ˛briːtʃ
ðən ði əb ˛zɜːvəns
aɪm 'nɒt ɪn ˛nɒt riːli ·ʃɔː wɒt

ˌregjəleɪʃn̩z ðər ˌɑː
fr̩ˌɪnstəns
ðɪː ə ˌtræfɪk ·laɪts
'red ˌred ·laɪts
'duː nɒt ə ˌplaɪ
fjɔː 'tɜːnɪŋ ˌraɪt
wɪtʃ ˌmiːnz ðət
'ɪf jə kʌmɪŋ 'ʌp tu ə ˌtræfɪk ·laɪt
'sʌmwʌn ˌstɒpt
huˌwɒnts tə ˌgəʊ streɪt ˌɒn
ɔː ˌtɜːn ˌleft
ən 'juː wɒnt tə tɜːn ˌraɪt
ðen ju 'pʊl ˌaʊt
ˌəʊvə ˌteɪk ðəm
ən ðen 'kʌt ə ˌkrɒs
ɪn ˌfrʌnt

Tape Unit 20

Exercise 1

1. I suppose the best thing is to try later.
2. If he's coming today there ought to be a letter around.
3. The world's greatest lawn tennis festival begins on Monday.
4. We've fixed for the repair man to come and mend it under guarantee.
5. The number's been engaged for over an hour.

Exercise 2

1. aɪ spəʊz ð bes θɪŋz tʰ traɪ leɪtə
2. ɪf ɪz kʌmɪŋ tʰdeɪ ðr̩ ɔːt tʰ bi ə letr̩ ɹaʊnd
3. ðə wɜːlz greɪts lɔːn tenɪs festʰvl̩ bɪgɪnz ɒm mʌndeɪ
4. wɪf fɪks fə ðə ɹpeə mæn tʰ kʌm əm mend ɪt ʌndə gærn̩tiː
5. ð nʌmbəz bɪn ɪŋgeɪdʒ fr̩ əʊvr̩ ən aʊə

Recommendations for general reading

References to reading on specific topics are given at the end of each chapter. The following is a list of basic books and papers recommended for broader areas of study: if you wish to go more fully into any of these areas you would do well to start by reading these. I would consider it very desirable that any library provided for students using this book should possess most or all of the books listed.

1. English phonetics and phonology

There are two major text-books in this area (sometimes irreverently known as the Old Testament and the New Testament): the older one is D. Jones, *An Outline of English Phonetics* (1918; 9th edition, Cambridge University Press, 1975); the newer one is A. C. Gimson, *An Introduction to the Pronunciation of English* (1962; 4th edition, revised by S. Ramsaran, London: Edward Arnold, 1989). Gimson's book is, not surprisingly, more up to date than Jones', and has the additional advantage of using almost exactly the same symbols as those used in this course. However, the Jones book contains much of value and of interest; both books are valuable sources of information for students who wish to go on to more advanced and detailed study after working through this course. A well-established and popular book at a much simpler level is J. D. O'Connor, *Better English Pronunciation* (2nd edition Cambridge University Press, 1980).

Two more recent books that approach the subject in rather different ways are G. Knowles, *Patterns of Spoken English* (London: Longman, 1987) and C. Kreidler, *The Pronunciation of English* (Oxford: Blackwell, 1989). There is a valuable collection of up-to-date papers on English phonetics in S. Ramsaran (ed.), *Studies in the Pronunciation of English* (London: Routledge, 1990), many of which give an idea of how research in this field is developing.

2. General phonetics

There are two good introductory books: one is P. Ladefoged, *A Course in Phonetics* (New York: Harcourt Brace Jovanovich, 1982) and the other is J. D. O'Connor *Phonetics* (Harmondsworth: Penguin, 1973). D. Abercrombie, *Elements of General Phonetics* (Edinburgh University Press, 1967) is also good, but less suitable as basic introductory reading. Catford, *A Practical Introduc-*

tion to Phonetics (Oxford University Press, 1988) is good for explaining the nature of practical phonetics. See also J. Laver, *Principles of Phonetics* (Cambridge University Press, forthcoming).

3. Phonology

Several books have appeared in recent years that explain the basic elements of phonological theory. P. Hawkins, *Introducing Phonology* (London: Hutchinson, 1984) and F. Katamba, *An Introduction to Phonology* (London: Longman: 1989) are the most basic. R. Lass, *Phonology: an introduction to basic concepts* (Cambridge University Press, 1984) is more advanced.

Covering both this area and the previous one in a readable and comprehensive way is J. Clark and C. Yallop, *An Introduction to Phonetics and Phonology* (Oxford: Blackwell, 1990).

The classic work on the generative phonology of English is N. Chomsky and M. Halle, *The Sound Pattern of English* (New York: Harper & Row, 1968); most people find this very difficult.

4. Accents of English

The major work in this area is J. C. Wells, *Accents of English*, 3 vols. (Cambridge University Press, 1982), a large and very valuable work which deals with accents of English throughout the world. A shorter and much easier introduction is A. Hughes and P. Trudgill, *English Accents and Dialects* (London: Edward Arnold, 1987).

5. Pronunciation teaching

A general book on the subject is MacCarthy, *The Teaching of Pronunciation* (Cambridge University Press, 1978). For English in particular, A. C. Gimson, *An Introduction to the Pronunciation of English* (4th edition, London: Edward Arnold, 1989), chapter 12 is worth reading. Among books written specifically about the teaching of English pronunciation, I would recommend A. Baker, *Introducing English Pronunciation* (Cambridge University Press, 1982), R. Hooke and J. Rowell, *A Handbook of English Pronunciation* (London: Edward Arnold, 1982) and J. Kenworthy, *Teaching English Pronunciation* (London: Longman, 1987).

6. Pronunciation dictionaries

Most modern English dictionaries now print one or more recommended pronunciations for each word listed, so for most purposes a dictionary which gives only pronunciations and not meanings is hardly worth having unless it gives a lot more information than an ordinary dictionary could. For many years the standard work has been the Everyman *English Pronouncing Dictionary* (originally by D. Jones; 14th edition revised by A. C. Gimson, London: Dent, 1977). The more recently published *Longman Pronouncing Dictionary* (J. C. Wells, London: Longman, 1990) contains much more information, and is recommended.

7. Intonation

Two important textbooks are D. Crystal *Prosodic Systems and Intonation* (Cambridge University Press, 1969) and A. Cruttenden *Intonation* (Cambridge University Press, 1986). Both of these deal with theoretical matters. Also recommended is E. Couper-Kuhlen, *An Introduction to English Prosody* (London: Edward Arnold, 1986). More practical guides are D. Brazil, M. Coulthard and C. Johns, *Discourse Intonation and Language Teaching* (London: Longman, 1980), V. Cook, *Using Intonation* (London: Longman, 1979) and J. D. O'Connor and G. F. Arnold, *The Intonation of Colloquial English* (2nd edition, London: Longman, 1973).

8. Stress

As suggested in the chapters dealing with this subject, E. Fudge, *English Word Stress* (London: Allen and Unwin, 1984) is a useful text-book on word stress. R. Kingdon, *The Groundwork of English Stress* (London: Longman, 1958) is still useful. On "sentence stress", see S. Schmerling, *Aspects of English Sentence Stress* (Austin: University of Texas Press, 1976).

Bibliography

Abercrombie, D. (1964) 'Syllable quantity and enclitics in English' in D. Abercrombie *et al.*, pp. 216–22

Abercrombie, D. (1965) 'RP and local accent' in *Studies in Phonetics and Linguistics*, pp. 10–15, Oxford University Press

Abercrombie, D. (1967) *Elements of General Phonetics*, Edinburgh University Press

Abercrombie, D., Fry, D. B., MacCarthy, P. A. D., Scott, N. C. and Trim, J. L. M. (eds.) (1964) *In Honour of Daniel Jones*, London: Longman

Adams, C. (1979) *English Speech Rhythm and the Foreign Learner*, The Hague: Mouton

Albright, R. W. (1958) 'The International Phonetic Alphabet: its backgrounds and development', *International Journal of American Linguistics*, vol. 24, no. 1

Arnold, G. F. (1957) 'Stress in English words', *Lingua*, vol. 6, no. 4, pp. 221–67

Arnold, G. F. (1967) 'Concerning the theory of plosives', *Le Maître Phonétique*, no. 125, reprinted in W. E. Jones and J. Laver (1973), pp. 29–32

Ashby, M. G. (1979) Review of A. Malecot, 'Contribution a l'étude de la force d'articulation en français', *Journal of the International Phonetic Association*, vol. 9, no. 2, pp. 74–80

Baker, A. (1982) *Introducing English Pronunciation*, Cambridge University Press

Bauer, L. (1983) *English Word-Formation*, Cambridge University Press

Bloomfield, L. (1933) *Language*, London: Allen and Unwin

Bolinger, D. (1951) 'Intonation – levels vs. configurations', *Word*, vol. 7, pp. 199–210

Bolinger, D. (1972) 'Accent is predictable (if you're a mind-reader)', *Language*, vol. 48, pp. 633–44

Borden, G. and Harris, K. S. (1984) *A Speech Science Primer*, 2nd edition, London: Williams and Wilkins

Brazil, D., Coulthard, M. and Johns, C. (1980) *Discourse Intonation and Language Teaching*, London: Longman

Brown, G. (1990) *Listening to Spoken English*, 2nd edition, London: Longman (1st edition 1977)

Brown, G., Curry, K. and Kenworthy, J. (1980) *Questions of Intonation*, London: Croom Helm

Brown, G. and Yule, G. (1983) *Teaching the Spoken Language*, Cambridge University Press

Catford, J. C. (1964) 'Phonation types', in D. Abercrombie *et al.*, pp. 26–37

Catford, J. C. (1968) 'The articulatory possibilities of man', in B. Malmberg (ed.) *Manual of Phonetics*, pp. 309–33, Amsterdam: North Holland

Catford, J. C. (1977) *Fundamental Problems in Phonetics*, Edinburgh University Press

Catford, J. C. (1988) *A Practical Introduction to Phonetics*, Oxford University Press

Chen, M. (1970) 'Vowel length variation as a function of the voicing of the consonant environment', *Phonetica*, vol. 22, pp. 129–59

Chomsky, N. and Halle, M. (1968) *The Sound Pattern of English*, New York: Harper and Row

Clark, J. and Yallop, C. (1990) *An Introduction to Phonetics and Phonology*, Oxford: Blackwell

Cook, V. (1979) *Using Intonation*, London: Longman

Coulthard, M. (1977) *An Introduction to Discourse Analysis*, London: Longman

Couper-Kuhlen, E. (1986) *An Introduction to English Prosody*, London: Edward Arnold

Cruttenden, A. (1970) 'On the so-called grammatical function of intonation', *Phonetica*, vol. 21, pp. 182–92

Cruttenden, A. (1986) *Intonation*, Cambridge University Press

Crystal, D. (1969) *Prosodic Systems and Intonation in English*, Cambridge University Press

Crystal, D. (1975) *The English Tone of Voice*, London: Edward Arnold

Crystal, D. and Quirk, R. (1964) *Systems of Prosodic and Paralinguistic Features in English*, The Hague: Mouton

Dauer, R. (1983) 'Stress-timing and syllable-timing reanalyzed', *Journal of Phonetics*, vol. 11, pp. 51–62

Davidsen-Neilsen, N. (1969) 'English stops after initial /s/', *English Studies*, vol. 50, pp. 321–8

Denes, P. and Pinson, E. (1973) *The Speech Chain*, 2nd edition, New York: Anchor

Fox, A. T. C. (1973) 'Tone sequences in English', *Archivum Linguisticum*, vol. 4, pp. 17–26

Fox, A. T. C. (1978) 'To 'r' is human?', *Journal of the International Phonetic Association*, vol. 8, pp. 72–4

Fry, D. B. (1958) 'Experiments in the perception of stress', *Language and Speech*, vol. 1, pp. 126–52, reprinted in D. B. Fry (ed.) *Acoustic Phonetics*, Cambridge University Press

Fudge, E. C. (1967) 'The nature of phonological primes', *Journal of Linguistics*, vol. 3, no. 1, pp. 1–36

Fudge, E. C. (1969) 'Syllables', *Journal of Linguistics,* vol. 5, pp. 253–86

Fudge, E. C. (1984) *English Word Stress,* London: Allen and Unwin

Gimson, A. C. (1960) 'The instability of English alveolar articulations', *Le Maître Phonétique,* vol. 113, pp. 7–10

Gimson, A. C. (1964) 'Phonetic change and the RP vowel system' in D. Abercrombie *et al.,* pp. 131–6

Gimson, A. C. (1977) *English Pronouncing Dictionary,* 14th edition, London: Dent

Gimson, A. C. (1989) *An Introduction to the Pronunciation of English,* 4th edition, revised by S. Ramsaran, London: Edward Arnold

Goldsmith, J. A. (1990) *Autosegmental and Metrical Phonology,* Oxford: Blackwell

Halliday, M. A. K. (1967) *Intonation and Grammar in British English,* The Hague: Mouton

Hardcastle, W. J. (1976) *Physiology of Speech Production,* London: Academic Press

Hardcastle, W. J. and Roach, P. J. (1979) 'An instrumental investigation of coarticulation in stop consonant sequences' in H. H. and P. Hollien (eds.) *Current Issues in the Phonetic Sciences,* Amsterdam: John Benjamins

Hawkins, P. (1984) *Introducing Phonology,* London: Hutchinson

Henderson, E. J. A. (1971) *The Indispensable Foundation,* Oxford University Press

Hogg, R. and McCully, C. B. (1987) *Metrical Phonology: a coursebook,* Cambridge University Press

Holmes, J. N. (1988) *Speech Synthesis and Recognition,* van Nostrand Reinhold

Honey, J. (1989) *Does Accent Matter?* London: Faber & Faber

Honikman, B. (1964) 'Articulatory settings' in D. Abercrombie *et al.,* pp. 73–84

Hooke, R. and Rowell, J. (1982) *A Handbook of English Pronunciation,* London: Edward Arnold

Hughes, A. and Trudgill, P. (1987) *English Accents and Dialects,* 2nd edition, London: Edward Arnold

Hyman, L. (1975) *Phonology: Theory and Analysis,* New York: Holt, Rinehart and Winston

Jakobson, R., Fant, C. G. M. and Halle, M. (1952) *Preliminaries to Speech Analysis,* Harvard, Mass.: MIT

Jakobson, R. and Halle, M. (1956) *Fundamentals of Language,* The Hague: Mouton

Jakobson, R. and Halle, M. (1964) 'Tenseness and laxness' in Abercrombie, D. *et al.,* pp. 96–101

James, A. R. (1988) *The Acquisition of a Second Language Phonology,* Tübingen: Narr

Jones, D. (1931) 'The word as a phonetic entity', *Le Maître Phonétique*, vol. 36, pp. 60–5, reprinted in W. E. Jones and J. Laver (1973), pp. 96–101

Jones, D. (1956) *The Pronunciation of English*, 4th edition, Cambridge University Press (first published 1909)

Jones, D. (1975) *An Outline of English Phonetics*, 9th edition, Cambridge University Press

Jones, D. (1976) *The Phoneme: its Nature and Use*, Cambridge University Press

Jones, W. E. and Laver, J. (eds.) (1973) *Phonetics in Linguistics*, London: Longman

Kahn, D. (1976) *Syllable-based Generalisations in English Phonology*, Indiana University Linguistics Club

Katamba, F. (1989) *An Introduction to Phonology*, London: Longman

Kenworthy, J. (1987) *Teaching English Pronunciation*, London: Longman

Kingdon, R. (1958a) *The Groundwork of English Intonation*, London: Longman

Kingdon, R. (1958b) *The Groundwork of English Stress*, London: Longman

Knowles, G. O. (1987) *Patterns of Spoken English*, London: Longman

Krashen, S. (1981) *Second Language Acquisition and Second Language Learning*, Oxford: Pergamon

Kreidler, C. W. (1989) *The Pronunciation of English*, Oxford: Blackwell

Labov, W. (1972) *Sociolinguistic Patterns*, Oxford: Blackwell

Ladefoged, P. (1965) 'The nature of general phonetic theories', *Georgetown University Monograph Series on Languages and Linguistics*, vol. 18, pp. 27–42

Ladefoged, P. (1967) *Three Areas of Experimental Phonetics*, Oxford University Press

Ladefoged, P. (1982) *A Course in Phonetics*, 2nd edition, New York: Harcourt Brace Jovanovich

Lass, R. (1984) *Phonology*, Cambridge University Press

Laver, J. (1968) 'Voice quality and indexical information', *British Journal of Disorders of Communication*, vol. 3, pp. 43–54

Laver, J. (1980) *The Phonetic Description of Voice Quality*, Cambridge University Press

Laver, J. (forthcoming) *Principles of Phonetics*, Cambridge University Press

Lee, W. R. (1958) *English Intonation: A New Approach*, Amsterdam: North Holland

Lehiste, I. (1977) 'Isochrony reconsidered', *Journal of Phonetics*, vol. 5, pp. 253–63

Lieberman, P. and Michaels, S. B. (1962) 'Some aspects of fundamental frequency and envelope amplitude as related to the emotional content of speech', *Journal of the Acoustical Society of America*, vol. 34, pp. 922–7, reprinted in D. Bolinger (ed.) (1972) *Intonation*, Harmondsworth: Penguin, pp. 235–49

Lieberman, P. and Blumstein, S. (1988) *Speech Physiology, Speech Perception and Acoustic Phonetics*, Cambridge University Press

Lisker, L. (1970) 'Supraglottal air pressure in the production of English stops', *Language and Speech*, vol. 13, pp. 215–30

Longman Dictionary of Contemporary English, 2nd edition (1987), London: Longman

MacCarthy, P. A. D. (1952) *English Pronunciation*, 4th edition, Cambridge: Heffer

MacCarthy, P. A. D. (1978) *The Teaching of Pronunciation*, Cambridge University Press

MacMahon, M. K. C. (1986) 'The International Phonetic Association: the first 100 years', *Journal of the International Phonetic Association*, vol. 16, pp. 30–8

Mortimer, C. (1984) *Elements of Pronunciation*, Cambridge University Press

Nolan, F. (1973) *The Phonetic Bases of Speaker Recognition*, Cambridge University Press

O'Connor, J. D. (1957) 'The fall–rise tone in English', *Moderna Sprak*, pp. 27–37

O'Connor, J. D. (1973) *Phonetics*, Harmondsworth: Penguin

O'Connor, J. D. (1980) *Better English Pronunciation*, 2nd edition, Cambridge University Press

O'Connor, J. D. and Trim, J. L. M. (1953) 'Vowel, consonant and syllable: a phonological definition', *Word*, vol. 9, no. 2, pp. 103–22, reprinted in W. E. Jones and J. Laver (1973), pp. 240–61

O'Connor, J. D. and Arnold, G. F. (1973) *The Intonation of Colloquial English*, 2nd edition (first published 1962), London: Longman

O'Connor, J. D. and Tooley, O. M. (1964) 'The perceptibility of certain word boundaries' in D. Abercrombie *et al.*, pp. 171–6

Palmer, H. E. (1924) *English Intonation with Systematic Exercises*, Cambridge: Heffer

Pierrehumbert, J. (1979) 'The perception of fundamental frequency declination', *Journal of the Acoustical Society of America*, vol. 66, pp. 363–9

Pierrehumbert, J. (1987) *The Phonetics and Phonology of English Intonation*, Indiana Linguistics Club

Pike, K. L. (1943) *Phonetics*, University of Michigan Press

Pike, K. L. (1945) *The Intonation of American English*, University of Michigan Press

Pike, K. L. (1947) *Phonemics*, University of Michigan Press

Pike, K. L. (1948) *Tone Languages*, University of Michigan Press

Pring, J. T. (1976) 'More thoughts on the r-link business', *Journal of the International Phonetic Association*, vol. 6, no. 2, pp. 92–5

Ramsaran, S. (ed.) (1990) *Studies in the Pronunciation of English*, London: Routledge

Roach, P. J. (1973) 'Glottalisation of /p, t, k, tʃ/: a re-examination', *Journal of the International Phonetic Association*, vol. 3, no. 1

Roach, P. J. (1979) 'Laryngeal-oral coarticulation in glottalised English plosives', *Journal of the International Phonetic Association*, vol. 9, no. 1, pp. 1–6

Roach, P. J. (1982) 'On the distinction between "stress-timed" and "syllable-timed" languages', in D. Crystal (ed.) *Linguistic Controversies*, London: Edward Arnold

Roach, P. J. (1987) 'Rethinking phonetic taxonomy', *Transactions of the Philological Society*, pp. 24–37

Roach, P. J. (1991) 'Transcription', *Oxford International Encyclopedia of Linguistics*, Oxford University Press

Sapir, E. (1925) 'Sound patterns in language', *Language*, vol. 1, pp. 37–51

Schmerling, S. (1976) *Aspects of English Sentence Stress*, Austin: University of Texas Press

Sharp, A. E. (1958) 'Falling-rising intonation patterns in English', *Phonetica*, vol. 2, pp. 127–52

Sledd, J. (1955) Review of Trager and Smith (1951), *Language*, vol. 31, pp. 312–45

Taylor, D. S. (1981) 'Non-native speakers and the rhythm of English' *International Review of Applied Linguistics*, vol. 19, no. 3, pp. 219–26

Trager, G. L. (1964) 'The intonation system of American English' in D. Abercrombie *et al.*, pp. 266–70

Trager, G. L. and Smith, H. L. (1951) *An Outline of English Structure*, Washington, DC: American Council of Learned Societies

Trim, J. L. M. (1959) 'Major and minor tone groups in English', *Le Maître Phonétique*, vol. 112, pp. 26–9, reprinted in W. E. Jones and J. Laver (eds.) (1973) pp. 320–3

Trubetzkoy, N. S. (1939) *Grundzüge der Phonologie*, Transactions du Cercle Linguistique de Prague, 7. (English translation: *Principles of Phonology*, transl. C. A. M. Baltaxe, Berkeley: University of California Press, 1969)

Uldall, E. T. (1960) 'Attitudinal meanings conveyed by intonation', *Language and Speech*, vol. 3, pp. 223–34

Uldall, E. T. (1964) 'Dimensions of meaning in intonation' in D. Abercrombie *et al.*, pp. 271–9

Vachek, J. (1964) 'Notes on the phonematic value of the modern English /ŋ/ sound' in D. Abercrombie *et al.*, pp. 191–205

Wells, J. C. (1965) 'The phonological status of syllabic consonants in English RP', *Phonetica*, vol. 13, pp. 110–13

Wells, J. C. (1970) 'Local accents in England and Wales', *Journal of Linguistics*, vol. 6, no. 2, pp. 231–52

Wells, J. C. (1982) *Accents of English*, 3 vols. Cambridge University Press

Wells, J. C. (1987) 'Computer-coded phonetic transcription', *Journal of the International Phonetic Association*, vol. 17, no. 2, pp. 94–114

Wells, J. C. (1990) *Longman Pronunciation Dictionary*, London: Longman

Wells, R. S. (1945) 'The pitch phonemes of English', *Language*, vol. 21, pp. 27–39

Windsor Lewis, J. (1975a) 'Linking /r/ in the General British pronunciation of English', *Journal of the International Phonetic Association*, vol. 5, no. 1, pp. 37–42

Windsor Lewis, J. (1975b) 'The undesirability of length marks in EFL phonemic transcription', *Journal of the International Phonetic Association*, vol. 5, no. 2, pp. 64–71

Windsor Lewis, J. (1977a) 'The r-link business – a reply', *Journal of the International Phonetic Association*, vol. 7, no. 1, pp. 28–31

Windsor Lewis, J. (1977b) *People Speaking*, Oxford University Press

Index